APPARITIONS OF MODERN SAINTS

Appearances of Therese of Lisieux,
Padre Pio, Don Bosco, and Others

Messages From God to His People on Earth

PATRICIA TREECE

*This is an abridged and updated version
of the book formerly entitled* Messengers.

CHARIS

Servant Publications
Ann Arbor, Michigan

Charis Books is an imprint of Servant Publications especially designed to serve Roman Catholics.

Selections have been taken from *DIARY, Saint Maria Faustina Kowalska, Divine Mercy in My Soul.* Copyright 1987 Congregation of Marians of the Immaculate Conception, Stockbridge, MA 01263. All rights reserved. Reprinted with permission.

Excerpts from *Dreams, Visions and Prophecies of Don Bosco* and *Biographical Memoirs of Don Bosco* have been reprinted with permission of the Salesiana Publishers, 148 Main Street, New Rochelle, New York 10802.

Excerpts from *Hasidic Tales of the Holocaust,* by Haffa Eliach, published by Oxford University Press, have been reprinted by permission of Miriam Altshuler Literary Agency. Copyright 1982 by Yaffa Eliach.

Excerpts from *The Way of Divine Love,* by Sister Josefa Menendez, are reprinted by permission of Tan Books and Publishers.

Servant Publications
P.O. Box 8617
Ann Arbor, MI 48107

Cover design by Paul Higdon, Minneapolis, Minn.

01 02 03 04 10 9 8 7 6 5 4 3 2 1

Printed in the United States of America
ISBN 1-56955-303-3

Library of Congress Cataloging-in-Publication Data

Treece, Patricia.
     Apparitions of modern saints : appearances of Therese of Lisieux, Padre Pio, Don Bosco, and others : messages from God to his people on earth / Patricia Treece.
          p. cm.
     Abridged and updated ed. of: Messengers. c1995.
     Includes bibliographical references and index.
     ISBN 1-56955-303-3 (alk. paper)
      1. Saints. 2. Apparitions. 3. Future Life—Religious aspects. I. Treece, Patricia. Messengers. II. Title.
     BL488 .T74 2001
     235'.2—dc21

                                                                                        2001002868

This book is an act of Thanksgiving to
DIVINE MERCY,
which hovers over every anecdote
in these pages

and an offering on behalf of my children and godchildren:
Christopher, Katherine, Joscelyn, Gilien, Candice,
Sabine, Elizabeth, Heather, Brina, Julianna,
Katherine Patricia, Joan, Maximilian, & Zachary.

Upon them, as upon readers and writer, I ask the blessing of
St. Francis' good comrade St. Clare:

May Almighty God bless us.
May he look upon us with the eyes of his mercy.
May he pour forth his graces upon us abundantly
And in heaven, may he place us among his saints.

CONTENTS

ACKNOWLEDGMENTS

During many years of research on this book, I have received the help of innumerable archivists, members of religious orders, journalists, postulators, personnel at shrines and other centers of devotion to particular saints, as well as individuals who believe they are alive, cured, or perhaps simply better people because God sent them a message carried by a dead saint.

Because I called on you so many times or asked for so much, I must mention several people by name: my deep gratitude to Mother Marie Lucile of the Lisieux (France) Carmel; Father Charles Fehrenbach, C.SS.R. of St. John Neumann's Shrine in Philadelphia; the late Father Joseph Pius Martin, O.F.M. Cap. of San Giovanni Rotondo (Italy); Sufi expert, writer Susan Fine of Rochester, Michigan; Angela Boudreaux and Father Joseph Elworthy, C.SS.R. of the Seelos Center in New Orleans; and Dr. Yaffa Eliach, founding director of the Center for Holocaust Studies and professor in the Department of Judaic Studies at Brooklyn College.

Trying to list all the others to whom I am indebted, I fear, will simply end in the embarrassment of leaving out one or more people who assisted me in important ways. If you helped in any way with this project, please be assured of my gratitude.

I also wish to thank those who read parts of the unabridged manuscript—or all of it—for style, clarity, or to verify accuracy. Included are many whose stories are in these pages, as well as Rolf Gompertz, Judith Hodgins, Cathy Schneir, and Katherine and Christopher Sariego. My original hardback edition editors, Jacquelyn M. Lindsey and Cathy A. Dee, deserve applause for hard work. And my thanks to my friend Bert Ghezzi of Servant Publications, who made this edition possible, and to Heidi Hess Saxton, who worked tirelessly to edit it.

Finally, I thank the friends—living and dead—who have prayed for this book. If it is of value to anyone, I know whom to credit.

PROLOGUE

Turin, Italy
The night of July 22, 1907

Twenty-eight-year-old Sister Teresa Valse-Pantellini lies awake, coarse linen sheets clinging limply to her modest nightdress. Without losing her peace of spirit, through the tedious hours she struggles to breathe under the weight of the hot, humid air pressing on her TB-riddled lungs. Slowly the noises of the city die away until the only sounds in the dark infirmary sickroom are her raspy breathing and the occasional whine of a mosquito entering by the open, screenless window.

Very late, the infirmarian looks in. Cautioned against talking because it brings on hemorrhages, Teresa smiles and nods she is OK and needs nothing. Closing the door, the infirmarian sighs as she pads down the hall on tired feet. She finds it hard to see someone die this young—even Sister Teresa, who *longs* to be with God.

Alone again in the dark, do Teresa's eyes close for a moment? Later, she will not be sure. But, if so, they open wide when her dark sickroom is lit by a bright light. In it Teresa sees a man. She has never met John Bosco, the holy cofounder of her order[1] who died when she was ten. But from the many photographs of Don Bosco[2] in circulation she recognizes the saint at once.

Rather short, he appears the same athletically well-built priest who outran and outplayed several thousand "slum boys" until his lungs, too, gave out. There is also no mistaking Bosco's square, firm-jawed face with its handsome features lavishly topped with dark curls. Nor his irresistibly warm smile. The only change, in fact, from his photographs, Teresa later explains, is that somehow—while unmistakenly Don Bosco—he looks "younger" and "more beautiful" now that life's cares have been lifted from those powerful shoulders.

Looking at her with fatherly compassion, Bosco—who joked that someone should get him a bellows when his own lungs went[3]—steps out of the light and approaches the dying, tubercular sister.

11

"Wait, Don Bosco!" Boldly, Sister Teresa sits up in bed and puts out a cautioning hand. Seemingly unperturbed by the dead saint's arrival in her sickroom, she exclaims hurriedly, "I'm not the one asking for a cure. It's Sister Giovanna."

"The next room," she adds, pointing the way to God's messenger as if he is some lost delivery boy.

Don Bosco stops. He grins at her; she later admits that. But we cannot expect any more from the woman whose secret motto is "to pass unnoticed." In fact, behaving just like the authentic saint she is reputed to be, Sister Teresa makes public *nothing* about what she and her dead visitor say to each other.

We don't even know how *long* they communicate. What is known is that at some point Don Bosco strolls out Sister Teresa's door and into the next room of the infirmary. The sick woman lying there, half-awake and miserable in the hot night, is Sister Giovanna Lenci. Seriously ill for years, she has been a resident of the infirmary much longer than Teresa. But unlike Teresa, Giovanna dreams not of heaven, but of health.

In fact, she is just finishing her third consecutive novena,[4] asking Don Bosco's prayers for her recovery. As the dead priest is about to be named "Venerable"—that is, one determined by his Church to have practiced virtue at heroic levels—the sister has hopes God will work a miracle in Bosco's honor. After all, once a Catholic is named "Venerable," the road to beatification and canonization rests on God speaking through miracles. Giovanna wants to be one of Bosco's.

The saint does not stay with her long. As he leaves, the nun springs out of bed with joy and rouses the house with her cries, "I've seen Don Bosco and I'm cured!" Puzzled medical men later verify the instantaneous return to health.

Does it last? It does indeed. It will be over thirty productive years before Sister Giovanna sees heaven.

That the dead saint hand-carried this miracle of God to Sister Giovanna is corroborated when Sister Teresa—whose good sense and rectitude they know—confesses she saw Don Bosco, too. Of course, when she admits—does the infirmarian groan?—that, longing for paradise, she forestalled any attempt to cure *her*, belief in Teresa's good sense wavers in some. Not even every nun is *that* otherworldly. And then, some chuckle, Teresa's cure would have provided such a bang-up double miracle to add to their celebration when—only two days after Bosco's Turin visit—his "Venerable" title becomes official.

Has Teresa extracted from her dead visitor precisely when her longing for heaven will be satisfied? Probably. For just over a month later, the sister in the late stages of tuberculosis sets her watch ahead for 7:00 A.M. without winding it. Asked to send a message about her condition to her family, she answers, "Let's wait 'til tomorrow."

At precisely 7:00 A.M. the next day, September 3, 1907, Teresa dies peacefully, letting slip that Don Bosco—accompanying Jesus and his mother—is there again, waiting for her. This time the visitors are seen only by Sister Teresa. But those around her bed see something of their glory in her luminous face.

<hr/>

The Master of the Universe plays love games with his saints. In this case, God snuck up on Teresa Valse-Pantellini even as the quiet nun believed she held off a miracle cure. Obviously God knew in advance what Teresa's response would be. But Don Bosco was sent to her as well as to Sister Giovanna anyway.

Think about it a moment. Knowing her motto, Teresa undoubtedly revealed she saw Don Bosco only to buttress Sister Giovanna's claim. But by Bosco's admitted visit to Teresa—which, you note, is so nicely validated as neither "a hallucination" nor "fever dream" by Sister Giovanna's cure and testimony—the cause of Teresa Valse-Pantellini for official sainthood, introduced in 1926, got an incalculable boost. Put simply, by sending a dead saint to chat with her, heaven called attention to Teresa, thereby nicely forestalling the young nun's desire to "pass unnoticed"!

Endnotes

1. The Daughters of Mary Help of Christians (commonly called Salesian Sisters).
2. Don is the Italian title for a priest.
3. He died of emphysema.
4. Prayer for a particular request said for nine days. Novenas (from the Latin for nine) take many forms and may be addressed to God directly or ask a saint's prayers.

Chapter One

IT'S GOING ON ALL THE TIME

Saint John Bosco appeared to two nuns after his death in two different rooms of an infirmary in 1907. Saints are also making after-death appearances now—that is, in whatever year you pick up this book. Nor are such appearances something new. Witnesses who spied on St. Francis of Assisi during prayer more than once saw dead saints—among them Peter, Paul, and John—speaking to him. After-death appearances of the holy in western tradition go back, in fact, to the beginning of Christianity and beyond into Judaism. It was, after all, two dead, holy, Jewish men who appeared to Jesus on the Mount of Transfiguration.

All spiritual traditions make a place for important appearances of the dead. The idea of the dead returning to do God's work then is not some weird Catholic notion, but a universal belief.

As for Christianity, as Paul says in the Bible, it is nothing—a gyp and a fraud—if Jesus Christ did not rise from the dead in his scourged, crucified body and appear to his disciples. No one has made more visits to the human family after his earthly life than the Savior. These, too, are always occurring.

I think of the little girl from Prestonville, Kentucky, mentioned in *Extension Magazine*[1] the summer I write this. Diagnosed with liver cancer and given six months to live, Mary Ann chatted with Father Joseph Muench, who visited the little Protestant in the hospital before she became a member of his St. Martha's Catholic parish. Asked by Father if she prayed, the six-year-old replied, "If I didn't pray every day, I wouldn't make it." Then she added, "I like it best when Jesus comes into the room, sits on the bed, and tells me what to say." Was the kid hallucinating? I don't know. But maybe Jesus did tell her "what to say," for the article reports her terminal cancer is inexplicably gone.

Lakota tribe member Harry Blue Feather won the 1992 Lumen Christi award for his evangelization work as a catechist. In the 1930s, Harry was a rough, tough, young guy "in trouble all the time." His life changed after Jesus appeared to him, bound and wearing the crown of thorns.

Distinguished novelist Reynolds Price teaches at Duke University, where he graduated *summa cum laude.* The former Rhodes scholar, fighting a life-and-death battle with a spinal tumor in 1984, had a mystical experience in which he found himself somehow with Jesus at Lake Kinnereth in Israel. Jesus forgave his sins and when Price asked, "Am I also cured?" the Savior said, "That, too." Against all odds, Reynolds Price survived.

Yes, Jesus Christ is still personally appearing—to all kinds of people—to change destinies. But, just as long ago in Galilee the Master sent others out to preach, teach, and heal in his name, the Lord still sends his closest friends as his messengers. This book is about them: the people called saints.

What do I mean by "saint"? I mean the people like John Bosco, who reach the heights of human development. "Whole" men and women[2] whose lives as much as their lips can say, with the writer of Romans: "... whether we live or die, we are the Lord's."

Of course all those in heaven (whether they achieved the purity during life to walk right in or entered following some after-death work) are legitimately called saints. But heaven is not a democracy where all souls are equal. To explain, let me borrow an illustration given to St. Therese of Lisieux when she was a little girl. Told people in heaven have different degrees of glory and joy, tenderhearted Therese felt bad. Her wise older sister got two glasses, one big, one tiny. Into each she poured water to the rim.

"See," she said, "they each have all they can hold."

In this book we are going to look at the big-glass folks, those who hold the maximum love and goodness. We will do this for the simple reason that when God uses human messengers, it seems to be his good pleasure to entrust the spectacular cures, the radical conversions, and the most beautiful gifts to their hands.

A second distinction: This book is only about *purposeful* apparitions, never sightings—even if they involve saints—originating, it appears, in psychic sensitivity. Hand a relic to someone sensitive in this way, and they might sense or even see the saint. In these instances, the dead are not messengers nor even present as we normally understand the idea. Instead the viewer somehow tunes into the past. St. Maximilian Kolbe, who did not have the gift himself, theorized the past is "out there" and that with the right technology one might see Jesus as he walked the dusty roads of Galilee. Maybe, but if that happens it won't be an after-death appearance!

Let twentieth-century Catholic Caryll Houselander illustrate. A mystic who had genuine supernatural experiences, the Englishwoman was also a natural psychic[3] who could hold a piece of folded paper, handwriting hidden, and give accurate information about the writer.

Perhaps because of her great sensitivity to others' sufferings, Caryll once had an experience of the type I mean. Glancing as she passed into an upstairs room of the English country house where she was visiting, the writer-therapist-artist glimpsed a little girl leaning against a dollhouse. Face ashen, darkly circled eyes shut in concentration, the child sighed with exhaustion as she struggled to pull off her boots. Mentioning the youngster downstairs, Caryll learned she'd seen a child found dead from undetected diabetes years earlier in that room. This was not a "haunted nursery," nor was the child a messenger of God, for she took no note of her observer. Caryll had somehow simply tuned in to the past.

Another distinction may be useful. This is the gulf between a *purposeful* visit by either a saint or a nonholy person, and the traditional ghost. The slain, the slayer, the mad, the lovelorn, the crazed suicide—with a few gentler spirits, the gallery of so-called ghosts is filled with troubled souls attached to sites where they played a morbid role. Pathetic figures generally, the ghost is a self-centered phenomenon. Real or imaginary, the specter signals human unwillingness to break away from past misfortune—some would say sin—and move on.

Thus you understand why saints do not "haunt" places: remorse, despair, the desire for revenge or refusal to forgive; unrenounced, unrequited (thus possessive) love—all the traditional emotions associated with ghosts—are long jettisoned by the holy. At death the saint, unfettered by such chains, simply flies to God. So do not consider dead saints as ghosts, please!

One other word before we begin. Whenever a Catholic writes about saints, the question always comes up: what about apparitions of the Virgin Mary? Having studied many reports, I believe that, after Jesus, no one gets around like his mother. The visits of the woman the Bible quotes as saying prophetically, "all generations will call me blessed" are extremely frequent in the modern era, both to groups and to individuals. The topic fills books of its own. So expect in these pages only occasional references to Jesus' mother. Fortunately I can sum up her appearances for you. Today, as at Cana, her message is, "Do as my Son tells you."

To appreciate the after-death appearances of saints—which are both the same and yet differ strikingly from other after-death appearances—we need to look first at after-death appearances in general.

Occurring to those who describe themselves as "not religious" or "rationalists," as well as to people of all creeds, they are as likely to be experienced by those who would never think of such things as those who do. Mostly, people keep mum about such experiences. But one woman I barely know (she worked in my pediatrician's office), learned I take after-death appearances seriously. She eagerly shared with me how her dead father appeared in a dream one night to warn her that her mother would die suddenly—and soon. "Of all my children, you understand this the least," he worried aloud. This totally unexpected dream, says my informant, made the shock of her mother's sudden death bearable.

I can also add two experiences of people I do know, thus whose stability and honesty I can vouch for. Lutheran professional woman and homemaker Eva Engholm—a true mystic—was one of my mentors and closest friends until her early death a few years ago. Eva was left a young widow with four children when her businessman husband died in the crash of a commercial airliner near San Diego. A down-to-earth woman who loved cooking and gardening, Eva confided in me how much it helped her cope when her dead husband appeared to her, consoling, "It was my time. Don't feel bad."

Another friend, talented, vivacious artist-designer Nancy Parker of Pasadena was once worried to the point of being physically ill over a teenage daughter's serious troubles. Having returned to school, one noontime Nancy was perched on her bed trying to tackle some homework. As she fought to keep her mind off her child, Nancy looked up, and there was her dead dad standing at the end of the bed. He gave his distraught daughter the strength to go on by assuring her everything would turn out OK—which it did. Raised a Methodist, Nancy had followed Christian Science for ten years, but at the time her father brought the message of hope, she had dropped away from any formal church affiliation.

Not everyone agrees with the politics of Jesuit peace-activist Daniel Berrigan. But his honesty has never been questioned. In his autobiography,[4] Berrigan reports that his troubled father appeared after death to Dan's niece in Minnesota, who was due to make her first communion. Her dead grandpa came only to ask the little girl for prayers, but the sudden sight of him so unnerved her that she screamed and fainted. The child's mother, who came running at the scream, attested again to the incident on her own deathbed.

In the late 1870s, Father Arnold Damen, another Jesuit, founded Holy Family Church in Chicago. Those who visit the old church, which stands on Roosevelt Road near the University of Illinois' Circle Campus, sometimes notice two unusual statues in the chancel area of altar boys facing each other. Father Arnold had them put there after he was summoned one snowy night by two boys who took him to their dying mother so she could receive the last rites.[5] The woman welcomed the priest but wondered who sent him. When he told her, she told *him* that her sons—altar boys at Holy Family long ago—were both dead.

Are such things rare? In one sense, yes. The full experience of *seeing the dead* is not something that happens to most of us. It certainly never has to me. On the other hand, many of those with whom I share deeply have had or know someone who has had—if not such a dramatic experience—at least something of a lesser degree. Feeling the unseen *presence* of a beloved dead person, for instance, is fairly common.

If you think—dramatic or otherwise—all this has to be imaginary, Episcopalian priest-author Morton T. Kelsey cautions that those "who believe we live confined in a completely rational and understandable world where nothing unusual ever happens ... simply haven't lived very deeply." Kelsey, who has done a lot of counseling, speaks of the "amazing experiences" people tell when, masks down, they speak from "the depth of their being."[6]

In many after-death appearances, like some of those mentioned, the dead help people deal with a loved one's death or bring help for the dying. Even more common, is for those who are dying or will die soon to see dead loved ones. To again mention something I have personal knowledge of, I recall a charming German-Swiss lady, mother of my onetime college exchange student roommate, and later my hostess in Zurich. A few days before the unexpected death of Mrs. Koch, she confided in my roommate's older sister, Elizabeth, that in "a dream of light and beauty" she had seen her own mother "coming and wanting to take her with her." Mrs. Koch said to Elizabeth that she felt eager for the reunion, but told her mother "to wait a little, until she had arranged all her affairs." A few days later, having made some last arrangements, Mrs. Koch was found dead of a heart attack. My nominally Protestant former roommate is solidly earthbound and not "religious" but she told me how much her mother's experience comforted her.

French Catholic philosopher Jacques Maritain, who taught at Princeton University, will be known to most readers as not only a confirmed Christian but a man of intellectual acumen, not associated with anything bogus or superstitious in spirituality. Jacques Maritain's sister-in-law Vera lived for many years with Maritain and his wife, running their house for them. After Vera was diagnosed with cancer, Maritain reports her "dream or vision" on April 10, 1959. In it her father approached her, "radiant with youth and with light." When she asked him, he said he had not come to take her "yet." That December, Vera died quietly at the Maritains' home, her last intelligible word "Papa."

Well-authenticated also are occasions where the dead "visit" the living before it is known the visitor is, in fact, dead. A later chapter will be devoted to such incidents among recent saints. But to show that this happens in the wider sphere, let me turn to Rabbi Herbert Weiner of Temple Sharey Tefilo-Israel in South Orange, New Jersey. The rabbi tells in his book *9 1/2 Mystics* of personally studying with a Kabbalist (an expert in Jewish mysticism) named Setzer.

Setzer, who lived on East Broadway in lower Manhattan, described himself as "a rationalist" but told his student he had to accept the following anyway because he *experienced* it. Quoting Setzer:

> I had two sisters. One of them ... became seriously ill. One day I was sitting alone in my room and suddenly ... I am a rationalist, but still, it happened ... I saw something dressed in black and it was my sister. She came close to me and kissed me, then suddenly dropped away. Then I heard a voice close by, whispering clearly in my ear, "Your sister died, your sister died." The whole next day I heard music, beautiful music ... so loud and clear that I was sure it was a radio or something which the neighbors also heard, but I found out that they didn't. Then I got a telegram telling me that my sister had died. I figured out the time and hour, and it was the exact moment when I heard the whispering.

Such experiences draw on the reality Catholics like myself call the Communion of Saints. Don't be misled by the word "saint." The reality is much more inclusive, referring to the supportive interconnectedness of not just the holy or even Christians, but of all those on earth and beyond who do not opt out of friendship with God—"beyond" including the blessed in heaven and those still undergoing growth and purification after death in preparation for heaven, a state we Catholics call purgatory.

When trying to explain this interconnectedness as it operates on earth, I'm reminded of an experience of a woman named Anne S. Watson.[7] Watson tells of a woman named Helen Hayden "who carried such a burden of (neurotic) guilt she seemed almost to apologize for being alive." Diagnosed with cancer, Helen lay in the hospital one morning waiting to be taken into surgery, while in another city Anne and a prayer partner knelt in an Episcopal church by the altar rail. As they prayed, they received an image of Helen "desperately trying to lift an enormous stone from her chest." So they used imaging to see Jesus help her. (Note this was not a vision but an exercise of their imagination, a meditation technique taught by St. Ignatius Loyola among others.) By imagination, they saw the Savior smile down at Helen, lifting the stone off her chest while saying, "This is too heavy for you; let me take it."

Helen at that time actually felt "utterly squashed," too depressed to even pray. When a hospital chaplain came in with communion, Helen protested with her usual outlook, "But I'm not worthy to receive it."

The chaplain sat down on her bed. Taking Helen's hand, he chided, "the worst sin is to believe you are the worst sinner." He urged her to accept forgiveness, "not to be freed of responsibility" for her actions but to stop dragging this unhealthy guilt with her.

"Suddenly," Helen later told Anne, "I felt as if a great stone had been lifted from my chest." As she received communion, she knew that she was a member of the "blessed company of all faithful people."

Or, as Catholic Cindy Cavnar puts it, "we are never alone and our prayers and sacrifices for one another do bear fruit." Anne Watson didn't have to be in the same city when she prayed for Helen Hayden, for distance is no barrier to our connection in the Communion of Saints. Neither, this book will offer ample evidence, is time or state of being. Ironically, since Christianity rests on Christ's return after death, some Christians deny there can be contact between the living and the dead, citing the story of Lazarus (see Luke 16:19-31). Read the story if you have such concerns. I think you'll see two things: 1) The abyss which cannot be crossed is not between life and death but between two conditions after death: those who are with God, like Lazarus, and those, like the dead rich man, "in torment" (probably purgatory since he cares about his five living brothers, whereas those in the state we call hell care for no one.) 2) Asked by the dead rich man to send Lazarus back from heaven to warn the rich man's brothers to change their ways, Abraham replies, "If they do not listen to Moses and the prophets, they will not be persuaded even if one should rise from the dead." That is an evaluation of the state of soul of five particular people, who have hardened their hearts against God and others. Abraham does not say "no one" would benefit from a visit by the dead. Or that the dead are not permitted to return. Christ who tells the parable will soon be both "risen from the dead" and visiting his living followers. As the Savior and his saints down the centuries demonstrate, if we are deep enough in God, as Cavnar says, "we are at one another's disposal—both in life and in death."

In this great interconnectedness of all people of good will, the veil between this life and the next, for *those with eyes to see,* can be very thin. And rent sometimes on deathbeds. I think of the dying mystical poet William Blake, who—with shining face and brightened eyes—"burst out singing of the things he saw in Heaven."[8]

Then there is the testimony of a child. Daisy Dryden was the daughter of Reverend David Anderson Dryden, a Methodist Episcopal minister who became head of the women's department of Santa Clara College, today Pacific University.

Daisy was one of those children who have great faith. When she was only five, her mother was so ill it was thought she would die. Finding her father weeping, Daisy told him not to worry: she would ask the Lord and he would surely make her mother well. From that hour the mother began to recover.

When Daisy was around ten, she herself became ill with typhoid. Recovering nicely, one day she told her father, who was struck by her expression of pleasure and amazement, that she saw Jesus and that he said she was going to heaven. Her condition suddenly deteriorating, during the last three peace-filled days of her life, Daisy saw clearly into the next world.[9]

Before Daisy's death, which occurred on the day and hour she foretold, a visitor remarked, "Well, Daisy, you will soon be over the dark river." After the visitor left, the dying girl commented to her father, "It is all a mistake; there is no river; there is no curtain; there is not even a line that separates this life from the other life."

If for most of us the veil between this life and the hereafter does not lift so readily, for certain people (not all) who live close to God, the veil is often breached during their earthly existence. Mystic visionary Adrienne von Speyr, for one, was told during a supernatural visitation when young that she would "live in both worlds at once." Her confessor, theologian Hans Urs von Balthasar, testified that the Swiss physician, wife of a University of Basel professor, frequently interacted with the dead—saints and others—until her death at age sixty-five in 1967.

Readers familiar with Franciscan stigmatic Padre Pio, who died in 1968, know he was visited by Jesus, the Virgin Mary, and various dead saints. Legions of dead who still had spiritual work to do also came to ask his prayers.[10] The Italian priest remarked in all seriousness that there were more (invisible) dead than living at his crowded daily mass.

The ordinary dead—as distinguished from the holy—are at times permitted or sent by God to reach out to those with whom they have a connection, almost always loved ones. Besides examples previously mentioned, such as my friend Eva's husband or my friend Nancy's father, there are even first-person testimonies of Holocaust survivors where after-death appearances of family members, usually in dreams, helped children and grandchildren survive death camps.[11]

While by far the greatest majority of after-death visitations of nonsaints are to someone known and loved while alive, some souls—I postulate those who have moved farther from ego concerns during life—appear to those with whom they have slighter ties.

An outstanding example—because it happened to a woman many of us regard as a saint and took place in broad daylight—is an experience of English writer, artist, and therapist Caryll Houselander during the tense days in 1939 before World War II. Wide awake, Caryll saw her dead family doctor plop down next to her on a London bus. Chatting matter-of-factly about the family's health, he referred to things *only* this doctor knew. Then he spoke of the coming conflict and what it would bring before hopping off with the remark "I won't vanish; people have enough to contend with." His appearance, Caryll said, made it possible for her to face the war.

Saints may be involved in all the types of after-death appearances sketched so far in this chapter. Thus, although this is probably rarer than with nonsaints, they at times appear to family members. Dead St. Maria Goretti, for example, saved her niece Isolina from lightning. Both St. Therese of Lisieux and Padre Pio appeared after death to various family members.

Much more often than the nonholy, saints appear, like the doctor to Caryll, to those with whom they were not intimate but had some earthly connection. St. Maximilian Kolbe, for instance, apparently appeared in the 1990s to Francis Gajowniczek, a former Polish army sergeant. Father Kolbe died in 1941 in Auschwitz, voluntarily taking the place of Gajowniczek when the father of two cried out for his wife and children as he was randomly marked for execution.

Like Kolbe laying down his life for an almost total stranger, in loving God to the degree they do, saints are connected to *all* people. Thus looking at the overall phenomena of after-death appearances, one finds a spectrum ranging from the self-absorbed dead (like those who come solely to request prayers for themselves) to the unselfish dead (like the boys God permitted to get a priest for their dying mother), all the way to the dead saint—the individual at the acme of human development—who loves *all* in and for God.

Like angels, dead saints are spiritually equipped to serve as pure, loving messengers to whomever God sends them. So in addition to the appearances mentioned above, saints may appear to: 1) people they never knew; 2) people who never heard of them; or, 3) those from whom they are separated by the widest barriers of culture, centuries, and—of course—death.

Thus Benedictine Sister Geralyn Spaulding told me about a friend of hers who doesn't want his name used. This young member of the Benedictine community in Pecos, New Mexico, saw dead St. Frances of Rome, who offered advice on what the monastery should do regarding a certain difficulty. Although he is an American male celibate and St. Frances was an Italian wife and mother most of her life, the dead woman and the young man she visited *are* linked by the fact that, in her final earthly years, widowed Frances became a Benedictine. Still, she has been dead since March 9, 1440—more than five hundred fifty years!

About here I expect a number of people to say, hey, wait a minute: how do we know this isn't a book about people's hallucinations of dead saints? After all, people's minds are capable of strange things, like the person reported in my daily paper as saying she was comforted by a living rock star during what she calls a near-death experience. Such bizarre incidents are fodder for those who insist after-death appearances and near-death experiences are purely interior events, defense mechanisms triggered in the brain in time of severe stress.

Guidance in such visions—say, where a saint appears to a combat soldier and instructs "Move!" just before the shell hits where he was standing—would come, in this view, from the hallucinator's unconscious intuitions and wisdom. Physical cures, like that of Sister Giovanna in the prologue, would be explained as the immune system's response to the hope stimulated by the hallucination.

Let's agree that some people *have* hallucinated a dead saint's appearance. This "event," creating expectation of a miracle, could then jolt the immune system as if by a massive electrical shock and set up biochemical responses that could indeed lead to "impossible" cures. If this is the way it works, we can only hope lots of people with terminal illnesses become hallucinators!

However, while I wish to follow ration as long as it can sustain the burden of evidence, there are a few problems with the theory that after-death appearances are all in the head. First, after-death experiences differ from near-death experiences. Speaking of near-death experiences on American television, British Professor Dr. Susan Blackmore spoke of the lack of oxygen and mind chemicals called endorphins producing visions and out-of-body experiences. But unlike near-death experiences, after-death appearances almost never occur when someone is suffering from lack of oxygen. As for the presence or absence of endorphins (secreted by the brain in certain emotional states) after-death experiences occur to people in the whole gamut of moods from the most banal to the most dramatic.

And there are other problems when one considers individual cases: take the two women in separate rooms in the infirmary. If they hallucinated, each did it without knowing the other was so engaged, and they didn't even do it at the same time but consecutively.

Consider also the very young child with cancer, who takes a sudden turn for the better, who begins asking for someone the family has never heard of. Later the family discovers a friend has been asking for the prayers of a dead holy person by the unknown name.

Then there is the recent Montana case involving St. Katharine Drexel (1858–1955). Withholding names because these people don't want to be harassed, let me just sum it up by saying a non-Catholic young mother was with her very ill baby, born with an "incurable" syndrome, in the hospital late one evening when a nun came into the room, introducing herself as "Sister Kate." The nun reassured the mother about the child, made the sign of the cross on the baby's forehead, then vanished. No one around the hospital had seen or knew of a nun in that particular habit. When the young mother confided in her Catholic mother-in-law over the phone about the eerie experience, they were both awed to learn that the mother-in-law was invoking the prayers of Mother Katharine, a dead American heiress turned nun (canonized in 2000) who used her fortune to aid those least apt to get a piece of the American dream—African and Native Americans. Until her death at age ninety-six, Mother Drexel wore the type of religious costume—now outdated for most nuns—sported by this "Sister Kate."

I could go on. But hopefully you see that the hallucination theory leaves a lot of loose ends that can all be accounted for if dead saints do simply appear when and where God wills.

Since my research has convinced me this is fact, the remainder of the book in your hands consists of what those who experienced them believe genuine after-death appearances of saints who come—like St. Frances of Rome and St. John Bosco—to help the living. To offer you the utmost in immediacy, I limit myself, with the occasional exception, to saints no further back from the present moment than the nineteenth and twentieth centuries.

Included will be a number of instances where dead saints have appeared to living ones. What these incidents offer, besides their intrinsic interest, is the greatest possible proof that this is an authentic event.

To be frank, lots of nuts—not all of them in mental hospitals by any means—think they have been visited by supernatural visitors. As I write this I have before me an article from a respected magazine in which artist Howard Finster claims his art grows out of visits "from the dead and from extraterrestrial life forms." Whatever you make of Finster, think for a moment of all the articles in those checkout stand newspapers full of outrageous claims. A researcher on the track of those who claim visits by dead saints must tread warily.

It certainly helps if a *bona fide* saint, while alive, leaves a testimony that she saw a dead saint because: 1) I know from her well-plumbed life before she was given the honor of official sainthood that she wasn't crazy. 2) I know she understood and valued truth so she was not a spoofer like those people who, for fun, created the famous photo of the Loch Ness monster, nor a con artist who stages after-death appearances for money and power.[12] 3) I know she knew enough theology to distinguish the dead from angels. There *are* faiths, such as Hinduism, that believe the dead become angels. But as a Christian, I go by the teachings of the Bible and tradition that an angel is a spiritual being created by God. To help someone out an angel may *pose* as a person,[13] but *always as a stranger or new acquaintance,* never as someone who is now dead. 4) I know she had enough humility to seek wise guidance as to whether this was, indeed, a real event, an imaginary one, or an illusion created by forces of darkness. Even saints can imagine something, one reason the Catholic Church will publicly canonize someone for heroic virtue, but never insist anyone believe in that saint's visions. And just about all the world's spiritual traditions join Christians in recognizing that "dark apparitions" do take place. Both St. Frances de Sales and Blessed Marie of the Incarnation (Madame Acarie) were involved with a young woman called Nicole Tavernier, who had many visions of Jesus. It was only as she became more and more self-enamored ("Look at me, how special I am since Jesus Himself delights in my company") that the saints saw clearly that while her visions and other gifts were real, they were not from God. "Jesus" was a dark spirit, playing on Nicole's egocentricity to incite her to the pride that turns one away from God in self-absorption.[14] 5) Finally, I know the saint has both the perspective and guidance not to go off half-cocked with interpretation of any visit.

If that last criterion sounds unimportant, consider how many cults, spiritual movements, and religions are rooted in a claimed visit by a spiritual being—whether perceived as outer space aliens, angels, or the dead. If you envision the world spiritual scene minus most groups that began this way, our human family would be free of many of its more bizarre theologies. Such "visits" then, judged by the aftereffects, may have more to do with forces of division than God.

If a Catholic saint appears to a nonsaint, while we cannot use the five helps to authenticity listed above, the fact that the "visitor" is a saint still provides more help at verification than if the visitor is nonholy. This is because if an individual claims to have seen a saint, the dead saint's postulator (if the Cause for beatification or canonization is still underway) will be interested in this claim—not with wide-eyed wonder or publicity in mind, but with a critical eye. Whether it is just seeing a dead saint or being healed while seeing a dead saint that is claimed, the claimant will be discreetly or forthrightly scrutinized. The more claimed, the more scrutiny.

Even after a saint is canonized, those associated with them continue to be concerned that claims are truthful. Knowing the topic of this book, Father Charles Fehrenbach of the Shrine of St. John Neumann in Philadelphia, for example, keeps an eye out for people who believe long-dead St. John Neumann has appeared to them. But while Father Fehrenbach passes on some information as worth an interview, he mentions other claims he "thinks we should pass on." Similarly you will note in the chapter on soldiers who claimed they were saved by appearances of St. Therese of Lisieux on the battle-field that the nuns receiving those testimonies requested corroborating material *on the credibility of the individual making the claim.* In their archives testimonies from those competent to make judgments about the claimant's honesty and stability rest alongside the testimony by the witnesses. Does that make you feel more assured in reading them? It did me.

Fortunately when an after-death appearance is really God-sent, there are aftereffects that speak for its authenticity. Called "the fruits of the apparition," especially where the claimant's honesty and stability are established, one or more of these is a powerful confidence booster that something supernatural may really be happening here. These possible fruits are:

1. *Physical healing* from serious, even terminal, illness.
2. *Emotional healing,* often with visible, radical personality improvement, particularly in behavior toward others.
3. *Spiritual growth* from egotism into greater other-centeredness. (Padre Pio, for example, judged by his directors one who authentically saw the dead, thought ever less about himself and more of God, urgently desiring that God, not Padre Pio, be known and loved, no matter what sacrifices this demanded. Contrast Padre Pio's humble gratitude for God's favors with Nicole Tavernier.)
4. *Rescue in a life-threatening situation,* either from natural peril such as fire or flood, man-made peril such as enemy troops, or self-destruction.
5. *New direction in life,* particularly regarding vocation.
6. *New acceptance*—even joy—in carrying some burden (including illness or facing one's own or others' deaths).
7. *Resolution* of spiritual questions or difficulties.

Having said all this, do you expect me to insist that no one has ever been fooled in this area? If so, think again. Even the nuns who amassed the many hundreds of testimonies on after-death appearances of St. Therese, Carmelites proficient at sniffing out the phony or sick might have been fooled now and then, in theory anyway. If some testimony in this book puts your hackles up, dismiss it. I have certainly dismissed from these pages incidents that smelled funny to me. My belief is there are enough instances in this book that even if you judge that one (or even several) got by the saint who experienced it, his counselors' discernment of it, the saint's postulator (who went over that saint's life with a fine-tooth comb), later guardians of his earthly affairs (like Father Fehrenbach), and/or my journalist's nose for the phony, the sheer bulk of the testimonies left will compel you to take the idea of after-death appearances of the holy seriously.

Endnotes

1. June 1994.
2. For more on how an individual reaches this point see my book *The Sanctified Body.*
3. Something apparently inherited like an ear for music.
4. *To Dwell in Peace*, Harper & Row, 1987.
5. Jean Glockler, Holy Family Preservation Society's administrative director, verified the statues' origin, citing parish archive material.
6. Quoting his article "The Transfiguration and Religious Experience," in September 1994, *Pecos Benedictine Bulletin.*
7. See her letter in *Bulletin of The Institute of Noetic Sciences*, Winter 1992–93.
8. According to a letter by his friend George Richmond.
9. That Daisy was not simply losing touch with reality is clear from the things she told visitors, things she could not have known, about their dead loved ones of whom she had never heard but now "saw" in heaven.
10. An entire book reports on this phenomenon: *The Holy Souls* by Pio's associate Alessio Parente, O.F.M. Cap.

11. See *Hasidic Tales of the Holocaust* by survivor Yaffa Eliach and this book's chapter 22.
12. See *The Psychic Mafia,* Dell, 1976, by reformed con artist M. Lamar Keene.
13. See the book of *Tobit* in the Bible for example.
14. Material on Nicole Tavernier comes from Dom Antoine Marie of Abbaye Saint-Joseph de Clairval who cites *Works* of St. Francis de Sales, vol. 18, p.325, Abbe Trochu's life of the saint, and J.B. Boucher's *Life of Bl. Mary of the Incarnation.*

Chapter Two

HOW DO THE DEAD COME BACK?

How do dead saints appear to the living? Appearances take many forms: a slim hand reaching out of dazzling light, a person who strides into the room, a figure briefly glimpsed when half-asleep, a stylized tableau, even disembodied voices, or appearances in dreams—where the telltale aftereffects follow, all may legitimately be called after-death appearances. And so may even odder things. For instance, since their deaths, many believe Therese of Lisieux and Padre Pio have made their presence known by wonderful odors.

As for the condition of the recipient of an apparition, appearances may be: 1) to a person fully awake and going about normal activity; 2) to a person in various altered states of consciousness, from those semiconscious states which immediately precede and follow sleep, to the deep relaxation of profound prayer, on into ecstasy and rapture; or, lastly, 3) to a person who is fully asleep. You note I do not mention someone attending a séance or otherwise "summoning up" the dead. Trying to call up a dead saint is a waste of time. Saints are God's servants and respond to only one call—God's.[1]

That dream appearances *are* included in these pages may make some readers shake their heads. Yet dream appearances by spiritual messengers are accepted in most spiritual traditions. Among the Greeks in the classical, pre-Christian era, for instance, devout individuals used to spend the night in certain healing shrines when ill, hoping for the gods to appear to them in a dream and heal them. At times healings did take place.

Among so-called primitive peoples, healers, such as the African shaman Dorcas studied by anthropologist Adrian K. Boshier, report being commissioned for their work through dreams. Dorcas' shaman grandfather appeared repeatedly in her dreams, cajoling and scolding until she accepted her calling. Both Judaic and Christian scriptures, too, are rich in numinous, guiding dreams (not often specifically after-death appearances, however).

Of course, important dreams arising from one's own unconscious change lives dramatically. Jung and other recent thinkers[2] address the question of when a dream ceases to be from the personal unconscious, coming instead from God, by proposing the depths of the mind open out into numinous realities ("the kingdom of Heaven is within you"). While I don't pretend to know the workings of God, it could be from these regions that God's messengers enter dreams.

Without ranking them in any way, here are forms of after-death appearances I've come across, including a couple too nebulous to play a role in this book. For each, adequately detailed examples will be given, mingling the holy and nonholy for again, I am not saying only saints make these appearances. Although admittedly in my years of research I've never found certain modes associated with nonsaints, such as the with-apparently-good reason named odor of *sanctity!*

1. *Seeing when one is fully awake something that seems perfectly "real,"* such as Caryll Houselander's experience on the bus. Caryll also "spoke of meeting St. Jude on a Chelsea street." When she was six, Adrienne von Speyr met St. Ignatius Loyola on the streets of her hometown, La Chaux-de-Fonds, Switzerland. The saint took the little Protestant child by the hand. He was "small, appeared poor, and limped a bit," Adrienne said.

2. *Seeing the dead in some obviously otherworldly, but still visual form.* This could be a tableau, such as the one by the gable wall of a small, rural parish church in Knock, Ireland, where Sts. John the Evangelist and Joseph appeared with angels, accompanying the Virgin Mary and Jesus (seen as the Lamb of God) on August 21, 1879. Over a dozen witnesses agreed the figures were "full and round as if they had a body and life," but they did not speak and no one felt impelled to speak to them. When a seventy-five-year-old woman tried to kiss the feet of Mary, she found nothing in her embrace but the wall.

   This type of appearance can include movement. For instance, early one morning in November 1917, fifteen-year-old Adrienne von Speyr saw in a golden light above her bed the Virgin Mary accompanied by angels and saints, among whom she recognized her old friend St. Ignatius. While Adrienne reported "the whole thing had the character of a picture," she also noted that the angels changed places and the golden light faded, letting the features of the Virgin Mary become more prominent.[3]

Two other forms this type of appearance can take: saints have appeared in an effulgence of light so great it is almost blinding, or they may appear in a kind of mental vision that only one or some of a number present see. For example, on July 17, 1918, sixteen-year-old Caryll Houselander was sent out by her mother to buy potatoes for dinner. Hurrying along a London street, she suddenly saw "wiping out the sky" what she later learned was a Russian-style icon of Christ as a crucified King, his face filled with grief and "ineffable love." That night or the next, on the same corner, Caryll saw newspapers reporting the assassination of Czar Nicholas II (canonized many years later in 2000 by his Russian Orthodox church). The face in the newspaper was the same as the crucified Christ the King of her vision. Speaking of her visions of this type, Caryll explains, "What do I mean by saying that I 'saw'? Frankly, in the ordinary way I did not *see* anything at all; at least I did not see ... with my eyes. I saw ... *with my mind* ... in a way that is unforgettable, though in fact it was something suddenly *known,* rather than seen. But it was known not as one knows something through learning about it, but simply by *seeing it* ... 'alive' and 'unforgettable.'" Theologians who distinguish among various types of visions call this mental vision one of the *least* apt to be hallucinatory.

3. *Seeing the dead in a dream,* like the pediatrician's assistant in the first chapter who dreamed of her dead father. Some canonization miracles involve dying people who saw dead saints in dreams and woke cured.

4. *Seeing the dead while one is in a strongly altered state of consciousness that onlookers can verify.* Such apparitions are often called visions. Mystic stigmatic Therese Neumann of Bavaria often went into medically verifiable ecstasy and saw various saints or the Lord. During this time, Therese was

observed out of touch with the reality around her, while caught up in another reality that usually included the full range of sensory perceptions—sight, hearing, touch, etc. Those present at such moments themselves saw none of what she experienced.

5. *Not only seeing but touching.* Caryll Houselander's dead doctor nudged her in the ribs when he sat down next to her on the bus. Similarly, St. Catherine Laboure rested her hands in the lap of the Blessed Virgin Mary during the two-hour-long conversation they had on June 6, 1830.

6. *Touch may occur alone, sometimes followed by cures.* In 1909 in Glasgow, Scotland, a widow dying of cancer, who was making a novena to Therese of Lisieux for a miracle, woke to feel a hand on her shoulder. That was her sole mystical experience; but the huge tumor was gone.

7. *The odor of sanctity.* Certain saints' visits, such as those of St. Therese or Padre Pio, are often associated with numinous odors. For instance, those with a woman expected to die after an automobile accident smelled a strong, unusual odor that could not be accounted for just before she unexpectedly came out of the coma. They had been asking the prayers of Padre Pio. Of course, if the only indication a dead saint is present is the odor of sanctity, there must be no possible natural source for the perfume and the visit must be followed by some strong "fruit," such as a cure.

8. *Hearing a voice only* (which again obviously must be authenticated by what follows, such as a cure, rescue, etc.). The sound may be heard exteriorly or purely interiorly. Padre Pio, when alive, as I mentioned, used to be visited by many dead people who needed prayer to help them with their after-death growth so they could attain the development necessary for heaven. One time during World War II, the friary had been locked up for the night with the door held in place with its two big iron bars. Yet in the downstairs entrance hall a group was heard shouting "Viva Padre Pio!" The Superior, Padre Raffaele, sent Brother Gerardo, the porter, down to

investigate. But there was no one there and the bars were intact. The next morning Padre Raffaele asked Padre Pio what was going on. The saint explained that a bunch of dead soldiers had come to thank him for his prayers.

9. *A feeling.* Of course, this is very hard to verify if it relates to the invisible presence of a dead saint and, for that reason, I rarely write of such things. But an example that may or may not mean *presence* is the priest's testimony in the *Bulletin* of St. John Neumann's shrine. Tracing his vocation to his visit to the saint's tomb as a youngster, the priest says "I *felt* him urging me on to the priesthood." Note this has been recalled for years as momentous, but for a researcher it is still nebulous.

10. *A knowing or sense of presence.* This occurs in varying degrees, from slightly more than a feeling to something that is kinesthetic. Thus a person making a pilgrimage to places associated with a particular saint can say, "I was never lonely," due to somehow experiencing "the company" of the saint. Episcopal priest Carl E. Buffington Jr. made a special pal of Chris Wright, a young hemophiliac who got AIDS from a tainted transfusion. Chris died in Houston's Hermann Hospital as Rev. Buffington, there with the family, massaged his feet. The next morning Buffington and Chris' father, Weldon Wright, were driving when the car was filled with a joy that "was persistent and overpowering." The Episcopal priest suddenly pictured Chris celebrating and worshiping God. Embarrassed to be so joy-filled, he glanced at Weldon and saw he was filled with this joy, too. "We were graced with a 'knowing,'" writes Buffington in 1992, "that Chris was better than okay."[4] Again, even at this level it is uncertain whether this was the "presence" of the dead boy or some other spiritual touch. During the WWII bombing blitz of London, among the extra jobs Caryll Houselander took on to help others was volunteer work in a London hospital. There one night in the fall of 1940, while Luftwaffe planes spewed death on the city, a friend's dead child gave Caryll the courage to keep up the spirits of patients too ill to move to bomb shelters. Caryll had been

terrified of the screaming bombs until, she says, she "became acutely and *unquestionably* conscious of the personality of a little child of three at my side—the child of a friend whom I never knew, but of whom I had heard constantly from this friend, and to whom I had often prayed." Caryll said that while she did not *see* the child, she felt her presence accompanying her through hospital halls the way one feels the presence of someone beside one in a pitch-black tunnel—a tactile-kinesthetic sensation. A couple days after the bombing attack, Caryll received a letter from the dead child's father, who lived outside London but had heard the deafening barrage. He wrote to say he had prayed to his child, Mary, to stay with Caryll through that terrible night.

11. *No perceptible presence in any way, even feeling, but signs of an extraordinary nature.* Mark Hoyle of Swansea, Massachusetts, is another hemophiliac teenager who died of AIDS in 1986. His father, Jay, in May 1988, was standing at his son's grave, "desperately sad." He said aloud, "Mark, if you can hear me, send a bird to land on your headstone." A bird appeared from nowhere and lit on the stone. "Send another." Immediately a second bird flitted to the tombstone. The dad asked for a third. It, too, came and perched on the headstone. "That's enough," Jay Hoyle said. During the next forty minutes not another bird came anywhere near.[5]

   In another instance where presence may have been indicated by a sign, a father and mother in May 1981 sat by the hospital crib of their unconscious thirteen-month-old child, Darren, who had bacterial meningitis. As the dad was asking the prayers of dead Padre Pio, he later wrote Pio's friary, "all of a sudden my head was lifted towards the ceiling by a strange force under my chin. I saw what seemed like a little blue light no bigger than a flash lightbulb come down from the ceiling very slow[ly].... [Coming] down to the novena leaflet[6] in my hand, it shot in a ball of light from the leaflet into Darren's back." Immediately the child's eyes opened and for the first time in a week he spoke. In a week he was home.

12. *Appearances in or out of dreams where the dead leave something material behind them.* For instance, Mrs. A.D. Allard of Providence, Rhode Island, told a strange experience to a priest named O.A. Boyer. In May 1934, Mrs. Allard had some kind of attack, losing consciousness. The doctor told her family she was dying.

A second doctor, called in, agreed there was no hope. That she was given what were called in 1934 "the last sacraments" testifies to these assessments. Three years earlier a local, French-Canadian Catholic mystic, named Rose Ferron, had given Mrs. Allard's ill daughter Clara, twenty-three, a red relic ribbon when praying for her. Clara was cured, but died fifteen months later of something else in a Rhode Island hospital, at which time the ribbon, which she always wore, was lost.

Now, as Mrs. Allard lay unconscious and dying, she dreamed her dead daughter came to her. The girl had the red ribbon, which she tied around her mother's head, telling her to keep it on for six hours. Mrs. Allard awoke. The ribbon was on her head. She got up—well—and went to assist her own mother on *her* deathbed. Of course someone could have secretly tied a second ribbon on the dying woman and she, feeling this, evoked the dream. Make of it what you will, the strange event is corroborated by witnesses who believed it supernatural.

Padre Pio and other saints left some things behind and carried away others during lifetime bilocations. With that to steady the mind, let me note that Mrs. Allard's experience is not as far as these things can go. On rare occasions, the dead have apparently left behind even more tangible physical souvenirs. At one time there was in Rome quite a collection of such "physical evidence." Believing much of the material questionable, a priest investigated each item. Only a few met his research standard. Among these I mention just two:

- On November 1, 1731, the dead abbot of Mantova, Father Panzini, appeared to Mother Chiara Isabella Fornari, prioress of the Clarisse Sisters of Todi, Italy. He left the imprint of his left hand and a crude cross burned into the wood of her worktable.

- In 1798, a Madame Leleux appeared to her son twenty-seven years after her death, begging him to change his ways. She touched his sleeve and left on it the scorch mark of her hand. Whatever anyone thinks of this melodramatic gesture, the son changed completely, living the rest of his life "in a holy manner" and even founding a religious order.

The table, sleeve, and a few other items some consider "proof" of after-death appearances may be seen in the annex of the Sacro Cuore del Suffragio Church on the Lungotevere Prati in Rome.

Having given you a dozen forms that after-death appearances may take, let me immediately add that these modes may be mixed, like the experience of Bavarian visionary Therese Neumann, who heard a voice that said it would help her sit up as she saw an effulgent light from which came an arm. The hand took hold of Therese and pulled her up in her sickbed. She was healed.

Regarding apparitions where a saint simply walks into a room, people ask, "Is that a real body?" Or assume a saint appearing in a dream is unequivocally nonmaterial. As always, reality is messier. The official miracle in the 1926 beatification of St. Jeanne Antide Thouret, for instance, involved a hospitalized child with cancer. Asleep and dreaming, she had a tactile sensation of someone pulling a tumor out of her body, and woke—screaming with the pain—healed. With such things going on, I can only quote my betters. St. Paul, whose own mission began when the risen Christ appeared to him, wrote, "there are heavenly bodies and earthly bodies." When teenage St. Dominic Savio appeared after his death to his mentor, St. John Bosco, reaching out to detain his spiritual son, Bosco grasped only air.

"Are you bodily here?" he asked.

Dominic answered, "This is how it is. If in God's Providence, someone dead has to appear to someone alive, he's seen in his normal bodily appearance and distinguishing characteristics. He cannot be bodily touched, however, since he is pure spirit. He ... [will only be] reunited with his [physical] body at the resurrection."

Catholic theologians state that because one is a saint does not mean every opinion, even those quoted from a dead saint, is either correct or covers all aspects of a truth. For one thing, reducing supernatural realities (the dead appear to communicate wordlessly, heart to heart) to language is tricky; for another, even saints do not always grasp everything said to them, and can innocently make mistakes. In this case, Dominic has not explained situations (or Bosco did not retain what he said) where a dead individual appears and, touched, is apparently just as much warm flesh as anyone alive. Christian mystical theologians add that such a warm body, too, just like one that proves only "air" when grasped, is not the original body.

Saints[7] even in warm, fleshly bodies, theologians continue, are actually in a temporary body that replicates—but is not the body that lies in the grave or has already returned to ashes or dust.

In the testimonies of individuals who believe they have experienced visits by dead saints acting as God's messengers, besides the various aftereffects (see chapter 1), these witnesses display something called *ineffability*—that is, the absolute conviction that this experience is utterly true, *totally real*, completely authentic. Thus they will underline, as Caryll Houselander did in speaking of the presence of the dead child during the Blitz, that the dead individual was *unquestionably* present. Or humbly admit, like Padre Pio, that the more he tries at times to consider that his visions may not be real, the more struck he is by their reality. Mystical theologians, who find this an important component of genuine spiritual experiences, say it comes from suddenly knowing something, no longer just intellectually, but experientially.

Unfortunately the fact that I can swear that something is absolutely true may prove nothing to you; after all, I could be sincerely wrong. All that can be said is those who believe they have been visited by a dead person often declare themselves willing to die rather than term the experience a fantasy, hallucination, or other product of their own mind.

An example: the three peasant children ages seven to ten who, in 1917, at Fatima, Portugal, claimed they were visited first by their country's angel and then by the Mother of Jesus. An embarrassment to their two sets of parents—only one of the four adults believed them, while the ten-year-old's mother beat her child repeatedly for "those dreadful lies you're telling"—the threesome's anxiety escalated to terror when they were kidnapped by an angry administrator determined to stamp out "senseless superstition." Each child was led separately before this ferocious, looming figure, who snarled down from his adult height that the only hope of avoiding immediate death by being boiled in oil was to admit their talk of apparitions of the Virgin Mary was a lie. Each terrified child, shown a dreadful, leering "executioner" who rubbed his hands, gleefully assuring the interrogator that the oil was "plenty hot," though fainting with terror, sobbed, "Kill me, but I saw her."

Endnotes

1. Séance transcripts are so boring, banal, and sans "soul food," I theorize because, to use St. John Vianney's term, only the spiritually undeveloped "low souls," if any, can be summoned up. Of course, most séances are cons (see endnote 12, chapter 1). And both Protestant and Catholic saints have found (see Appendix) dark spirits posing as the dead in séances they investigated.

2. See, for instance, Morton T. Kelsey's *Dreams: A Way to Listen to God*, Paulist Press, 1978.

3. That Adrienne did not just have a vivid dream is apparent from the fruits, including a permanent wound under her left breast left as a sign of her mysterious connection to God.

4. May-June issue, *Acts 29*, Episcopal Renewal magazine.

5. May 13, 1990 interview with Hoyle by Tricia Hempel in *Our Sunday Visitor* newspaper.

6. For explanation of novenas, see endnote 4, prologue.

7. The Virgin Mary and Elijah would be exceptions, assumed and snatched up to heaven respectively in their physical bodies.

Chapter Three

THERESE AT WAR

August 1914
France

Parents, wives, and sweethearts of able-bodied young men look glum. Only forty-four years ago—in the 1870 Franco-Prussian conflict—German sabers cut down the flower of France's manhood. Now France and Germany are at war again.

Soon, it appears, the Germans will again take Paris. When that happened in the earlier war, the Virgin Mary appeared at Pontmain, promising, "My Son will show mercy." An unexpected peace followed.

This time the Virgin will not show herself publicly in France. And the new conflict will be much worse. Over four times as long, it will engulf so many nations it becomes the first "world" war—hell on earth to many. A so-called lost generation, by the war's end, will be shorn of all faith in supernatural realities. But the same war will bring others closer to God. They see his hand everywhere. To many of them, bands of angels and human "angels of mercy"—alive and dead—are at work as God's messengers, on bloody battlefields and in pain-wracked hospital wards.

Among the human angels of mercy between 1914 and 1918, none is more prominent than a young dead woman. Only twenty-four at her death just seventeen years before 1914, this Sister Therese was a Carmelite nun in the provincial town of Lisieux. In her after-death appearances she often is recognized, or that it was indeed she verified by the pictures of her in wide circulation.

Judging by the letters of thanks and petition pouring into the Lisieux Carmel as 1914 starts, Sister Therese is already known all over the world for favors like the one in 1910 to the old fellow in the Lisieux Home for the Aged. His tongue eaten away by gangrene, Ferdinand Aubry listened as the home's doctor patiently explained that, sadly, the human body cannot regrow the missing parts of a tongue. An ignorant old man who lacked proper respect for medical knowledge, Aubry obstinately turned to the dead Carmelite, who had already obtained his cure from gangrene. He *told her* he needed a new, *whole* tongue.

And she went to the Father and got one for him.

The flabbergasted physician himself formally attested to that, attaching a photo of Ferdinand Aubry's restored appendage to the declaration.

No wonder that four years and hundreds of such favors later, wives and mothers press tiny relics or medals of the dead nun on men departing for the front or urge soldiers to "put yourself under Sister Therese's protection."

Devout young men—there were still some in 1914 France—accept with alacrity. Another type grimaces and squirms, accepting the medal or relic only as a sop to some teary-eyed woman. Let the women and old men weep, they think. Their new uniforms sharply creased and boots still shiny, this breed is impatient for action and glory.

Let us follow some of these strong young men, the devout and the less devout—Paul-Henri Joly, Joseph Martin, Roger Lefebvre, Auguste Cousinard, and nameless others—into bloody battles and rat- and rain-filled, disease-breeding trenches. We go with them through their letters or more formal documents.

When the individual is not named, it is not because the reports are unsigned but because, in a more spiritually modest age, the individual has asked the nuns at Lisieux in whose archives I worked to make public only his initials. Such accounts, too, I assure you, come with corroborating statements or attestations of good character.

From the archives, here is only the barest sampling of the World War I work done by the messenger of God's mercy today known as *Saint* Therese of Lisieux. Yet this was no Joan of Arc, but a quiet, cloistered nun who had no visions, healed no sick, and passed without a ripple through her world. After living quietly, barely out of her teens, she died quietly. If people knew about her, it was because as she was being eaten up by tuberculosis, she had written a couple of notebooks about her very unsensational inner life at the request of two of her blood sisters.[1] The focus of that life had been a gospel-based reliance on God's boundless love and mercy and her burning desire to respond with love and surrender. That Therese of the Child Jesus should be noticed at all, let alone that it was she to whom millions were turning as a great intercessor, is as flabbergasting as Ferdinand Aubry's tongue!

But on to the testimonies. To make space for more incidents, character references and other attestations of veracity that accompany these reports are omitted. If you believe that mentally balanced young men of good character and sincere devotion to the truth may still hallucinate in extreme situations, what good are such documents? Conversely, if you believe that by diverse—and sometimes unusual—means God responds to the prayers of people in crisis, then to you what others call a "hallucination" may well be "of God."

Speaking of God, some of you will have problems with God sending a warning to one soldier so he can save his life by killing another, or with the fact that a praying soldier may still *die. I* can only remind you that we all die and, from God's view, that may be as much gain as loss. Therese, for instance, lived only twenty-four years and found greater work and happiness after death. As to why one man is tagged to die young and another live long, that lies in realms I cannot chart, but I can affirm my own belief that the one who dies is as much in God's love and mercy as the one who lives.

Let us now flip our mental calendars back to October 1917. The Second Company of the Sixth Regiment of Sharpshooters from Tlemcen, Algeria, a group often used as scouts, is in possession of one sector of the woods of Courrieres and Bezonvaux, facing the enemy lines. This is a perilous position, as the sharpshooters are sixty meters (more than two hundred feet) in advance of their own main line.

Taking up this position on October 3, for the next eleven days, one Sergeant Diez notes, they are "exposed daily to intense bombardments and to poison gas attacks." That Diez himself has been spared to this point he attributes to the intercession of the Servant of God, Sister Therese.

At the moment the squad the sergeant commands has a highly important assignment: They are guarding the opening of the communications trench that leads over those sixty meters back to the French lines.

Surprise German attacks on other squads under cover of darkness in these woods have been frequent. Diez remarks to his lieutenant that they should expect one day to be awakened by such an attack themselves. Now let me translate from his French the sergeant's own account:

On October 14, about 3:30 in the morning, I was at my habitual place, [guarding the head of the communications trench] when I was dazzled suddenly by a great silvery light. To my stupefaction, before my eyes I saw Sister Therese [looking] like an angel. She went from left to right, holding in her hand a very short saber. I felt no choice. I had to follow her and found myself facing a swamp that served as a kind of natural defense for us and was situated behind our lines. [Watching her] I rubbed my eyes, I pinched myself, and I said to myself, "You're not sleeping. What does this mean?" I went back and took up my former position only to see with astonishment the vision repeated.

Then I understood that this was a warning from heaven. At that, I didn't lose a minute; I made a rapid inspection all around my post and I pulled the pins of my grenades[2] to be ready for a sudden attack.

After this, I checked my watch and saw it was 4:00, just the time when the Germans usually made their surprise attacks. I didn't say anything to my men—except to keep a good watch and be on the alert.

Not two minutes later, I was surveying the side of the swamp when I saw a creeping shadow, then two, then three [approaching] Indian file. At first I thought it was the arrival of the patrol, which was to relieve my men and so I called out to them in Arabic "Who goes there?" For answer I heard the bursting of a grenade, which, happily, fell outside the parapet of the trench. "Here's the Boches!" I cried.

[I ordered] "Fire, gunners!" and immediately I threw three grenades. Then I saw a German advancing on me. Without hesitation, with my automatic pistol, I killed him cleanly and he fell at my feet.

From then on, it was a heavy exchange of grenades and nearly hand-to-hand combat. I didn't lose courage, I kept ordering my men, "Fire!" even though I was soon wounded. Then the enemy fire stopped. Not being able to do more [due to the wounds], I sat down on the side of the parapet. Everything was calm again. I was relieved by my superior officer, who arrived to reinforce us, then evacuated to the aid station with four of my wounded men.

I didn't forget to thank my Protectress, whose celestial warning had saved us....

The sergeant was hale and hearty, and had pinched himself and rubbed his eyes to be sure he was awake at the time he believes he saw Therese.

Another soldier was in a military hospital, with pneumonia, about to become one of many WWI soldiers who died of disease from long days and nights in sodden, rat-infested trenches. Knowing his condition was worsening, in these preantibiotic days when pneumonia even in the young was often fatal, the soldier asked to see a priest to receive the last rites. Told there was no priest around, the very ill young man turned to God and Sister Therese, asking for the grace to "suffer patiently." Taking up his testimony:

The following day (Jan. 6, 1917) my fever went still higher. I was suffocating little by little [as his lungs filled up].... In a crisis ... my body stiffening and trembling ... at moments I couldn't breathe at all. But I didn't lose consciousness. I recall very well that a Red Cross nurse took my pulse and then, turning away from [my bed], said to her buddies who were playing cards in the hall, "He's dying."

But all at once, I perceived in front of my bed a great light: at first I thought it was my feebleness that was giving me vision trouble, but when the night had completely come, I saw the same light and then the little Sister Therese with a halo. I experienced a happiness that I could never express. I don't hesitate to say that this night was the most painful of my life due to the great [physical] sufferings I endured, yet at the same time it was also the happiest time of my life.

Having written this shortly after his unexpected recovery, the soldier fulfilled a promise to come to Carmel and share more details of his extraordinary night. Leaving out some repetitious material about his pneumonia, his fuller report continues, as the mother superior took it down on April 10, 1917:

After the bitter crisis of which he spoke in his letter, he found he could sit up in his bed, aided he felt by an invisible hand; by himself, he was absolutely incapable of making such an effort. He saw above the bed a great brightness, then that disappeared and Sister Therese showed herself to him. She had a halo but he only saw her within a mysterious penumbra, which still did not keep him from perfectly recognizing her [from the image he had been given by a fellow soldier]. He experienced a joy beyond telling.

Vehemently he insisted that he would gladly suffer again—even if it should be for years—as he suffered that night to pass again a night like that one.

"But did you see Sister Therese all night then?" the mother superior asked.

"Yes, from ten hours in the evening to five hours in the morning, and she instructed me the entire time. We conversed together. I had doubts on the truths of religion and she made me understand everything; it was as if she taught me catechism. She said to me that this life is nothing, that there is a better and that anything that one has to endure on earth is nothing in comparison to the happiness with which we will be recompensed. As I was very chagrined at how I had fallen away from God, she consoled me, assuring me that if I had repented and had confidence [in God] the good God would forget everything, and I could still be pleasing to Him. She brought to mind several saints who had been sinners before they became holy.... Everything [she said] was as if the words were imprinted on the very depths of my heart. I felt a courage to suffer no matter what in this life, as long as I could serve the good God and go with Him to Heaven. And this courage has not left me. I'm returning to the front Friday and I'll be in the front lines but that doesn't make me at all afraid. If I die I'll go to Heaven, Sister Therese promised me.

Carmelites are not credulous. The mother superior suggested that perhaps all this took place in a dream. Certainly anyone who has ever been very sick with a high fever knows what strange "fever dreams" one can have. But the soldier insisted that during his night with Therese he was sitting up in his bed, just as completely awake as now talking to the mother superior. Then he confided that he had wished very much to die that night. But Therese had replied "No," with a shake of her head.

Fever dream or a visit by a messenger of God, in the morning the young soldier was out of danger, fever fallen and drowning lungs drained so he could breathe freely once more—in a word, "convalescent" rather than "dying," as the nurse had pronounced.

His body saved, the soldier's spirit had been remade, too. Before leaving the Carmel, he remarked that if anyone mocked religion, he now knew how to respond. Not that it mattered to him what others thought. He understood, he said, that if he told his fellow soldiers about his experience, they wouldn't believe him. But "when you've had this kind of experience yourself," he added, "I assure you, one believes and would never forget it if one lived to be a hundred!"

There are many other "change of heart" reports. Take macho Auguste Cousinard, who hadn't darkened the door of a church since his first communion. His wife begged him to prepare his soul for war by going to confession. Not he! He would have been ashamed before the world, he said later (though he squirmingly accepted a relic). That stance lasted until he was pinned down under artillery fire in a trench at Gotha (near Reims), where he began to think about his wife and children, and called out to Therese. In his words:

Hardly had I completed this prayer than I saw a cloud open up and the visage of the saint appear against a blue sky. I thought I was hallucinating. I rubbed my eyes, several times ... [but] the face became ever clearer and more resplendent.... How beautiful her eyes were as she appeared to look up to heaven in prayer!

After this visible prayer of the dead nun for him, Cousinard not only left the trench alive: he no longer cared what other macho-types think of men who go to confession. Putting what he told the Carmelites personally into an official written testimony, Cousinard adds he will be proud to have his name made public.

I think also of the sublieutenant who didn't believe in God until a sweet voice three times said, "Get out of there!" in ever more urgent tones. He left his position just seconds before a shell wiped it off the map. His loved ones had been praying for Therese's intercession and she had not only saved his life but opened the eyes of his soul, he said, on November 30, 1919, when he left his Cross of the Legion of Honor at Carmel in thanksgiving.

A soldier of the 229th Infantry Regiment, Paul-Henri Joly, described as "a very serious fellow," writes from Abbeville on September 14, 1916. By this time the war has gone on two full years. From its beginning Joly has carried on his person, "with the most profound respect" a precious relic of Therese. He has had "some bad moments" so far, he writes, but "always my little saint shows up to save me."

That he means this literally is clear in the long letter, picked up as he begins to speak of the fighting in the Somme, where Germany lost five hundred thousand men and the Allies, six hundred thousand:

Among the dangers I've run, above all I have to mention this July 30th and the days following. We were then in the Somme ordered to reinforce the first line of troops. I was serving as liaison and we were under terrible bombardments during four long days as we successfully repulsed enemy attacks. One evening, August 2, we were cowering—a whole half platoon—around a tumble-down cottage that was being blown to pieces under the rain of machine-gun fire.

Fellow soldier and Christian Brother Jean-Baptiste Vidal gives more detail:

The Germans [were] bombard[ing] us with an unbelievable violence and the roof timbers of our shelter were going to pieces. We were all squatting in the dust, covered with phosphorescent sulphur; one could have said our clothes were on fire.

Things were so bad that Vidal says, "I encouraged my poor comrades to make an act of contrition, then we said the rosary together." Returning to Joly's account:

... praying in our peril, which was ever mounting, ... my buddies were saying the rosary. As for me, while praying to the Virgin, I invoked Sister Therese, calling her with confidence to our help. Suddenly, about eleven o'clock, while the battle raged on, I saw her standing at the foot of a machine gun that was there. She looked at me and blessed us all. Then she said to me, smiling, "Don't fear anything. I've come here to protect you."

Terribly moved, I called to my companions, "I see Sister Therese. She's [over] there! We are saved!" And, in fact, not a single one of us was hit and we soon emerged from that dreadful situation healthy and safe.

Something else in Jean-Baptiste Vidal's corroborating report cannot be omitted. The Christian brother writes that while the men said their acts of contrition and rosary,

Paul Joly was calling out in a loud voice invocations to Sister Therese when around eleven o'clock in the middle of the din of shells, I heard him cry out, "I see Sister Therese; we are saved!"

Writing books, I've run into the phenomenon of those who seek notoriety by claiming association with dead heroes or saints. So for those of you, like me, whose cynical bent makes them wonder if soldiers sometimes made this stuff up after the fact, note that Joly does not confide *after the battle* that he saw Therese. There he is, calling out *aloud* to her in front of the whole half platoon as hell rages around them! Truly no spiritual shrinking violet, when he sees her he bellows that out, too! Some people may still claim he hallucinated, but no one can claim he made this up after the battle. And those who believe his testimony can point to an impressive fact: after he claims Therese blessed all the men, not a single one was lost or even hurt in a situation where troops who had been in combat for two years estimated the situation called for acts of contrition in preparation for death.

Joly made it home alive, writing the sisters at the end of the four terrible years, "she is always with me."

Another soldier sends a report "from the front" on September 10, 1916. His perilous job at dreadful Verdun was to carry messages by bicycle without protective escort. On May 22, as the French took the fort of Souville from the Germans, he found himself under enemy bombardment. It was tough going between shell holes and debris from destroyed buildings until he got to the main road to Verdun. Hope that conditions would be better on the main artery died at once. An easy artillery target, this road was under such heavy machine-gun fire that, "enveloped in an ocean of lead and fire," as he puts it, the bicyclist felt himself lost and wailed, "Come here, Sister Therese!"

Immediately, he says, she appeared, "all luminous and aureoled." She held up an arm and the enemy fire stopped instantly. The grateful cyclist continues, "not a single shell was fired until I had entered [the town of] Verdun."

Those on the home front also felt they had helpful "visits." A Paris doctor and his wife, the Freysselinards, have left their long, written testimony about what happened on July 7, 1918. They had two sons in the war. The elder, a lieutenant, had been missing in action for forty-three days. Like parents immemorial in such a position, they were, as the mother puts it, "in mortal anguish," but the wife clung to hopes for help through Sister Therese.

That morning about 9:00 A.M., her husband was in the corridor that led from their living quarters to his consultation rooms. He smelled a very agreeable odor there, a mix of roses and violets. But there were no flowers around. Still he attached no importance to this. It was not an olfactory hallucination (if such is possible!) because his wife, discovering her husband sniffing around the hallway, verified the reality of the unseen "bouquet."

An hour later, Madame Freysselinard was in their dining room when she was struck by a wave of fragrance. This seemed to be violets. Again, no flowers were around. She called her husband and they searched among the things there for some natural explanation, but found none. A man of science, Doctor Freysselinard grew disturbed. As for his wife, welling up in her was a growing conviction that Sister Therese was announcing good news regarding their missing son.

"Would you believe in the perfumes of Sister Therese as symbols of her protection of us, if we get good news about our son?" she asked her physician husband.

"Yes, I would," he replied without hesitation.

The following morning the mail brought a letter from the missing son. A prisoner, he was still safe and sound. *He* later told his parents a long, hairy story about his experience on March 13, 1915, near Beausejour (in Champagne), where at only eighteen he won the Cross of the Legion of Honor for his valor. That blood-soaked morning, sixty men were cut down all around him in one of those "over the top" attacks on the German trenches. He alone was left alive. Pinned down in a shell crater only twenty meters from the enemy, he later told his parents that he did not cease to invoke Sister Therese's help, from eleven in the morning until six in the evening. Only then, in the early dark of that time of year, did he manage to slip away and rejoin the French forces.

Another French family felt that both those at home and their man at the front *saw* Therese in dreams. The wife's testimony, written May 31, 1916, from Bourg-Saint-Andeol in the Ardeche area:

My baby was three years old when he came down with whooping cough [this was May 1915]. I confided him to Sister Therese of the Child Jesus and I began a novena. Now the last night [of the novena] I had particularly asked the saint to watch over my son during his sleep. In the morning, when he woke up he said to me he had a dream. He said, "I saw a beautiful lady, dressed like a nun; she was sitting near my bed smiling at me." When I showed him the image of Therese, my little angel at once recognized her as "the beautiful lady." And, moreover, his illness was aborted immediately.

By a coincidence which is, at the least strange, my husband who was in service at the same date and therefore far away, unaware of all this, on the same night also had a mysterious dream. He saw himself in great danger of losing his life, when at his side a young Sister appeared with angelic features and the dress of a Carmelite nun. She stopped her horse, which was ready to dash away, and raised her hand in a gesture of protection. This dream turned out to be a prophetic sign. I attribute to the humble saint my dear [husband]'s return [alive] from Verdun and his having been protected when he took part in the artillery struggle at the Argonne.[3]

This is all very pious and nice about the husband's dream. But it becomes much more intriguing by a detail the husband adds. After getting home safe and sound, he authored what the Carmelites call "a philosophical book" on the war. A lawyer—therefore by profession one engaged in looking at events critically with an eye for "evidence"—the ex-soldier wrote that sometime after his unusual dream he arrived at Verdun, which was to be one of the horrific battle sites of the war, where French casualties were 540,000 and German, 430,000.

At once he recognized certain prominent landmarks, such as the old fortress, not because he had been to Verdun before, but because *he had seen them in the mysterious dream.* Later he ran into a picture of this Sister Therese so many people were talking about and recognized the nun of his dream. You make of it what you will, of course, but this family had no doubt: God had somehow used the dead nun to shepherd the husband safely home.

This lawyer-soldier was a rational man. I cannot make the same claim for Roger Lefebvre, a twenty-nine-year-old roofer from Saint-Aubin-du-Thenney in the Eure. But see what you think ...

In spite of being the father of a family, Lefebvre was off to war in its first month (August 1914) as a soldier in the 224th Infantry. He carried a little relic of the saint and said he "invoked her at least twenty times a day."

On September 17 at La Neuville near Reims, about 4:30 in the afternoon on a battlefield where enemy shells seemed to be falling as thick and fast as raindrops, Lefebvre was hit six times. His head was wounded, as were his face and thigh. Several veins in his neck were cut and he had a terrible gash on one foot. Collapsing, he lost consciousness.

He came to in the freshness of the evening bathed in his own blood, which continued to flow from his open wounds. He felt weak to the point of death. He cried out "with ardent faith" to the one whose relic he carried and whose protection he was constantly invoking: "My Sister Therese, come help me!" At once he saw right by him the "little saint," as so many of these soldiers call Therese. Beautiful and gazing on him compassionately, she held in one hand a large crucifix. With the other she grasped the dying soldier's right arm and lifted him to his feet. Then she smiled at him and disappeared.

A hallucination by a man whose mind is naturally fuzzy as he slowly bleeds to death?

Maybe.

But the blood had stopped flowing "as if a celestial hand had bandaged the wounds." And he who had been weak to the point of death a moment earlier now "no longer felt the least suffering." He *ran* to the first aid post, which was four hundred meters (a quarter mile) off the battlefield.

Although he had to have more than one operation on his foot, he never suffered after seeing Therese. When he visited the fellow Carmelites of Therese, completely hale, on February 4, 1915, he confided, "my heart still leaps when I think about it."

He was heading back to the front with aplomb, he told the mother superior, telling everyone what had happened and certain that "Sister Therese, who protected me once, will protect me always."

Perhaps because of such perfect faith in the intercessory power of one of his saints, God just couldn't let him down. At any rate, there is more to the military history of Roger Lefebvre, who on December 15, 1915, was returned to the front lines, this time with the 24th Infantry. Still alive and uninjured, he returned to Lisieux (he visited Therese's tomb on every leave) in May 1916.

On this visit he told his dead friend that he had only one fear: being taken prisoner. He asked her for death over captivity. Then rethinking this request, he modified it: If he had to be taken captive, let her see that he was severely wounded so he would have a good chance to be repatriated.

This prayer is why I make no claim for the clear thinking of Roger Lefebvre! Be careful what you pray for, they say. In his mysterious wisdom, perhaps sometimes shaking his head, God answers some pretty dumb prayers. Just a month after this one, on June 1, 1916, Roger Lefebvre found himself surrounded by Germans, the French badly outnumbered. Something seemed to command him to resist, he reported later, although surrender seemed the way to go. So ignoring the enemy's offer to let them throw down their arms, he and several buddies went on fighting. He later wrote:

After no more than a minute, two of us were dead and I had taken a bullet in the right shoulder. But I threw two more grenades with my left hand. Then I was hit again in the right side and the left shoulder and I fell on my back, unable to move. Soon my last comrade went down while the captain, refusing to surrender, was killed at point-blank range. A German soldier aimed at my cheek to finish me off, but an officer stopped his arm. I stayed thus for three days, stretched out, unable to move. It was clear that my holy Protectress did not abandon me. I lay in a narrow trench, which the enemy was advancing, taking ground. Past me marched hundreds of German soldiers in solid ranks but not a single one walked on me. All of them, on the contrary, at risk of being killed, stepped up on the edge of the sloping [trench wall] in order not to touch me.

However I was at the end of my strength and suffering so much that the third day I asked Sister Therese to free me from my pains by letting me die. At that very instant, without my being able to explain how, because by myself I couldn't move at all, I found myself suddenly upright in the trench and able to walk.

[I set out to seek help and] I ran into some Germans and one of them gave me some coffee to drink, rather than giving it to a wounded

German, who wasn't very happy about that but the officer who was giving me the drink told him that I was more badly wounded than he and he only got water. Then they sent me on to an aid station. Since the bombardment by our artillery continued without letup as we tried to regain the ground we had lost, when I got to the post, a German military chaplain there had me get down, with a warning which deeply touched me, into a nearby shell crater. Eventually they took me to the rear to a hospital because I was so severely wounded and I was operated on at once. After that they transported me to a hospital in Stuttgart where I found some good nuns who took care of me very well.

I stayed in Germany until December 15 when I was repatriated via Switzerland as a severely wounded, although I was almost completely recovered. It was there that I knew the soldier Latus. [He tells of teaching this comrade to seek the intercession of Therese and how Latus, very ill with tuberculosis, was suddenly cured, and mentions another very sick soldier for whom he prayed that he either be cured or die happy and how Therese, he believes—before Lefebvre knew of the death—came via the lovely odors which often signal her favors, to report that the soldier died happy.]

Because Lefebvre could not use his right hand, and had developed abscesses on his right elbow following surgery on it, he began to make novenas to Therese. Nine faith-testing novenas later, nothing. But Lefebvre did not give up, and after novena number ten the abscesses were cured and he regained the use of his right hand. From then on, he had no more suffering.

Home for good, he returned to Lisieux at various times, wife and children in tow. There the Carmelite nuns noted with pleasure that, despite his stiff elbow, he was able to return to his physically demanding prewar job as a roofer.

Another soldier's special relationship with Sister Therese preceded the war by several years. He put himself under her care when he marched to war with the Sixth Company of the 150th Infantry regiment. And he felt she "often" protected him on the battlefield. Then, having almost made it unscathed to war's end, on July 15, 1918, at Bois-le-Roi (some kilometers from Reims) during a great allied offensive drive, he was "mortally wounded in the chest." Picked up by compassionate Germans, he was evacuated with them as they kept retreating until he finally arrived, in skeletal state, at a German camp from where he was sent to a hospital at Germersheim.

Finding himself in moral and physical distress over the "hopeless" prognosis of the doctors, it was natural to him to turn to his longtime spiritual friend. In spite of the doctors' grim prediction, he suddenly overflowed with joy and confidence when he heard Therese tell him, "You shall see your parents and your dear France again!"

He returned home alive and well and was studying for the priesthood when he wrote the nuns.

But what about the hundreds of thousands of soldiers who died? Near-death-experience studies indicate God does not let anyone die alone. To some are sent angels. For instance, in a May 1994 television special on angels, a medical doctor who was stabbed more than thirteen times and left to die reports angelic beings surrounded him with love and light until he was discovered and restored from clinical death. Many other testimonies imply that God often sends to the dying person loved ones who have gone before them. To some WWI soldiers it appears God sent Therese.

Here are two other suggestive events. First, military chaplain Father Chevalier of the 24th Infantry Regiment gives a detailed account of the death of a corporal, Robert Pochet, at which Chevalier assisted. Pochet believed Therese was helping him die. And when he asked her to lessen his suffering, the chaplain observed his pain lessened. Was this a coincidence? Or was Therese there? The busy chaplain took the time to write the nuns in belief that *somehow* Therese helped Pochet. But he does not report the dying man *saw* her.

There is also this incident:

Carmelite nuns have personal friends just like everyone else. A family that included a married sister and a single one were "well known" at the Lisieux Carmel. The two sisters put one's strange experience in writing for the nuns so it could become part of the official data being accumulated on Therese.

Among the two women's friends was another family with a twenty-one year-old son. "A true apostle" in his work for an organization called Catholic Youth, the young man went to war[4] and the sisters joined his family in calling upon Sister Therese to watch over him. Everyone waited for news from the new soldier, but none came.

Just after eleven in the morning on August 24, 1914—so the war had barely broken out—the unmarried sister was in her room when she suddenly saw a mysterious spectacle, distinctly, but as if at some little distance. Their soldier friend was in the arms of Sister Therese. Celestially beautiful and smiling, with one hand the little saint supported the young man; with the other, she presented to him a palm. Both of them were looking upwards, with expressions that were radiant and triumphant.

The brief vision was deeply moving. At its end, the viewer ran to tell her sister, adding that she was certain their young friend was dead or going to die. The sister who claimed to have just seen Therese was believed because, as her sibling later wrote, she was known to be neither given to flights of imagination nor a seeker of "spiritual experiences."

And most importantly, the vision proved prophetic: Two weeks later, on September 7, the young man was killed at La Fere Champenoise, struck by a bullet in his forehead, after he had just been cited for heroism and promoted to sergeant on the battlefield.

Why did Therese appear this way? Perhaps because by her "visit" to a family friend, as the sister writes, the devastated father found comfort and even a sort of sorrowful pride in what the vision said about his only child.

Did God use Therese to help only the French? Since they turned in droves to this descendant of French military men, obviously God could use Therese mightily in France. German soldiers undoubtedly didn't as often ask the prayers of an "enemy" nun. And if they did, they could hardly send a letter to her French Carmel. Nor were French wartime publications—even by Carmelites—going to headline Therese's miracles for the other side's soldiers! If Therese appeared to any Germans on the battlefield then, it was out of the public eye. But there is some evidence that, as you would expect, when

German military men asked for her help, she responded.

For instance, before the war the father of Bavarian mystic Therese Neumann obtained some relics of Sister Therese for his family. When the devout Catholic tailor was drafted, his wife and children asked Therese to bring Ferdinand Neumann safely home. The Bavarian soldier did not see the saint but he came home alive and well.

Moreover, on March 14, 1980, an elderly Sister of Divine Providence in Alsace wrote Carmel regarding various favors to her family. Among these is a "miracle" in favor of her uncle Joseph Mathis de Housch, a WWI noncommissioned officer in the Germany Army. On the battlefield, Mathis saw every one of his men fall. Shot in the lungs himself, he fell to his knees invoking Sister Therese and somehow survived. Nine years after the war, he died a saintly death looking at an image of Therese, his last words of her.

I've chuckled over one German wartime cure of a civilian. Therese made an after-death appearance *immediately* after a mother superior stood over the dying individual—a young nun—and taunted that, since they were at war, French Therese probably wouldn't help a German!

Because it is so brief, a letter the Carmel received in 1919 can close this limited sampling of Therese's work during WWI. Let it stand for the appearances Therese made on non-French battlefields. Carmillo Cessi writes October 20, 1919, from Bassanello in Italy.[5]

> I'm carrying out the sacred duty of a grateful soul. For a long time my family has had great devotion to Sister Therese of the Child Jesus; but when war came, our confidence and our supplications [for her prayers] redoubled. My wife and my children never quit praying for her intercession and I felt myself protected on thousands of different occasions, above all at Mt. Frikoptel, at Mezli, and particularly at Mont Noir. At this last I believed I would fall on the battlefield but at the moment of most greatest peril, I heard the voice of "Little Therese." She told me that she was watching over me and that I had nothing to fear. This sort of thing one doesn't forget. Being now returned to my loved ones, I want to give great witness to my gratitude to the saint of miracles.

He closes with his permission to publish "these humble lines" with his signature. "The saint of miracles," he calls her. Doesn't sound exaggerated to me.

Endnotes

1. Now known as *The Story of a Soul*, Therese's autobiography has sold many millions and appears in every major world language.
2. According to an interview by A.J. Daly with Master Sergeant Soister of the U.S. Marine Corps Weapon Training Battalion, these must be the type that have both a safety lock and the pin, which once pulled, permits the grenade to explode. Diez obviously has pulled only the safety lock!
3. A huge battle area of the 1918 period as the Allies pressed Germany's Siegfried Defense Line with horrible casualties on both sides.
4. Some readers may wonder that an "apostle" was not a pacifist. In WWI for good Catholics going to war when called was part of "rendering to Caesar." This does not mean the Church favored the war. Pius X tried desperately to stop WWI and died, grief-stricken, ten days after it began.
5. Italy was by treaty allied to Germany, then switched sides and fought with the Allies.

Chapter Four

ALL THE WAY FROM HEAVEN

On July 5, 1969, a Syrian Melkite-rite Catholic from Brooklyn named Margaret (at their request, these are not their real names) married a widower with a half-grown daughter. Eddie, a Maronite-rite Catholic born November 2, 1919, in Beirut, Lebanon, had been in the United States twenty years, since arriving as a seaman. Four years after their marriage, Margaret became pregnant. This was great news but, at the same time, Eddie became ill. His stomach bothering him more and more, X rays finally diagnosed an ulcer.

On March 24, 1974, as her stepdaughter began college, Margaret gave birth to a girl. Her joy mingled with anxiety because the infant had a heart murmur.[1] As she lay in her hospital bed, recuperating from a cesarean delivery, Margaret was most worried, however, about Eddie. In spite of treatment for his ulcer, each week he grew paler and felt worse. Picking up her bedside phone, she called for the results of his new X rays. As she feared, the news was not good: Eddie's condition had only grown more serious.

Over the next six months, although he followed the doctor's orders, Eddie continued to get sicker. When baby Katie was six months old, a third set of X rays revealed that Eddie—now a very sickly color from losing blood internally—was "much worse."

"You'd better see a surgeon," the couple was told.

On September 17, at the Methodist Hospital in Brooklyn, the surgeon operated. As Eddie was coming out of the anesthesia, the grave-faced physician's words to the patient's wife made it, Margaret still recalls with emotion, "the worst day of my life."

There was no ulcer.

Instead a five-pound tumor had been removed, along with a full three-quarters of Eddie's stomach. Worse, Dr. A., the surgeon, told Margaret with regret, this was no benign tumor, but "cancer in a very advanced stage."

Although he tried to encourage her to have faith in God, medically speaking the surgeon could give his patient's wife no hope of Eddie's recovery. His doctors would try a ten-week course of strong chemotherapy, but without any real hope. Due to the misdiagnosis, things had simply gone too far.

Eddie, an outgoing man who had a positive attitude toward life, took the news much better than she did, Margaret recalls. He wasted no energy on anger over the misdiagnosis, nor did he become depressed. Accepting his situation, he said, "If it's not my time, I won't go." And he was able to smile and joke with the hospital staff.

Margaret was devastated. At only three weeks old, she had lost her mother. Her father had died before her marriage and her stepmother soon after. Now she was about to lose her husband. And just as Margaret never knew her mother, their little Katie would never know her dad.

Back when she was only fourteen, Margaret had been a patient in St. Anthony's Hospital, run by the Franciscan Sisters of the Poor. She became friends with one of the nuns she believed a holy person. Now Margaret shot off a letter to this Sister Fidentiana, desperately begging prayers for Eddie.

Sister Fidentiana wrote back an encouraging letter: the foundress of the Franciscan Sisters of the Poor, Mother Frances Schervier (pronounced SHURE VER) had been beatified that April. "Let's ask her prayers," she suggested, enclosing a novena booklet. Also in the nun's letter was a little touch relic[2] of the tenderhearted Frances, who had died in 1876.

Margaret began the novena and tucked the relic in her husband's shirt pocket, telling him to keep it with him at all times. The Brooklyn housewife knew nothing of Blessed Frances. But she was to learn that this frail, nineteenth-century nun, fiercely protective of the poor and needy, had "done it all."

A sampling:

- Mother Frances took in thirty prostitutes who wanted to turn their lives around, despite flak from "good people" over a nun associating with "fallen women."

- In an epidemic, she bent consolingly over dozens of smallpox victims, nursing them devotedly with complete disregard for her own rotten health. Amazingly, she survived unscathed.
- Often she companioned the condemned, whom she did not send off with pious blessings, but accompanied all the way to the end—serene, indomitable—staying close enough that the axe severing her spiritual charges' heads more than once spattered her brown habit with their blood.

Along the way, the daughter of well-to-do Germans reluctantly founded a religious order, collected a Cross of Merit from the King of Prussia for her nursing work on bloody battlefields (her nuns did the same in the United States' Civil War), built hospitals and homes for her beloved poor, and, as the vice-postulator of her cause wrote, "mothered all alike"—including Protestants and Jews—"without distinction and without letup."

Margaret learned that Mother Frances had been to the United States twice, where in five years her sisters, sent as missionaries, had spread out from their first assignment under the bishop of Cincinnati into Kentucky, Indiana, Illinois, and New Jersey. Maybe she had even passed through Brooklyn!

Eddie had never heard of Mother Schervier either. But he is from a devout family in Beirut, where a sister is a nun. As a child he experienced what he believes a dramatic rescue by his guardian angel: as he began to slip into a deep trench, invisible hands grasped him under his armpits, hauling him back, to the gasps of astonished onlookers. He knew what God can do.

Not a reader, he never read nor joined Margaret in using the novena booklet, nor did he look at the relic she transferred each day to the pocket of his next shirt. But he assured his wife, "I'm praying to that nun from the Bronx." By which he meant Blessed Frances, who was actually from an area that at one point belonged to France—her town then called Aix-la-Chapelle—and today, as part of Germany, is known as Aachen. Eddie referred to Blessed Frances as "the nun from the Bronx" because he has no memory for names but he knew her order has a hospital and home for the aged there—a place named for Frances.

The ten weeks of daily chemotherapy was tough. Eddie says in an understatement, "It made me very tired. I didn't have the energy to walk." Yet Margaret points out her husband still insisted on climbing on the treatment table himself to spare the nurses' backs.

In his formal testimony he writes: "I finished the treatments on December 5. On Saturday, December 7, I was too tired to get out of bed and I had severe chills. I was due back at work on Monday the 9th, but my wife begged me to wait till January, hoping I would have my strength [back]...."

That Sunday, December 8 (for Catholics the Feast of the Immaculate Conception), Eddie managed to drag himself to a special mass for the sick of their parish. He stood the whole time in the back of the church because it "was all old ladies" going up to be blessed and that made him feel out of place. Without receiving a blessing, he returned home, "completely exhausted." Margaret pleaded with him again not to try to work the next day. But with the quiet heroism of the world's working men with families to support, he intended to try. His testimony continues:

That night I went to bed about 10:00 P.M. My wife turned out the light. I turned on my right side. The room was pitch-dark. I saw a nun kneeling next to me, her elbow resting on the bed. There was a white arch around her face with a black veil. I lifted myself up to get a closer look at her eyes. The closer I got the deeper her eyes went. I saw her habit was brown. Her stockings and shoes were black. Her shoes had laces with a rounded toe and her foot was small. She told me to relax. She had a round metal box in her hand. She opened it and took a small host, rectangular shaped with a green cross in the center. She told me to open my mouth and placed the host on my tongue. Then she asked me where I had my operation. I unbuttoned my pajama and pointed to my stomach. She took another host and made the sign of the cross on my stomach. I felt it on my skin (later he says this sensation was of being touched with something sharp as she blessed his flesh with the rim of the wafer.) She said, "You're cured" and disappeared. I went into deep sleep. The next morning I woke up feeling well. I put in a full day's work with no tiredness and have since felt very well.

To this written testimony he can add a few more details: as she rested her arm on his bed, his visitor knelt on one knee with the other leg stretched out behind her. When she put the host on his tongue he felt it but it disappeared— absorbed mystically, somehow, as in certain saints' communions—without his swallowing. The sick man saw the nun's clothing very clearly, but her body was somewhat hazy, the flesh slightly blurred. The eyes, for instance, which drew him in "deeper and deeper," he can fix at no particular color.

Perhaps because he went into such a deep sleep, when the alarm went off at 5:30 the next morning, although excited to feel well, Eddie did not immediately recall the nun's visit. He rushed off to work to Margaret's final plea, "Please if you don't feel well, come home early."

Through all ten weeks of her husband's radiation Margaret had been fervently asking Mother Frances to beg God for "a sign that Eddie would be cured." On the previous day, knowing he was determined to try to work the next day, she had prayed especially hard for a sign—above all, for the sake of their six-month-old baby.

Still when Eddie left for work his wife was sadly sure—after all, he'd been exhausted just standing up in church the day before—he'd never finish his workday. Not in the physically demanding job of a truck driver who lifts heavy loads in and out of his truck and does a lot of walking besides. That particular day, Eddie did even more walking than usual, covering the whole length of the pier at Port Elizabeth in New Jersey. Yet he felt equal to everything.

When he came home after a full day's work they discussed with joy how well he felt—he wasn't even tired. Margaret recalls, "I was so happy I told him how hard I'd had been praying for a sign."

That triggered his memory.

"You know, I saw a nun," he replied.

"What do you mean, you saw a nun!" Margaret exclaimed.

Then he told her about the sister who had knelt by their bed the past night. When he described the nun's clothing, Margaret ran for the novena booklet. She placed the picture of Mother Frances before him.

"That's her exactly!" he said.

His wife searched for another explanation. "Maybe you saw her picture on the relic?" Mary Ann suggested.

Eddie shook his head. "No, you put it in my pocket and I never took it out. I just prayed to her."

Later it was realized that in his careful description of Mother Frances and her clothing, Eddie also detailed the stockings and shoes, *which do not show in the novena picture.* And one of the nuns, Sister Rose Margaret, confirmed, "yes, Mother Frances did have a small foot."

Dr. A., Eddie's surgeon, is a Syrian Orthodox believer. When he began his professional career he was moved by a portrait of Mother Frances and asked the saint to help him succeed in his practice. Gratefully Margaret says the surgeon tried to give his patients hope, reminding her and Eddie that whatever the situation, humanly speaking, regarding the cancer, they should remember Christ said: faith moves mountains.

Now they came back to this "believing" doctor—Eddie alive and bursting with good health—for a six months' checkup. Her husband's surgeon told Margaret that for Eddie to even be alive, let alone well, six months after surgery had bared his desperate condition, was astounding. "That's a miracle!" he said.

The sisters were interested, too—to a point. Because it costs money for doctor's fees to pursue the detailed medical investigation by specialists that can lead to an officially designated miracle, money they believe is better spent on the poor, the sisters are opting not to pursue canonization for Blessed Frances. "That's how she'd want it," they feel. And Eddie's cure might not make it as a canonization miracle because for some people—not Dr. A., who saw his interior—the radiation treatments could get credit for the cure.

Assume for a second that radiation did cure Eddie, against all medical expectations when others in his condition died whether they had radiation or not. God's role is in no way negated. Blessed Frances announced a cure; she did not go into how God was bringing it about. Those who believe that "radiation" is not the best answer to "What cured Eddie?" point to something significant: Eddie went to bed on December 8 in sad shape and woke up December 9—a dead nun having dropped in on him during the night—a new man.

The recipient of a miracle (official or not), as he sees it, Eddie asked God to let him see Blessed Frances one more time. On July 13, 1975, that prayer was answered. The saint came to his bedroom again. This time the red-cross emblem on her brown robe stood out more, perhaps in deference to those nuns who worried that he had not noticed it before. But she did not touch or speak to him. He saw her in a static type of vision, sitting in a chair next to a table on which were three books.

In her own life Mother Frances, whose frailty never kept her from arduous work for the sick, was miraculously cured of asthma at Lourdes (the French healing shrine inaugurated by appearances of Jesus' Mother to St. Bernadette Soubirous). From the time of her asthma cure, Mother Frances placed her congregation under the protection of the Blessed Virgin Mary. Perhaps that is why when Frances came to Eddie a second time, apparently wanting, saint-like, to get the spotlight off herself, it focused on the one who brought *her* miracle. At any rate, Blessed Frances disappeared and Eddie saw the Mother of Jesus, radiant with a heavenly crown, in garments of white and blue. Mary blessed the Lebanese-born truck driver. Then she, too, disappeared.

Twenty years have passed. Eddie is now seventy-five and retired. From the night of Blessed Frances' first appearance, he has been able to eat anything he wants. At first, with only a quarter-stomach left, he could take in only small quantities at one time, but gradually his stomach expanded until even quantity was no longer a problem.

When he became anemic again some years ago, doctors, suspicious of malignancy, immediately ran a new series of gastrointestinal tests. These showed some intestinal bleeding—but in a perfectly normal, cancer-free intestinal tract. Eddie was having a problem common among those who take aspirin for arthritis, one solved by simply laying off aspirin.

Margaret was not surprised. As she says, when a saint comes all the way from heaven to say, "You're cured," you can count on it.

Endnotes

1. Several years later rediagnosed as a more serious defect, the problem was then successfully corrected by surgery.

2. A first-class relic is something like the bone of a saint; a second-class relic is something like the saint's shirt or prayerbook; a third-class or touch relic is something touched to a saint's relics. In the book of Acts, we see people healed through this type of item, called in many translations "a prayer cloth."

Chapter Five

"CHEER UP, LADY!"

Vacationing in St. Louis when she was sixteen, Mary Wilson, a Presbyterian born in 1846, attended her first mass at St. Louis University, a Jesuit-run institution. Miss Wilson was swept away spiritually and, after a series of instructions, was received into the Catholic Church on May 2, 1862.

Not a tolerant century, her Protestant family immediately disowned the young woman just as Catholics would have done had matters been reversed. Four years later, Mary joined the Society of the Sacred Heart, the order founded by St. Madeleine Sophie Barat. Because the young convert's health was poor, her superiors wanted to spare her harsh climates and snowy winters. They sent her briefly to a convent north of New Orleans, then to their Academy of the Sacred Heart (still operating today) at Grand Couteau in southern Louisiana, where the climate is optimal.

On the evening before she graduated, so to speak, from postulant (the first phase of becoming a nun) to novice, Mary collapsed with terrible pains in her side, vomiting blood. Had guilt over her family's rejection caused her body to prevent her taking an even more definitive step away from them? Possibly. In a similar situation, Venerable Francis Libermann developed epilepsy. Whatever the cause, it appeared Mary Wilson was not long for the world. A Jesuit from the local college was hastily summoned. Hurrying over, he gave Mary the final rites. To the surprise of all, for the next month the dying twenty-year-old lingered, neither dead nor alive.

Since, however precariously, she clung to life, the sisters decided to make a novena to Jesuit Blessed John Berchmans. Why they picked Berchmans I don't know. But in choosing him, they were asking the prayers of a young man born in Flanders in 1599—that is, 265 years earlier—who had studied there, then in Rome in order to be ordained a Jesuit priest. Known for cheerful humility,

71

holiness, and trying to do little things as perfectly as possible for God's sake, Berchmans never reached his goal. Still a Jesuit novice he died on August 13, 1621, at twenty, the same age that Mary lay dying at in 1866, 245 years later.

Death, it is wisely said, is the final healing. As the novena progressed it seemed it would help Mary out of her sufferings by helping her die. For during the last three days of the nine-day prayer, her limbs grew cold while her tongue swelled and bled until she could hardly talk. Again she received the last rites.

Somehow she managed to communicate that she was asking Blessed Berchmans "for a little relief and health. Otherwise, that he give me patience to the end. I am resigned." Left alone at one point, she lay a holy card[1] of Berchmans across her mouth, whispering, "If you can work miracles, I wish you would do something for me."

"Open your mouth," came a young man's voice.

She obeyed and felt a finger on her swollen, bloody tongue. The same voice continued, "You'll get the desired (novice's) dress. Be faithful. Have confidence. Fear not."

Opening her eyes, Mary Wilson saw a luminous figure by her bedside. "Is it Blessed Berchmans?" she croaked.

"Yes," he answered. "I come by the order of God. Your sufferings are over."

Later that same day when her Superior came in, Mary astounded her by speaking clearly. The astonished Mother Martinez was afraid this improvement was the somewhat common respite before a dying person's final moments. So she ordered Mary to stay in bed. The postulant obeyed. But when a sister came to redo her bed that evening, the patient could stand it no longer: With a chair for a partner, Mary danced merrily round the infirmary.

When physician Edward Millard made his daily call the next morning, Mary Wilson opened the door. He almost fainted, the account says, and was teased by Mother Martinez that they better get him a chair before he keeled over.

Recognizing the magnitude of what had taken place, formal documents were drawn up with depositions from all the witnesses. Mary Wilson, of course, had to write her testimony, too. Perhaps because she had been so ill she was very concerned about whether her report was totally accurate. Berchmans reappeared at this point to the healthy young woman and assured her she had everything right. He also told her that just as he had died before he completed his novice period, so would she.

The documents, which included not only medical records but the depositions of thirteen people who had been involved, were sent by the Archbishop of New Orleans to Rome, where the miracle, accepted as genuine, was used for the canonization of John Berchmans in 1888.

As for Mary Wilson, after some months of a healthy, happy, fervent novitiate, on the Eve of the Feast of the Assumption (August 14) she suffered a stroke. At her death three days later, observers believed (although they saw nothing) that Blessed John Berchmans came a third time to assist her.

Today on the Academy's second floor a shrine open to the public marks the spot where a young man, dead almost three hundred years, brought God's healing to a young American woman in a nation that didn't exist when he left this life.

This chapter is a sampling of cases like Mary's where people with serious ailments were cured, they believe, through the prayer intercession of a dead saint—who actually showed up to announce the cure or trigger it with a compassionate touch or word. Some of these people believe the healing brought them through the saint was imposed from without by God's "fiat"; others would say the sight of the dead saint, in God's design, set off the body's inner healing powers in a sudden mega-explosion. But all cured credit God as the source.

For greater immediacy, all cures are from the last 135 years. Moreover, the first cure—that of Mary Wilson—does double duty: It also stands for hundreds of dead saints *who died longer ago than the past 175 years,* the limits of this book, but who are still appearing as God's messengers.

Maria Marazzi was born in the middle of the nineteenth century in Castel Gandolfo, the little Italian town where Catholic popes retreat from Rome's summer heat. Gazing at their newborn, Maria's parents noted with concern a wen on the baby's right eyebrow. This proved so large as the child grew that she could not see out of that eye. Surgery for such things was so crude at the time that the little girl's mother could not bear to subject Maria to that possible remedy. So the child lived, essentially one-eyed, until she was five.

Then her mother took Maria on a pilgrimage to the tomb of a dead priest in Albano. During his lifetime, Father Gaspar del Bufalo was used by God in astounding ways: whether preaching on a crowded plaza while straightening out individual souls in the confessional (bilocation at its highest form), converting armed thugs sent to kill him, or drinking poison without harm. That until his death in 1837 he worked miracles and healed the sick—both the physically and mentally ill—goes almost without saying.

Now as the disfigured little girl peered with her one usable eye at the marble tomb, into her half-range of vision came a priest dressed in a rose-colored chasuble.[2] Walking up to the child, he suddenly bent to touch the grotesque wen with his right hand. Dizzily, little Maria suddenly saw the world out of two eyes. But there was no priest there. He had vanished—apparently carrying the wen with him. For it, too, was gone.

Ecstatically, the mother and child returned to Castel Gandolfo, where the parish priest, who had known Father Gaspar personally, interrogated the little girl about the appearance of the priest who had touched her. Ingenuously, the child—who had never seen Gaspar—described him feature by feature.

Another healing visit by this wonder-worker took place in 1861, also at Father Gaspar's tomb in Albano. Clementina Masini was a local woman who had an absolutely terrible problem: chronic suppurating peritonitis aggravated by a purulent cyst, which perforated the wall of her abdomen and her intestines. The doctors of the day did not even have an antibiotic to offer her and could only sadly diagnose her situation as "incurable."

Clementina Masini turned to God. She witnessed:

I went to the tomb of the Venerable (Gaspar) and from the heart I recommended myself to him. Night and day I prayed without losing faith. During the night of January 21 (1861) while I was lying in my bed, Venerable Father Gaspar del Bufalo appeared to me.

I begged, "My holy advocate, obtain this grace from God for me." He responded, "Cheer up lady. Don't be anxious. Tomorrow morning you'll get up with nothing wrong."

After saying this he lifted the baton he held in his hand and touched the part of my body where the cyst had its mouth. Then he disappeared. After he was gone I said some Our Fathers and Hail Marys in honor of the Venerable. After a little bit, I fell asleep. I got up the next morning about five o'clock cured of all illness.

Clementina Masini went right back to a normal life, which in her case included hard physical labor. The illness never returned.

Sezze, Italy 1934

About seventy-five years after Clementina's cure in the area where a century earlier Father Gaspar broke up gangs of Mafia-type "bandits," Ursula Bono, a widow from the town of Sezze, lies bedridden. Before her malignant abdominal tumor got this bad, she has traveled to Rome to consult cancer specialists there. But the doctors refuse to take the widow's money for surgery since, as they tell her, "yours is a hopeless case."

No longer able to retain any nourishment, Bono is now too weak and wasted to get out of bed. Without hope of a natural cure for their mother, her two daughters—nuns in a group called the Sister Adorers of the Precious Blood—think of a beatified saint, a spiritual friend of theirs, who needs God to speak on his behalf through miracles[3] of canonization calibre. At her daughters' recommendation, Ursula Bono has been asking the intercession of this Blessed Gaspar del Bufalo.

On the night of the twenty-third or twenty-fourth of May, the bedridden, emaciated widow is alone when a priest strides into her room. "Oh, Father Francisco," she says gratefully to her parish priest.

"No, it's not Father Francisco," the priest replies in quite a different voice than she expects. "I'm the Blessed Gaspar."

Ursula Bono bursts into tears. Between her sobs she begs her visitor either to help her get well, or to help her die, "because I can't live any more like this."

"Courage!" encourages the dead saint, placing his hand comfortingly on Ursula's forehead. "In a short time you'll be healed," he promises the terminal patient. Then, without walking, out he disappears.

Does she sleep at once the sleep of a child whose terror is over? Or does the widowed cancer victim weep, laugh, and praise God for joy all night? Such things are missing from the rather clinical report. But it does tell us that the next morning the nuns' dying mother was completely cured except for the kind of weakness associated with fasts of many days. Two or three days of eating normally—which she could do now with grateful gusto—and her strength returned.

Careful palpitation and tests revealed that the big tumor was completely gone. Her doctor's verdict: "This is a true miracle!" Specialists in this type of cancer (whose religion—or lack thereof—is never an issue), asked by the Congregation for the Causes of Saints to examine Mrs. Bono, agreed. The healing is one of the official miracles for Gaspar's 1954 canonization.

In 1927 in Naples, a holy physician, apparently in good health, told his friend he was going to die. A few hours later, he did just that.

During his lifetime, gentle, kindly Dr. Giuseppe Moscati's favorite patients were those too poor to pay for his help. While accepting modest fees at times to maintain their dignity, he was known to tuck money under patients' pillows when no one was looking.

Like spiritual giants of all cultures, this twentieth-century physician understood that physical health is intimately bound up with psycho-spiritual health. He felt he was saving souls by caring for bodies and at the same time he counseled his patients on the importance of having their spiritual life in order to stay healthy—counsel often accepted, not because of the doctor's undisputed brilliance, but because of his kindness. Beatified in 1975 and canonized in 1987, he has appeared to various sufferers as a harbinger of graces and cures.

Costantino Nazzaro, for instance, in 1954, was a mess. Addison's disease had not only made him weak and turned his skin brown, it had atrophied most of his body. In his misery, Nazzaro often asked the selfless, dead physician to pray for him. Then one night Dr. Moscati came to him in a dream. The dead doctor placed his hands, which had comforted so many patients during his lifetime, on the diseased body. Then he gave a verbal prescription: "Return to living peacefully and don't take any more medicine."

A funny dream? Maybe. But Costantino Nazzaro woke up feeling awfully well. Doctors confirmed he was completely healed—and this cure, too, became an official miracle before Giuseppe Moscati's beatification.

In 1951, attorney Francesco Belsani of Naples had some kind of illness that appeared to be influenza. After twenty days of fever he was put on penicillin and given another drug to make him sweat. If anything, he grew worse. With a temperature of 104 degrees, he suffered so many violent coughing spells, accompanied by fierce hiccups, that his heart was eventually affected.

Finally doctors discovered this was not just a flu: Belsani had a cancerous growth near the right lung. Unfortunately, by this time the lawyer was too weak to withstand an operation. During the night of August 23, the sick man entered a crisis where the fever, the coughing, and the hiccupping brought him to the realization he was "in immediate danger of death."

Choking and with his damaged heart pounding furiously, Belsani turned to a tenderhearted pope who died of grief in 1914 as his spiritual children prepared to slaughter each other in WWI. This was Pius X—the first pope to be beatified in centuries. Belsani was devoted to Pius—even had his picture hung over his bed. Now he begged the saint's intercession fervently. To his amazement, Pius X appeared at his bedside. The dead pope clapped his hands, as if giving an order, and told the suffering man that the next day he would be well.

As the early hours of the new day began, without any medical intervention or explanation, Belsani was perfectly cured of cough, hiccups, fever—and the tumor. The cure was accepted by the investigating arm of the Congregation for the Causes of Saints as one of Pius X's formal canonization miracles.

A nun also believes her miracle was delivered by the same dead pope. Daughter of Charity Sister Maria Luisa of Palermo came down in 1952 with meningoencephalomyelitis (deadly meningitis made worse by inflammation of the brain and spinal cord). Her hands and legs were paralyzed, her vision clouded, and there was little hope for her life.

Her fellow Daughters of Charity began a novena to Blessed Pius X. They prayed their hearts out for nine days, and the only result was: not dead but no improvement. Nuns who work with the poor and sick know how to not give up. The Daughters prayed another nine days with the special intention of restoring Sister Maria Luisa's health.

She got worse.

The indomitable nuns were on their third novena and Sister Maria Luisa was continuing to deteriorate. But her faith in Pius' help remained firm. She not only had a framed picture of the white-haired, gentle-faced priest over her bed, she tied an image of him around her neck, a kind of improvised locket photo. Pius X was Sister Maria Luisa's spiritual hero, and she was positive he was going to help her by his prayers.

They say that kind of faith moves God to respond. At any rate on June 18, 1952, still paralyzed and half-blind, Sister Maria Luisa suddenly saw a large Eucharist suspended in midair above a chest near her hospital bed. She reports:

It filled the room with a brilliant light. With indescribable joy I tried to move but couldn't. Then I saw a figure dressed in white moving slowly toward my bed, and I heard a voice,... "Rise, my child, and walk!"

Popes, of course, wear only white. He did not announce he was Pius X, but Sister Maria Luisa had no doubt. She was paralyzed, but her hero, in the presence of God in his effulgent *Shekinah* light and Eucharist, was telling her to get up.

What's paralysis in a moment like that? Get up—how, she admits she has no idea—she did. Dressing herself, she raced down to the nun's chapel, where her appearance stupefied the community, which, seconds later, erupted in cries of joy and thanksgiving. This healing, too, was approved as a formal miracle.

———•◦•———

Not every pope is holy. But in recent times, Catholics have been blessed with pope after pope who truly live as "other Christs." Of no one is this truer than of Pope John XXIII, the rotund, peasant-born Italian who called the Second Vatican Council.

John died soon after that historic event began. Three years later, in 1966, another nun was dying in Naples. Although she was still a young woman, Sister Caterina Capitani's troubles went back to years of internal bleeding from ulcers. As a radical remedy, three-quarters of her stomach and her spleen had been removed in 1965. In May 1966, the quarter stomach she had left developed a peptic ulcer complicated by a fistula, that is, an open, running sore that broke through her abdomen, emitting everything she ate. Her pulse weak, breathing labored, and temperature high, and the fistula making normal nouishment impossible, Sister Caterina was close to death. She received the last rites and, at her request, was left alone in her hospital room to pray. Saying her rosary, she suddenly felt a hand on her ravaged stomach while a man's voice said her name.

The sudden touch and voice frightened her, as she had heard no one enter. Nervously she rolled over and saw Pope John, "smiling and indescribably beautiful," at her side.

"Don't be afraid," he reportedly told her. "It's all over. You're well."

They spoke together for about ten minutes, although much of what was said remains Caterina's secret. But it is known that the dead pope told the nun the fistula would close up and she'd be able to eat anything she wanted.

When he left, the ecstatic sister found her pain, temperature, and all other symptoms gone, too. As for the fistula, a tiny black dot pinpointed where it had been, as if to aid medical men in judging this miracle (a fistula can close, but not instantaneously).

Joyously, Caterina leapt out of bed, calling for something to eat. Within forty-eight hours nourishment restored her strength to the point that she went back to her demanding work as a nurse. From that time on, she has had none of the digestive problems that ought to remain in her case. Her cure was proclaimed the official miracle at John's September 3, 2000, beatification.

———•◦•———

St. Charbel Makhlouf (1828-98) is the first canonized saint of the Maronite rite.[4] In his lifetime he was one of those thousands of quiet monks who pass through the world in great sanctity without being noticed beyond their own monastery or, possibly, the immediate locality. This is no tragedy, for it isn't God's purpose to hold up every saint as an example through beatification and canonization. Some feel God lets the greatest saints—the ones who, as Hasidic Jews put it, "hold the world together"—pass among us completely unknown. But God decided otherwise with Charbel (also sometimes spelled Sharbel).

After his Christmas Eve death in rural Lebanon, so many strange phenomena took place—inexplicable light hovering over the gravesite, the unembalmed body found floating completely incorrupt on a sea of rainwater and mud, a mysterious oil with apparent healing properties that oozed for years from the lifelike corpse, and "miracle cures" that it became obvious God was saying, "Hey there; take some notice of this friend of mine!"[5]

Among many miracles, let me mention two of them where believers claim they saw the saint.

One day in 1937, Alexander Thomas Oubeid was walking with a relative through the Lebanese countryside near his village of Baabdat. Carelessly the other man let a cypress tree branch swing back into Oubeid's face. The retina of one of Oubeid's eyes was torn. In spite of treatment at several hospitals, including American Hospital in Beirut, the retina did not heal. Oubeid could see from that eye only if he was lying down. By 1942, even that much vision was gone. The complete blindness might have been bearable—after all, he had another eye—but he also suffered intermittent pain in the injured area and the misery of migraine headaches.

When it became public knowledge that tremendous healings were taking place at a holy, old monk's tomb, Oubeid's wife made a pilgrimage there. Her husband stayed home but he made four novenas, seeking guidance as to whether he should go to the trouble and extra pain of a trip to the monastery. Nothing he saw as a sign to seek Charbel's intercession occurred until he was given a piece of cotton saturated by the strange, bloody sweat exuded by the saint's incorrupt corpse. He put this on his eye. He slept and dreamed a monk said to him, "If you don't come to me, you won't be content."

That, Oubeid felt, was the sign. He pilgrimaged to Charbel's grave and spent the entire night in the monastery church. The next day he returned home, his condition unchanged. Except for one thing: he had somehow gained great faith in God. Still he only got worse. Due to blocked tear ducts, a large swelling bulged out below the injured eye. The pain became so bad he could neither sleep nor continue his work as an ironsmith. He could only lie around, moaning.

Finally one night, in exhaustion, he slept. Again he dreamed. This time he was back at the monastery delivering some iron but a man threw a piece of it, which hit his bad eye. The pain caused Oubeid to scream and awaken. This is commonplace: we are in some physical distress and fit a dream around it.

He slept once more and dreamed again that he was at the monastery. This time he was drilling through a wall and some of the dust got in his sore eye, paining him badly. He did not wake up this time though. Instead in the dream he went to the monastery well and washed his eye. Then he sat down outside the church.

An old, emaciated monk came along.

"What's wrong?" he asked Oubeid.

The ironsmith explained how the dust had aggravated his injury. The monk fetched some medicine with which to treat the eye.

"You'll be healed," he told Oubeid, "but only after you've suffered severely from the swelling caused by that blocked tear duct." Then he put the medicine in the injured eye. Immediately he disappeared.

Oubeid searched the area fruitlessly. "Did he go away because I did bad work?" the dreamer asked himself. Wondering, he went to look at the wall he was drilling. On it in Syrian letters he saw the words *The Servant of God Charbel.*

Trembling, he awoke and immediately was aware of the swelling, bulging painfully beneath the blocked tear duct. Moved by the numinous dream, he picked up a picture of Charbel and kissed it. Then he drew it across the painful, blind eye. With that simple motion, Oubeid says, his sight returned, after thirteen years.

Doctors may have pursed their lips at tales of dead monks appearing in dreams, but they did know Oubeid was blind—their records were clear on that and on their inability to help—and now here he was before them able to see. After inquiry by two physicians and seven professors from related fields, the cure met all criteria for a miracle and was so proclaimed at the Servant of God's beatification in 1965.

Twelve years later, in 1977, reporter Joe Alex Morris Jr. of the *Los Angeles Times* described a quest for healings through St. Charbel that followed on the heels of his canonization. In the city of Beirut, Morris wrote with dismay of people in a religious frenzy, weeping mothers practically forcing crippled children to walk only to have them fall. The reporter saw others grubbing in the earth for what they called "miraculous incense," which Morris suggested was simply rock impregnated with soap from a defunct factory. Hawkers worked the crowd, selling everything from the "incense" to St. Charbel medals and calendars. Meanwhile in the war-torn country, Christian militia patrolled the site with guns, using this massing of Christians in a Moslem area of the city to establish a new political beachhead.

Reading Morris' article, most *Times'* readers must have concluded that if God exists he would surely have nothing to do with such blatant credulity, downright cruelty, and cynical exploitation. Yet Morris mentions that in one night three miracles were reported at the site. They followed, he said, the event that started the whole circus. Writes the *L.A. Times* reporter:

One evening last week Charbel[6] is said to have appeared before a blind child who was praying to him [for his prayer intercession with God]. The saint reportedly told the child to get incense, to light it and to pray, and that his sight would be restored.

As the story goes, the boy told the saint that he had no money to buy incense, and Charbel told him to go to a place next to the church of the "Sabteeya," as the Seventh-Day Adventists are called here, and to dig there. The boy got his mother and they went to the place, where they dug up a soft stone that smelled like incense and burned like incense.

The boy regained his sight.

Endnotes

1. Usually a pocket-sized picture of the saint with a prayer for his or her intercession on the back.
2. The outer garment shaped rather like a poncho worn by priests. Colors varying with liturgical seasons, rose represents joy.
3. The seven criteria given in more detail in my *Nothing Short of a Miracle* include that the cure be instantaneous, complete, permanent, and not explainable by any medical treatment or other natural cause.
4. The Catholic Church has a number of these ancient rites, with varying liturgical languages, rites, and customs.
5. Seven witnesses left their astounded testimonies of this April 4, 1999, event, four months after Charbel's death. Every other body deposited over many years in the monastery burial cave decomposed rapidly due to the climactic conditions. The supernatural lights which led to the grave being opened were seen by Muslim and Christian laity, including the Prefect of Polic as well as the monks.
6. He spells it Sharbel.

Chapter Six

"I WILL COME DOWN"

Just before TB sent Saint Therese of Lisieux to bed for good, her blood sister Marie, also a Carmelite, came across her little sister forcing her disease-racked body to pace back and forth in the cloister garden.

"Why are you doing that?" Marie cried in exasperation at Therese's obvious exhaustion.

The infirmarian told her to take some exercise, Therese responded. She didn't mind, Therese assured Marie, because "I'm walking for a missionary." She figured, she explained to her sister, that somewhere far from France one of them was exhausted. To lessen his weariness, she was offering God hers.

Marie probably was not surprised. All the Martin family knew how much their youngest member loved the missions. Soon she would beg them not to buy flowers for her coffin, but to send that money—where else?—"to the missions."

Only illness prevented Therese herself from sailing off to Vietnam, where she had volunteered to join an understaffed Carmel. Shortly before she died, someone chuckled, "Those nuns are probably still expecting you." With all mail traveling by boat, undoubtedly they were. But Therese only remarked offhandedly, "Oh well, I'll be with them very soon."

Before Therese's illness, her prioress had assigned the young woman to be the spiritual backup of two missionary priests. Therese had ingenuously turned many of her most monotonous chores—doing laundry or sweeping spider-infested stairs—into prayers for these two men.

In her last letters to them, she promises she'll "return" and "come down," after her death, urging they believe "your little sister will keep her promises." Did the missionaries think these pious platitudes? If so, they misunderstood. Therese staked her whole life on a belief in supernatural realities that would let her work for God even in places far from France, "'til the end of time." Not from megalomania. But because with a loved child's certainty, she trusted heroically that her "immense desires ... to make God loved everywhere" came from God, whose work it would be, therefore, to see them fulfilled.

Can one go too far? Trust God too much? Therese thought not. And God's response to that trust—her greatest claim to fame, when you think about it—indicates she was not simply as naïve as those claims to come back might imply. Therese was barely dead and her unassuming little autobiography (written in obedience to others, not on her initiative) barely in circulation when reports of miracles linked to her began to arrive in the Carmel letter box from places like Madagascar, the East Indies, and China. Soon that mailbox was receiving fifty letters a day, then hundreds. The nuns remembered then that Therese had said another older Carmelite blood sister—her "second mother," Pauline, called Agnes of Jesus in Carmel—"would find consolation through the letter box" and "be kept so busy with me she'll scarcely suffer [grief] at all."

How busy was Agnes of Jesus (and the other Carmelites)? Consider, for only one indication of many that could be given, that in the first twenty-eight years following Therese's death in 1897—that is, just up to her canonization—more than thirty million pictures and seventeen million relics were sent out by the Lisieux Carmel of about twenty nuns in answer to requests from all over the world.

Only thirty years after her death as an unknown, cloistered sister who never put a foot out of Europe, God had used Therese to work so many miracles—including many involving after-death appearances—*in the missions* alone that the pope, by a 1927 Pontifical Decree, made the young nun equal patron (with the great Jesuit missionary St. Francis Xavier) of all missions and missionaries. I like to ponder that as an example of the many things in this world that make sense only when we take supernatural realities into account.

There are statues of St. Therese in most Catholic Eskimo homes. They are there, three-dimensional photos, so to speak, because she is loved for the many proofs of her friendship across snowy wastes and eye-stretching tundras. This friendship began five years *before* Therese was made an official saint.

In 1917, a French Jesuit fifteen years older than Therese was named the first Catholic Bishop of Alaska. By then the entire Catholic world knew God was pouring out favors in missionary lands through Sister Therese. This, no doubt, explains why when one morning as the new bishop, Joseph R. Crimont, ate breakfast and a prune pit slipped into his throat, she came immediately to mind. Choking to death, he called on Sister Therese for help, promising—was he a prophet, too?—to make her patroness of all the Alaska missions, if she would save his life.

When she came to his rescue, Crimont kept his promise.[1] He encouraged others to ask her prayers. When they received cures or other favors, the bishop himself sometimes fired off the reports to Lisieux. And as soon as the Church officially recognized her holiness, he put up a statue of Therese at St. Mary's Mission chapel in Akulurak.

(Statues, by the way, for those who wonder, are a visual prayer aid growing out of a universal human desire: When you love someone you like to have their likeness where it can remind you of them. Museums are full of busts the rich had sculpted of their loved ones; we Catholics do likewise for our saints. Seeing such statues reminds us of those who love us in God and are willing to pray on behalf of anyone—non-Catholic, too—who asks.)

St. Mary's Mission Chapel also served Eskimo children who, leaving their villages to receive an education, boarded at a Catholic school in Akulurak. To one of them Therese appeared two years before Bishop Crimont's death. Chronicled in *The Alaskan Shepherd* (publication of the current bishops of northern Alaska), 1992 September-October issue, here is the eyewitness account of Sister Lucy Daly, O.S.U., who was thirty-seven at the time:

On the feast of St. Therese, October 1st, there was always much celebration ... [including a Mass with] usually twenty-five altar boys. After Mass all pupils and people of the village were invited to go up the river on the large mission boat to pick berries ... on the tundra....

In 1943, the day before the feast ... one of our little girls [in the school], Christine, had a nosebleed. This was not unusual among the

Eskimos, but our Sister Superior thought that, because there was a sheet of ice on the river and it was already cold, Christine had better not go up the river, especially since the Eskimos at that time were susceptible to tuberculosis. Christine did not have the disease, but was susceptible to it.

The warmest place in our cold building was in bed so our Superior told Christine she should stay in bed while the other girls went up the river. This was hard for poor Christine, but she understood. She was eight years old, spoke very little English, had not yet made her first Communion, and was my pupil in second grade.

After returning from berry-picking, the girls went to the dormitory.... As soon as they entered the dormitory, Christine very excitedly called them to her bed. The girls began to talk with great excitement in Eskimo, which I did not understand.

Then the girls began to tell me what Christine had said: that St. Therese had talked to her for a long time and told her that, in honor of the feast, she would bring her to heaven that evening. St. Therese had surely communicated in Eskimo, because Christine knew very little English.

I certainly did not believe the story and neither did our Superior, Mother Mary Louise Ronnenbaum. When she told it to Father Segundo Llorente, S.J., he replied, "All Eskimos have visions of one kind or another."

Since I had charge of the dormitory at that time, I brought up Christine's evening meal. She was very happy and talked enthusiastically, though I did not understand her dialect, having been in Akulurak only two years. When I returned for the tray, she seemed unconscious, with the pallor of death on her face.

I rushed to Mother Superior with word that Christine seemed to be dying. She and Father were both shocked.

That was at 7:00 P.M. Five minutes before midnight, after five hours of suffering, Christine slipped peacefully into the next life. Sister Lucy ends her account by mentioning that the other Eskimo pupils, including the eight-year-old's sister and brother, were filled with joy that "Christine is in heaven."

In 1934, of course, Therese was already official copatroness of the missions.

Let me now back up to give a 'round the world sampling of those early favors that led to this honor.

July 20, 1909, is the date on one letter received at Therese's Carmel from China. A missionary priest writes that a native non-Christian woman dreamed of "a radiant and mysterious being who showed her heaven" without saying a word. Probably because the "being" looked European, the woman rushed to the missionary and described all this in great detail, including the garb of the celestial being.

The missionary was struck that what he was hearing from a Chinese non-Christian, who should know nothing of the details of nun's dress (almost every group of nuns has distinctive garb), was a description of the clothing of the cloistered Carmelites. Digging around, he found a picture of Sister Therese, who in 1909 had been dead only twelve years and was neither beatified nor canonized. He showed the picture to his visitor and she exclaimed at once, "Yes! That's it! That's exactly it! I recognize her!"

Immediately the excited woman arranged both to begin studying Christianity and to put her two children in the missionary's school. The report does not say if she came from another faith tradition or was one of many in every culture who ignore spiritual realities. All that is known is that God called her in this way and she responded.

In Dahomey, Africa, Therese was also at work before official recognition by the Church. In 1915, a young black tradesman in Calvai, who was studying to become a Christian, was severely bitten by a normally tame dog. Adrien Metamehou Quenum was toting his collection of fetishes—rather uneasily, having been threatened that they would take their revenge—determined to "give them up" to Bishop Francis Steinmetz.

Although Metamehou (who went by his middle name) was "built like a Hercules," the dog bite did not heal quickly. Whether because he was the victim of a shaman's curse or his body responded to the thought that he was, something like blood poisoning set in and he began to wither away with ceaseless fever.

One of the missionary priests, Father R.P. Barril, meeting him at the hospital at Godomey in August of that year, decided to interest Sister Therese in Metamehou's case. He gave the young tradesman one of those seventeen million relics of Therese and encouraged him to confidently ask her prayers.

A few days later the sufferer—uncured but still joyful, he insisted, in his new faith—visited Father Barril. The priest had a large picture of Sister Therese on his wall. Metamehou went up to it and, speaking aloud, asked her to obtain his cure.

That was August 29th. When night came, Metamehou—as every night now—tried in vain to sleep. Finally toward four in the morning he fell into a heavy slumber. But this was no ordinary sleep, for the sick man dreamed he saw Jesus Christ, at whose side was the young nun whose prayers he had begged that day. Jesus presented her, radiant and beautiful, to the sick African and she put her hand on his head. "I'm the little Sister Therese of the Child Jesus," she told him, "sent to cure you. I've prayed for you and you are delivered from your trouble."

Speaking his language and using a figure of speech very understandable in his culture, she explained that she had a lot of credit with God she could draw on to help him. She also told Metamehou, "The good God has made me powerful, because, out of love for Him, I knew how to make myself very small."

"Soon," she predicted matter-of-factly, "He's going to glorify me and do still bigger things." Metamehou, of course, was not yet even baptized. His mind did not turn to things like beatification or canonization or, rarest of all, someone being named a universal patron of the Church. But when he repeated her words to Barril and other priests (the bishop and three of his clergy signed the deposition sent to Carmel), beatification did come to their minds. In their deposition they affirmed that Therese was not only "known, loved, and invoked" in Dahomey, but that they were praying "to hasten" her beatification.

Far more important than things like beatifications to young Metamehou was another fact: When Therese's dream visit ended, he woke up filled with joy and perfectly healthy. Was this a case of a mind substituting, as more powerful, one "fetish"—devotion to Jesus and Therese—for an older one? Some nonbelievers may look at it that way. But Metamehou felt he had freed himself from a religion that controls by fear, for something that brought him healing and love.

Baptized that September 8th, he already had "in every room of his house," according to the priests who took down his story (he could only sign with his "X"), "... a portrait of Sister Therese." The joy of his encounter with the dead French Carmelite even drew into her faith Metamehou's mother and entire family—the very people who had heaped curses on his head when he went to "turn in" his fetishes.

From Tunisia came another cure testimony. This was the case of an eleven-year-old girl. In September 1911, she was gravely ill with typhoid fever—a great killer in that era—complicated by deadly peritonitis. The family's doctor had called in other medical men but—remember this is before antibiotics—they could only echo she was "beyond human remedy."

The doctor tried to prepare the child's father that she could not make it through the night. As he struggled to deal with the coming loss of his child, a woman whom the signed testimony identifies only as Madame B., placed a picture of Sister Therese of the Child Jesus near the delirious child, who had recognized no one for two days. The sick girl at once said, "Sister Therese turned her head toward me and smiled at me." Weeping and praying by her daughter's bedside, the mother paid no attention. Who would? The child was delirious.

Then the girl began to look fixedly at a point in the room as if someone were there. Her face expressed astonishment succeeded by joy. After several seconds like this, she spoke again to her mother. This time she said, "Mama, don't cry anymore. Sister Therese has come to cure me. I've seen her; she came near me with angels around her. I was surprised at first but then I felt so happy. I smelled the roses. And I still smell them now."

More delirium? Who can say? But something definitely was happening in the girl's dying body. When the doctor arrived for his next visit, he exclaimed to the parents, "What have you done? It's a miracle to find this child in this state!"

As for the perfume of roses the child claimed to smell, strange as it may seem, it does not appear to have been an olfactory hallucination. A number of people who came to visit the "little miracle child" before she was allowed out of bed sniffed, following a belief of the times, "Roses in here! You'll give the child a headache!" From the strength of the odor, they failed to observe there were no roses in the bedroom, nor in the entire house.

Recovery was quick and permanent. When the formal testimony of this cure, written by "a close friend of the family" (probably the self-effacing Madame B), accompanied by written attestation as to the report's accuracy by the child's father, was submitted to Carmel on April 3, 1913, the only after-effects of the girl's "fatal condition" were gratitude toward God and "tenderness without limits" toward the dead messenger of her cure.

In Khandwa, India, a cure of a woman born Catherine Augert (on October 26, 1888, at Fontcouverte in Savoy, France) was considered so remarkable that the local head of the Church, Bishop Coppel of Nagpour, made a formal inquiry into it and sent a complete account to the Carmelites.

In her late twenties, in 1915, Catherine was a missionary of the Sisters of St. Joseph, renamed Sister Emma.[2] Besides mentioning Sister Emma's qualities that indicate good mental health, the bishop's report states explicitly that she does not have any "sign of eccentricity or nervous symptoms," a formal way of saying that whatever happened to her should not be attributed to her being a nut!

We also have the briefer first-person testimony of Sister Emma herself, which she sent to her brother Joseph, a missionary priest stationed in Fribourg, Switzerland. He contributes his attestation, too.

Reduced to the basics, this is the story: Ever since arriving in 1911 in the portions of India under British administration, Sister Emma's "stomach troubles" that were already evident before she left Europe, grew worse. Various British military doctors—majors and colonels all named in the bishop's report—treated her for what they diagnosed from symptoms as a bad stomach ulcer wherever she was assigned over the next four years. Typical of the treatments—which all failed—was having her eat nothing whatsoever for eight days except for a few spoons of water. This to give the ulcer a chance to heal by eliminating further irritation from digestive acids or from the food itself.

By 1915, in spite of all that medicine could do, the young nun's digestive tract could tolerate only eggs beaten in milk. Then she had to give up the eggs. That April she was in terrible pain and her doctors concluded the ulcer was "incurable." Her order did not give up. They called in a new doctor.

Same verdict.

Things were so bad Sister Emma was hoping to die.

Then on the seventeenth of that month, she was inspired to try a novena for the prayers of Sister Therese, whom she admired as a model Christian. She also had one of those millions of relics people were requesting from Therese's Carmel and, having begun the novena, laid the tiny object on her chest. With new confidence she fell into a light, intermittent sleep.

Neither dead to the world nor awake, she saw in a sort of dream Sister Therese, who, smiling, took her hand and asked, "What do you want me to do for you?"

Sister Emma immediately requested good health, adding, with a confidence reminiscent of Therese's own, that she "knew" Therese could obtain this for her. She awoke immediately and understood that she was completely well.

Nuns tend more to the skeptical than the credulous. When Sister Emma bounced in and announced her cure the next morning, her superior says she simply "attached no importance to her declaration." But when the nuns sat down to eat and Sister Emma sat down, too, and—spurning her usual diet of several drops of milk—ate with gusto *everything* served, even meat, the superior's own spoon dangled in astonishment, as did those of the other sisters present.

A bite or two of the foods Emma was wolfing down should have put her in agony leading to death. Instead there were no ill effects whatsoever.

Even the skeptical superior had to agree with the Bishop's verdict that Sister Therese had hand-carried a miracle to British India.

In the South Malabar region of East India in 1913, another nun had a visit. She was Sister Marie Cornelia of the Sacred Heart. A native of the area, she entered as a novice the Carmelite Convent of Saint Joseph at Ambazhakad on the Malabar coast, only to become tubercular. After three years' attempts to cure her, on February 7, 1913, her doctor threw in the towel and said the nuns should call a priest to prepare Sister Cornelia for death. Two days later, death imminent, the chaplain of the nuns, Father Anthony Kachapully, gave her the last sacraments in the presence of the nuns and two other priests, who later signed his report as witnesses.

Sister Cornelia almost at once lost consciousness but suddenly was heard to speak in a low voice, as if with someone invisible, her face showing now joy, now sorrow as the conversation progressed. Trying to gauge her level of unconsciousness, someone brought pictures of St. Therese and the Virgin near her face. Unexpectedly she reached out at once, grabbing and kissing them with great reverence. About an hour later, her face became sad and, at the same time, she lost even her former level of awareness of what was going on around her, the pictures falling from her hands while she rested immobile a long time, apparently in some sort of deep trance state.

Rather than lapsing further into unconsciousness and dying, however, she eventually returned to normal awareness. To her Superior's question, the report says, she replied that the Virgin Mary and Sister Therese appeared to her and told her not to be afraid because she was not going to die of this malady. They said she would get worse this day and the next but that Sister Therese would always be with her to sustain her until her cure, which would take place suddenly.

Some deathbed hallucination! Except that while she did get worse, she didn't die (and remember, she was already dying, so "worse" should have meant only one thing). And those who were there say they felt "a supernatural presence" in the room, which they credited with sustaining the dying nun, even though whoever was there remained invisible to everyone present.

On February 11, Sister Cornelia fell again into that mysterious state in which she claimed to have seen Therese and the Mother of Jesus. This time there were several priests, including a Carmelite father, joining the sisters as witnesses.

As the church bell of the parish church tolled the hour Catholics of the day knew as the Angelus, the deathly ill nun again returned to complete consciousness. Questioned by Father Kachapully, she said that Mary, this time with the Child Jesus, had appeared to her again, accompanied by Sister Therese. Sister Therese had repeated that Cornelia's illness was going to end this very evening.

And "in effect she was cured," the priest continues, "with no more symptoms whatsoever of tuberculosis." The doctor, he adds, "affirmed that he attributed the cure to supernatural intervention."

In Calavi, Dahomey, where she cured the young tradesman, Therese also paid a visit to a missionary nun who was a widow with four children. Her oldest son had just drowned and she asked Sister Therese, whom she addressed—thinking of her spiritual maturity, not her chronological age, as "little mother," to obtain the strength necessary to bear her grief. On the night between the fourteenth and the fifteenth of October, 1916, the nun was awake around 4:00 A.M., her heart racked with sorrow, when she saw Sister Therese by her bed.

"You'll be consoled," she said simply, "if you unite your pain to the pains of the holy Virgin [who lost her son] and your tears to those of Jesus when he wept over the tomb of [his dead friend] Lazarus."

That was the whole visit. But as God who sent his messenger obviously knew, it was enough: no sooner had the sister followed Therese's advice than peace filled her soul to such an extent that she later commented "resignation" was not the right word; what she felt, she said, could only be called "supernatural joy."

The Carmelites also heard from Father R.P. Seraphin, the superior of a Catholic missionary effort in what is now Ethiopia. He dated his testimony April 4, 1919, sending it from the Church of Notre Dame in Addis-Ababa. In December 1918, he writes, he came down with the pernicious flu that killed twenty million of the world's people in a year. When he felt himself definitely near the end, he decided to receive extreme unction, at that time a once-in-a-lifetime event.

He placed a relic and picture of Sister Therese on his bed's bolster, hoping in his weak condition—whether through thinking of Therese's life or invoking her help, he does not say—to muster up some devotion so he "could make a good end." But while thinking only of how to die well, he heard an interior voice reproach, "Why are you thinking of abandoning the mission this way? Why not have compassion on the Apostolic Vicar? Better to ask for a cure." (The Apostolic Vicar was the priest who would have the difficult job of replacing the missionary.)

A man after my own heart, Father Seraphin was cautious about this voice. After all, he was very sick and could be prey to something like a "fever dream." So he made a mental pact with Sister Therese. If it wasn't an imaginary voice, but really the saint, she should see that he was much better by Friday (this was Tuesday). If that did not occur, he would take the last sacraments.

To his astonishment, by that very evening his condition had improved dramatically. On the second day there was no longer any danger of death whatsoever. Relapses are common in influenza. But when Father Seraphim wrote three-and-a-half months later, he had not experienced a moment of ill health since the voice reproached, "It'd be better to ask for your cure...."

A similar experience took place at Lokandu in the Belgian Congo in the fall of 1919. The same terrible influenza hit a missionary who had worn himself out during the war years. In June 1919, with WWI over, this Father Mulder had been told to return to Europe to recoup his strength. He stayed at his post because the new young missionary sent out to help him did not yet grasp either the native language or the Africans' customs.

By July, Father Mulder later wrote, he was "exhausted, at the end of my strength." Taken ill with the dread disease, he began vomiting, and then experienced bloody urine, a very bad sign. With no doctor in this remote outpost, he turned to Therese, "asking her prayers out of pity for the poor mission." Two days after his appeal to Therese, he was better. Not well, but well enough by July 15 to travel to his regional missionary superior, with whom he was in touch by radio.

Arriving there, Father Mulder learned that a doctor was at Kindu, some sixty-two kilometers from Lokandu. This medical help was summoned, arrived, and prescribed a dozen injections of arsenic. Did this help or sabotage the recovery? All we know is that on August 2, after returning to Lokandu, the missionary had one of the relapses, so common and so often fatal, of the deadly virus. This time he had bloody urine, then couldn't urinate at all, while he vomited, was racked with "an agonizing cough," and experienced all the miseries associated with a very high fever. "The doctor and everyone else," he writes, "judged me lost."

But Father Mulder was a fighter. He mobilized his young assistant to get the entire parish together daily for a novena asking Sister Therese of the Child Jesus' prayers, "that I might recover if it was useful for the good of the mission." Using imagery to represent mysterious realities, he had them place a picture of Therese by the tabernacle so she could "plead my cause."

He put another of her pictures, he relates, where he could see it, lest he forget in his misery to keep supplicating her prayers. Translating his French precisely here:

On the second day of the novena, on August 4, at six o'clock in the evening, while my faithful flock prayed in the church and I united myself to their efforts, the image of Sister Therese that I had where I could see it grew in size and appeared as if alive; then I heard a voice say to me very distinctly with a sweet tone: "No, my father, you won't die yet; it's necessary that you continue to work...."

He reports honestly that he couldn't control himself at that point: he began to weep. However, there was no change in his condition at all: every deadly symptom persisted. But he seems to have had that sense of ineffability in regard to his experience that makes doubt impossible. For when the next morning the provincial of his religious order proposed he receive the last sacraments, Father Mulder refused, confiding "the heavenly promise" he had received. Typically, the provincial was skeptical but he agreed to let Mulder wait a bit. The novena continued and on its last day, Mulder notes joyously that the provincial had "a happy surprise" when he saw his head man at Lokandu "out of danger."

By August 24, Mulder writes, he was able to attend Mass. There he could not contain himself. Probably still too weak to be speaking, he got up and, "with a voice half cut by sobs and tears" because he felt he was not worthy of the grace, a humility that indicates to me he was one of those "pure as crystal" priests after Therese's own heart, he told his flock, "the secret of my cure"— that is, about the visit of the dead nun he calls "the dear little BIG saint."

In the last portion of his long testimony, Father Mulder notes he has talked about his cure to three doctors, two of whom have been practicing tropical medicine for more than fifteen years. All three, he says, are in accord that "they have never seen a cure where there was bloody urine and then urinary failure for five days."

The doctor who personally treated Father Mulder urged the priest to leave *at once* for Europe to avoid another relapse. But "today," the recovered priest boasts in his testimony, "six months after my cure, I'm still here and I'm working as if I'd never been sick."

Blessed Arnold Janssen (1837-1909) is the German-born (in Westphalia) founder of three missionary groups—an international group of priests and brothers, an order of nuns, and a women's contemplative branch to provide the spiritual power behind the other enterprises.

Saints come in all kinds of personalities. Janssen, a mathematician and expert in the natural sciences, had the rather cool and reserved personality associated with not only mathematics, but those born in the Prussian part of Germany. Even his own secretary acknowledged, "It was only after his death that we recognized what a great saint we had in our midst." His personality is the only clue I find to one of St. Therese's strangest after-death appearances, for in the miracle that was accepted for Janssen's beatification—that is, attributed to *his*, not her, prayers—she apparently played stand-in for this saint. Quoting the authenticated account furnished by his order:

It was during the severe winter 1928-29. As a result of frostbite Missionary Brother Kostka [born Joseph Wasel at Allrath on March 23, 1863] began to suffer from a serious leg ailment. At the time Brother Kostka was living at St. Wendel Mission Seminary. Both feet became numb. Both legs were badly swollen up to and above the knee. Blisters and boils began to form. Although the bandages were changed daily no improvement occurred. Brother Kostka relates that one day he heard a noise behind him. He turned around and saw the figure of a Sister, who looked like the picture of St. Therese of Lisieux. She smiled at him and, pointing to the picture of Father Arnold Janssen, said, "You could pray to your founder [for his intercession with God] and ask that your legs be healed." Then the figure waited a short while, as if to assure herself that he had understood her. Then it disappeared.

Looking at the picture, Brother Kostka now prayed for the cure of his leg ailment for about ten minutes. Next he heard a voice saying to him verbatim, "Now go into the water. Your legs will get well. Moreover you will never again have any trouble."

When Brother Infirmarian Juventius came to the room a half hour later and heard what Brother [Kostka] had experienced, he immediately removed the bandages and to his great astonishment observed that both legs had a normal appearance; in place of the previous boils only smooth scars were visible. No trace of the swelling remained. Standing and walking did not cause the least pain. Brother Kostka could immediately take a bath.

As patroness of the world's Catholic missions, St. Therese has some claim to appearing *for* a missionary *to* a missionary. But it still raises a chuckle that, even dead, Blessed Arnold was too reserved to come himself.

Endnotes

1. The bond between the missionary bishop and Therese held until the former's 1945 death: he had himself buried at a shrine to Therese north of Juneau.
2. Receiving a new name when entering a religious order symbolizes beginning a radically new life; today many orders keep birth names since the continuity of lives is more emphasized.

Chapter Seven

A SMILE FROM HEAVEN

The hustle and bustle of day has subsided to late-night's near silence as a well-dressed traveler pays off his cab before one of Europe's great hotels and follows the bellboy through the whirling door into the lobby. That luxuriously appointed area appears empty as the traveler—an important French industrialist in this era before WWII—strides toward the night clerk's desk.

Suddenly, to his amazement, a young nun crosses his path. Wearing a white cloak against the night chill over her brown nun's robe, the young sister does not meekly lower her head as she passes. Instead she looks the traveler directly in the eye, her broad face breaking into the full smile of one meeting a friend. Instinctively, he responds with the manners of the time by lifting his hat as he continues toward the night clerk. A second later, he cannot help looking back, but she has gone.

As he signs the register he asks the night clerk, "Who was that nun?"

"I beg your pardon," the night clerk replies with barely concealed surprise.

"That nun—the one who just smiled at me—who was she?"

Clerks at great hotels are schooled to never tell travelers they are out of their minds. But this one treads perilously close to the forbidden territory. Eyebrows arched, he says with some asperity, "You're mistaken, sir. A nun in a hotel at this hour! Nuns don't wander around town smiling at men."

"I know they don't!" the industrialist retorts with exasperation. "That's why I'm asking you to explain who that was that just came up and smiled at me *now* in this lobby."

Stiffly the night clerk replies, "Sir, *you* are the only person who has come in or out of this lobby in the last half hour."

Over the next days the traveler dismisses the night clerk's obvious inference that he was crazy or hallucinating because he cannot doubt what he has seen.

At the same time, he does not know what to make of it. Later, upon visiting the house of some friends, the industrialist is shocked to see a photograph of the nun who had given him that frank smile of friendship. Even more shocking, he learns that she is dead. She is, his friends explain, a recently canonized saint named St. Therese of the Child Jesus, sometimes called St. Therese of Lisieux.

Some time later, the man tells the story—and its aftermath—to famed Trappist author and mystic Thomas Merton (1915–68). As Merton reports in his book *The Waters of Siloe,* the former traveler was no longer an important French industrialist too busy to think about religion or to attend Mass. And he no longer took taxis or stopped at the world's great hotels. Head shaved and beard long, he was working on a tractor when Merton came upon him. He had become a lay brother in the Trappist abbey of Aiguebelle.

The former industrialist now understood that a smile from heaven had invited him to join Therese as one of those contemplatives who fast, pray, read, and keep great silence in order to seek God with one's whole mind and heart. Or, as Merton might say, the one-time traveler had responded to the invitation of God's messenger to join those who hold our world together with sacrifice and prayer.

This story is a clear example of how God uses saints to guide ordinary people—that is, we who are not holy (or not yet!). These guiding visions—involving saints or other special messengers of God—are part of human spirituality. In Catholic tradition they occur from early Christianity, when apostles like Peter and Paul had such experiences long before they were holy. Only space considerations limit examples here to the past two hundred years.

Other after-death appearances by St. Madeleine Sophie Barat appear later in this book, including a whole chapter of the French educator's appearances to simple Spanish visionary Josefa Menendez. But here is the place to note that Josefa's mother, Lucia Menendez, also had a visit from the foundress of the Society of the Sacred Heart.

It came about in 1907, in Madrid, when one of the Menendez family's four children died. Both Lucia and her husband took their young daughter's death so hard it seemed they would die of it. One came down with typhoid, the other with a lung illness. Josefa, the oldest child, struggled to support the family as a seamstress while running the household and nursing her parents.

Some teaching nuns came to the rescue. Besides tactfully providing means by which Josefa could earn more money, they proposed that the devout Menendez family join them in a novena to their foundress, Mother Barat. Its purpose: to petition for the healing of Josefa's parents, particularly the mother, who lacked the psychological and spiritual strength to go on and seemed certain to die.

In the middle of this novena, Lucia Menendez called her girls to her bedside and said, "Don't cry anymore. Mother Barat has just been here to visit me. She told me I'm not going to die because you still need me." The saint did not leave behind an instantaneous cure. But dead Sophie's encouragement turned the tide in the mother's battered spirit. And since spirit and body are somehow one, by the next day she was completely out of danger and lived many more years.

Because she received a miracle cure through an after-death visitation by a saint, it may encourage someone to know Lucia was a good wife and mother, but definitely not a holy woman. In fact, lacking in gratitude after this miracle, she impeded her oldest daughter's vocation to Mother Barat's order not just once but a number of times, caught up in her own needs, rather than thinking of what was good for Josefa. Lucky for her—and the rest of us—God doesn't love only the holy or bighearted!

In 1940 Catherine de Hueck, a Russian-born Catholic servant of the poor and apostle of racial justice, married Eddie Doherty, who was a household name in the United States as an exceptionally talented star reporter, magazine writer, and Hollywood screenwriter. Catherine and Eddie—both of whom may be beatified one day—soon founded Madonna House in Combermere, Ontario, Canada, as a retreat house and residence for those committed to living the gospel. Eddie died in 1974 as an ordained priest with a reputation for holiness.

Catherine lived on until December 14, 1985, when she was about ninety. Those closest to her (including her mostly lay followers now living in twenty-five locations) characterize her spiritual legacy to be:

- *incarnational,* that is, rooted in simple day-to-day tasks,
- *all-embracing,* that is, reaching out to every sphere so that nothing is ungraced except sin, and
- *rooted in the Cross of Christ,* which plunges one into the pain of the world as a carrier of God's healing, transforming mercy.

This is the spirituality Catherine was living when a local Ontario farmer came up to her one day as she worked in the community garden. His wife, very ill with cancer and being cared for at home by a daughter, needed someone who could come daily to give her a shot of morphine. The nurse doing this was no longer available, he said, and he could find no other. He had heard Catherine did some nursing. Would she take on this daily job? Especially, he wondered, would she—a Catholic—do it for a family of "Protestant Orangemen," as he put it?

She would—gladly. Daily the farmer picked up the lay evangelist and drove her up an old, rutted lumbermen's road to his remote farm. On the first visit Catherine read the doctor's notes left for the previous nurse. The cancer was located in the wife's intestines and alimentary canal, too far advanced to do anything except ease pain with what Catherine said was "the highest dosage of morphine I have ever seen prescribed for a patient."

Daily, Catherine climbed the farmhouse stairs to the bedroom, gave the shot, tried to make the woman comfortable, visited a bit, and "consoled her the best I could." This went on most of the summer—about two-and-a-half months. Then the husband failed to show up for a few days. Catherine assumed that the first nurse, a niece, had been able to come back.

Then, again one day, the farmer, George, came looking for Catherine. Agitated, he said, "Ma'am, I want you to phone them Sisters. My woman wants them back. I'll pay for the call."

Catherine was flabbergasted. He seemed to mean nuns. No nuns could drop in on such a remote farm. None were even in the area. She asked George to explain. Quoting Catherine's account from her book *A Cricket in My Heart*:

He had been milking, he said, and had been late with his chores. It was past seven o'clock when he finally got to the house for supper. He found his daughter Ella in the kitchen quite perturbed. She said she had gone upstairs and found her mother looking fairly well from what she could see through the door—but it seemed her mother was talking to two nuns! They had their backs to Ella. She would have gone in, she said, but Mom looked so happy that she didn't want to intrude.

George joined his daughter in waiting uneasily for the nuns—strange and fearsome creatures, indeed, to Orangemen—to come downstairs. Father and daughter agreed they had not seen or heard any car arrive. They concluded the Catholic nurse (Catherine) must somehow have dropped them off. Hours passed and no one came down the stairs. Neither father nor daughter felt able to go up and deal with something so out of their experience. Eventually each went to bed (due to his wife's pain, George, like his daughter, was sleeping downstairs now), still without anyone having descended the stairs.

The next day George talked to his wife, whose face, he told Catherine, was shining.

She said that from the time those nuns had come to see her, all her pains had left her. She felt especially good when the young one had held her hand. She said they didn't talk much.... The older one remained in the rocking chair. The young nun simply sat on her bed and held her hand. She was a powerfully good person. She took the pain away.

Because of her illness, the wife had been able to take only a few sips of water or suck on ice. Now she wanted strong tea with cream—and it stayed down. In days past, moving her pain-wracked and bedsore-ulcerated body even slightly had caused her agony; now she wanted a bath and a fresh nightgown—and could be comfortably moved to have them.

The next couple of days continued this peacefully. Then the pain returned and the wife sent her husband to Catherine with the urgent request those sisters visit again.

George described the pair to Catherine. The older of the two, his wife said, was the most beautiful woman she'd ever seen. The young one had a round face, dark eyes, and a soft voice. They wore rough brown robes with black "aprons" tied up high, white around the necks, and sandals on bare feet. Catherine says she became physically dizzy when it hit her that St. Therese had apparently sat on the woman's bed while the Mother of Jesus sat in the rocking chair. This made sense in a supernatural way: These two were Catherine's patron saints for nursing. When she made a house call, she always asked Our Lady of the Visitation (a title for Mary, based on her helpful visit to her cousin Elizabeth) to go with her, and she always asked St. Therese to stay on as night nurse when she left.

Catherine says she tried hard to convince George that she couldn't phone those nuns, at the same time trying not to sound as if anything too unusual had happened. She asked him what he thought about "the mother of our Lord." Did he think she would be powerful enough to help people?

George did.

That gave Catherine the opening to offer him a medal with a picture of Mary on it, telling him that Mary was better than any nun and it would be nice for his wife to have this.

To her pleased surprise, he took it.

Two weeks later he was back. He had given his wife the medal. Oddly enough, the Protestant farm wife did not seem distressed at this odd substitute for the requested visit. She put it on her nightdress. Then she slept. In the middle of the night, she called George. Her pain once again was gone. She could even sit up a little.

Theirs had been a happy marriage. Now she wanted her husband to hold her while they reminisced about their years together and thanked God for them. They kissed and with her head on his shoulder, she quietly, painlessly died.

Therese also made appearances at times to give information about her own Cause for Beatification and, it seems, saw that a bishop carried an interest in

God's works through her back to the Philippines.

The first of these two instances requires a little background: When a saint's Cause reaches a certain point, the body must be exhumed, identified, and then reburied in some place, such as inside a church, where it cannot readily be dug up and made off with. If this sounds weird, consider it was common in the early Church for cities to fight over—and, yes, kidnap—the relics (remains of a saint), which is why we end up with the rather grisly state of affairs of one city having the head of a saint, another the heart, while some lesser place "makes do" with a toe bone! Later (helping bring on the Protestant Reformation and the Counter Reformation), selling relics—often fakes, of course—flourished in spite of condemnation by the Church. If you think people today would never try to filch a relic, never try to sell one, and never dream of offering a spurious object as a holy one, you will not understand exhumation but the rest of us do.

The official exhumation of Therese's body was scheduled for September 6, 1910, in the Lisieux cemetery; then the remains were to be reburied in the church of the Lisieux Carmel. With so many miracles involving Therese, there was talk that her body would certainly be found incorrupt, as has occurred in the twentieth century with a number of saints. That she had said during her lifetime, when someone commented on this possibility, that they would find only "a little skeleton," and another time remarked she would prefer to be reduced to ashes, was taken not as prophecy, but saintly humility that God would surely override.

During the night between the fifth and sixth, God sent Therese on an after-death visit on just this question—but not to Lisieux. It was the prioress of the Carmel in Gallipoli, Italy, Mother Carmela, who had no idea this exhumation was even going to take place, who saw her. Therese's "countenance ... very beautiful and shining, her garments glitter[ing] with ... light as of transparent silver," in Mother Carmela's description, the dead saint came to tell the Gallipoli prioress "only my bones will be found."

This announcement helped ease the disappointment when that indeed proved the case. There could be no accusation that the three biological sisters of Therese in the Lisieux Carmel engineered this apparition, as would undoubtedly have been said had she appeared to a Carmelite in Lisieux.

In life, Therese said another time she would not want to be incorrupt, because she wanted in everything not to be extraordinary. But perhaps God, while honoring this wish, just had to do a little something for the occasion. At any rate, the palm branch buried in her coffin was found fresh and green, as if it had just been cut, while a number of people who turned out to watch her coffin carried from the cemetery back to her Carmel received miracle cures, including a disabled World War I veteran.

Therese was canonized on May 17, 1925. Her cause had moved with unheard-of speed due to the outpouring of miracles with which God signaled his interest in its success (once heroic virtue is determined by the investigation, it waits upon miracles, which are God's vote in the saint-making process). That September 30th, Lisieux celebrated the first Feast of *Saint* Therese of the Child Jesus. Eager to participate, more than forty abbots, bishops, and cardinals descended on the small city. Among them was Bishop M'Closkey of the Philippines, who confided to Philadelphia's Cardinal Dougherty a strange experience.

Dropping in at the Carmel in Lisieux, the bishop entered the public Hall of Relics, where various items pertaining to the new saint were on display. To his strong surprise, a Carmelite nun joined him and explained the exhibits. He was so surprised because in that era, once Carmelite nuns crossed the cloister threshold, they sacrificed the freedom to go outside the Carmel the same way they gave up meat, dressing as they liked, and other good things. Unless she entered as an extern sister, a Carmelite generally planned to go outside her walled enclosure only in a hearse. Later in the day, Bishop M'Closkey had an opportunity to speak with Mother Agnes, the blood sister of the saint, who was now prioress. Through the visitors' parlor grill, which both kept the public out of the cloister and let the nuns sacrifice touching their loved ones, the bishop questioned the prioress about the nun who had shown him the exhibits. In turn, *she* questioned him, knowing that none of her flock had been outside what Carmelites call "the enclosure." Finally, hearing his description, Mother Agnes reported to the bishop her conclusion: "the one who explained the souvenirs was none other than St. Therese of the Child Jesus herself!"

In the opening pages of this book, I mentioned that St. Maximilian Kolbe, the martyr of charity at Auschwitz, appeared many years later to Francis Gajowniczek, the man for whom Kolbe had died in 1941. About 1988, Gajowniczek, who traveled around the world for years speaking without fee about the man who laid down his life for him, was in an accident and pronounced dead. Before he revived, the elderly Pole found himself on the road to heaven, but saw Father Kolbe, who told him it was not yet his time.

Father Kolbe also appeared to a dying woman in Trinidad, according to a testimony sent from a hospice there to an American group of the saint's Conventual Franciscan order in Libertyville, Illinois. I condense the testimony from the Winter 1994 newsletter of the Shrine of St. Maximilian Kolbe.

A native of Trinidad and the ninth of ten children, this woman had married a man who beat her. She took her three children and left him, and married a kind man who was good to her and her family. Years passed and she got breast cancer, which in spite of treatment proved impossible to cure. A compassionate Catholic woman cared for her each day while the husband worked. This woman knew that both the sick woman and her husband had prior marriages that had never been annulled.

I mention this because it *may* mean—coupled with the sick woman's later complete lack of recognition of his name—that at the time Kolbe was officially proclaimed a saint in 1982 with worldwide publicity, due to her marital situation, the woman may have been one of the billions who pay no attention to whom the Catholic Church canonizes. She *may* then never have heard of St. Maximilian Kolbe.

As death neared, the dying woman was brought to a hospice for the sick run by a Catholic charismatic community. It was then she began telling the nursing staff that a strange man was walking around her bed. He said he had come to take her to "the banquet" (of heaven). He also told her to have the hospice staff gather around her bed and pray for her husband and children.

The staff did this willingly, although they wondered if they were dealing with a hallucination. So they counseled the dying woman to ask the man his name if she saw him again. She did and reported his name was "Maximilian."

Because these details are "skimpy," this is one of those cases I was going to throw away. I present it to you for one reason: Whatever was going on that to me, as an American investigator, is not adequately detailed as to names of the staff, dates this took place, etc., was compelling enough to the hospice staff that they went to their bishop. And whatever they told him seemed meaningful enough that he came over and dedicated that hospice to St. Maximilian.

———————

Another group of Franciscans, those who lived with Padre Pio in San Giovanni Rotondo, Italy, received a testimony of an after-death appearance that involves only the sense of touch. The writer of the testimony asked to remain anonymous, but Father Joseph Pius Martin of San Giovanni Rotondo vouches for the story's veracity. The anonymous writer reports:

> On July 3, 1984, my mother died suddenly. I was crushed and broken and never having suffered grief before I thought I would surely die in despair.... I asked God each night to call me home. On the night of July 20 of that year I prayed to Padre Pio [This sounds idolatrous but it isn't; such "prayers" always ask the saint's prayers to God the same way one phones a friend to pray for one.] using the little prayer leaflet. I was sitting up in bed at the time. After finishing the prayer I eased my way gently under the covers. I had just settled myself into a lying position when in the silence of the night my two hands were taken gently and held by two very large hands. At once I stiffened ... but [realized] ... that someone wanted to comfort me....

The mourner kept wondering during the next days whose hands had offered that comforting touch. Could it have been Padre Pio? Then one morning this individual picked up the day's mail and found a publication with a cover photo of Padre Pio's hands. "I think," the writer continues, "Padre Pio was saying, 'Yes, it was me.'" What is believed a saint's visit didn't wipe out all grief, as it sometimes does; the writer adds that it wasn't until All Souls' Day, several months later, that the weight completely lifted. So the after-death touch eased, but did not eliminate, the natural grieving process.

———————

A priest I know to be eminently dedicated to the truth is the Jesuit pastor of Sacred Heart Church in Hsinchu, Taiwan. Over roughly half a century, Jesuit John Baptist Palm has taken many hundreds of written and taped testimonies about Rose Ferron, a stigmatic from Woonsocket, Rhode Island, who died in 1936. Many people are directly petitioning both Rose's present bishop and the Congregation for the Causes of Saints to investigate her possible heroic sanctity based on the favors, cures, and after-death appearances by which they believe God is speaking on her behalf. While I don't know if Rose is a saint, I do know Father Palm is a great lover of God and I don't believe he has made up the several thousand pages of material he has shared with me over the years. Here is one of those stories.

When he left for China in 1948 to become a missionary, Father Palm knew it was *forever*, since Jesuit missionaries didn't get home leave. But he is a very devout man who puts the things of God ahead of even those he loves. Before departing from the United States, on his way to Baltimore, Maryland, to say good-bye to his family, he made a private pilgrimage to Rhode Island to meet the family of Rose Ferron and visit her grave. After the brief visit, which increased his certainty that Rose was a genuine saint, Father Palm says, "I said good-bye forever to the mother of little Rose." Two other Ferron daughters drove him to his train. He told them "good-bye forever" too. He writes:

> On their return when their mother asked them why they seemed so sad, they answered, "We'll never see Father Palm again." Mother Ferron said, "He will return before he goes to China." They said, "No! He said he would not come back forever!" "Yes, he will return...."

Much later Father Palm would learn from the daughters how their mother comforted them by explaining she had had what she referred to as "a dream." In it, Rose told her that the young priest would return to Woonsocket and when he did, her mother should give him the crucifix that Rose had held in her hand as she died. Meantime, Father Palm recalls:

On the three- to four- hour train ride to New York I kept smelling the sweet fragrance of rose powder and at the same time kept hearing, at each turn of the wheels ... the insistent *you must return! you must return!*

Since he had only a limited time to spend with his family for what he thought would be the last time, the last thing the Jesuit wanted to do was make another trip to Woonsocket. But the "voice" was so insistent that finally he cried, "OK, I surrender. I'll go back." And he somehow fit it in. He writes:

When I did return, Mother Ferron placed this crucifix lovingly and slowly in my hands, pressed her two hands against mine, and said, "Little Rose told me to give you this crucifix, that it would do more good in China than here."

This time when he left, Mrs. Ferron again told her daughters that the priest would return, "but I'll be gone." Due to the Communist takeover in China, Father Palm's life took an unexpected course and he did return to Woonsocket in 1959, Mrs. Ferron having died in 1956.

Who can insist Rose really returned after death to give her mother advice and prophecies? I can tell you only that I have read many testimonies by those who knew Rose's mother and who considered her a holy woman. Holy women don't lie. Of course, the holy may be mistaken or deceived. At any rate, the aftereffects of what Rose Ferron's crucifix accomplished in China fill a large book written by this Jesuit missionary. In it are testimony after testimony by foreign and Chinese Jesuits, as well as by Chinese lay people, of cures, conversions, and other favors—most of them involving the so-called odor of sanctity similar to that Father Palm experienced on the train—that took place whether Father Palm or someone else had possession of Rose Ferron's crucifix.

A second incident involving Father Palm and, it appears, Rose Ferron, grew out of the years 1941-44 when Father Palm was stationed at Our Lady of Lourdes Catholic Church in Bethesda. Not yet an ecumenical era, the 1940s were a time when people schemed, sweated, and prayed to get a Protestant to turn Catholic, or a Catholic to turn Protestant. It may not edify you but it is not odd then that one of Palm's parishioners was determined her non-Catholic husband, Evan Scholl (who ran Scholl Cafeteria in Washington, D.C.), was going to become a Catholic. For fourteen years the woman fasted and prayed just for this. Young Father Palm, who years down the road would discover ecumenism, tried to help by arguing with Scholl about religion. That did about as much good as arguing usually does. In short, Evan wasn't buying. Then in 1948 the priest came by the Scholl home to say "good-bye forever." In his enthusiasm for Rose Ferron, he told the couple about her. Boldfacedly he said he would ask Rose's prayers for Evan's conversion and advised the wife to do this too.

Weeks later, in Nanking, a letter arrived from Bethesda. Right after Father Palm left, Evan Scholl was enveloped in a cloud of fragrance as if from masses of fresh roses. The odor was not heavy or cloying. Instead it filled him with a very cool and refreshed feeling. Accompanying the odor, repeated like a mantra, was the message, "you must become a Catholic."

A fairly trivial incident. But Evan was absolutely, one-hundred-percent sure (remember the quality of ineffability) that this was supernatural. He demanded to be baptized that very day. Of course, that wasn't possible. He had to study all the teachings of the Catholic Church and make sure he could assent to them, a matter usually of many months. But he never wavered in his sudden resolve. He became a fervent Catholic who, Palm says, "lived to bring others into the Church" where he had discovered so much spiritual wealth and who gave so much of his time and money to help others he was eventually knighted by the pope for his charities.

And speaking of his charities, it was in search of money for a good cause that Rose Ferron, Evan Scholl believed, paid him a second visit.

Again Father Palm was involved. Having been expelled by the Communist regime from mainland China, the priest was working in Taiwan—as he still is—when his bishop sent him back to the States in 1959 to give talks in churches to raise money for the Jesuit order's Far-Eastern seminarians. While home, Palm also had permission to contact his personal friends and family for money to build what is today Sacred Heart Church in Taiwan. Father Palm visited the Scholls in Florida and asked if they would help. Generous though he was, Evan had to tell the visitor that times were tough. He didn't see how he could contribute to this appeal too.

At that point, the host took a swim in the ocean, only to have a large sea nettle wrap itself around him, poisoning him in many places. Taken to the hospital, Evan heard the same voice he remembered from his earlier, never forgotten experience. This time it was saying, "You must help Father Palm to build his church!" There were two aftereffects: Evan Scholl received a complete physical healing on the spot and Father Palm received twenty-five thousand dollars toward the church—five thousand from Scholl and the rest from four friends the businessman persuaded to match his gift.

At the end of Evan Scholl's life, after a funeral attended by many priests, religious, and bishops, including Scholl's good friend, retired Cardinal O'Boyle, the Cardinal wrote a letter to the bishop of Providence asking him to consider looking into the case of Rose Ferron, who played such an important role in the life of Evan Scholl, a man who, in turn, touched so many others.

Chapter Eight

SAINTS NEED GUIDANCE, TOO

People striving for holiness need guidance, too. So it is no surprise to find in most spiritual traditions those who yearn to live completely for God who encountered some kind of supernatural guide. A figure may appear in dreams, like the unidentified being who once told the three wise men of some long-vanished faith not to return to King Herod (see Matthew 2:12). Shamen, like Black Elk in his pre-Catholic days, may learn in altered states of consciousness such as visions from "spirits," perhaps angels, often appearing as animal figures. Angels are almost universally acknowledged guiding messengers. And so are the dead. From Hasidism to Hinduism, dead holy people have appeared to guide the living. In Christianity, such events go back to the long-dead Moses and Elias helping point out Christ's glory to three awed apostles. While such events have taken place in every century, the examples here begin and move forward from the nineteenth.

———◆◆◆———

Anyone who thinks that seeing a dead saint is always a blissful experience has never read the life of Venerable Cajetan Errico. As a young priest, Cajetan made a yearly retreat at a college of Redemptorists, an order founded by St. Alphonse Ligouri, who died in 1787. In 1818, praying on one of these retreats, Errico got the idea to found a congregation similar to the Redemptorists. The modest priest dismissed the thought as presumptuous and a temptation to pride.

But on Errico's next retreat, St. Alphonse himself appeared to command him, in God's name, to found a congregation of missionaries. He even told him what to name them. Then the dead priest told the living one that God would enable Errico to build a church dedicated to Our Lady of Sorrows in his hometown of Secondilliano, where Errico was a parish priest. When the church actually was built, this would be the sign Errico should proceed to found the new order.

A wise person, Cajetan Errico did not rush out to follow those instructions. Aware that he might be slipping a mental cog or that this might be a vision from dark spirits, he sought counsel from various religious authorities, including his spiritual director, who knew him like a book. Their consensus: Wait and pray. If this is the real stuff, you'll get more confirmation.

So he waited. And confirmation kept coming in the form of more visits from St. Alphonse, who, on the last of several appearances, was insistent: Do as God wants *now!* But Cajetan sagely continued to balance what the dead saint ordered with the advice of his living spiritual advisers and superiors. All meshed when he received permission in 1827 to build the church.

After that everything should have been easy. But this is real life. When he broke the good news to his townsfolk and began collecting money for the church, all hell broke loose. He was accused of extorting money from the poor. He was accused of diverting monies to enrich his family, in order to marry his sisters above their station. He was reported to the church authorities, accused of supplanting the town's main parish church with a church where Cajetan would reign supreme. He was accused of hurting local businesses because he bought up and demolished houses on the site for the new church. And on the side, so to speak, for "being so dumb" as to give uninvited talks about God inside taverns and other places where preachers aren't exactly clamored for, he was tied to a tree and beaten with clubs. Surprisingly, none of this killed him.

Did his friends and family stick by him? Well, sometimes. At times his timid confessor said, "Right on." Then let the criticism reach a fever pitch and he would suddenly say, "Stop!" Cajetan's mother and sisters were more consistent: They never supported him. Instead they nagged at him to give up this nonsense; it was an embarrassment to them.

"Take a pastorate somewhere else," they begged. You can't choose your relatives, of course. Unfortunately his friends, too, suggested he back off, and called St. Alphonse's visits "your bad dreams." As for his enemies....

But that old ineffability factor was at work. Cajetan Errico had taken a long time to be convinced, dead saint's orders or no. Once convinced, he commented, "As soon as we know the will of God, we must fulfill it, even if we die."

So he kept going. And one day St. Alphonse appeared again with the Virgin Mary. They provided a little comfort. But it was in suffering and struggle that the church was built. But built it was and the Missionaries of the Sacred Heart founded. In spite of Cajetan Errico's understandable early death—he certainly had enough stress—the order can be found today as far away from Secondilliano as Linwood, New Jersey.

Could the visits of St. Alphonse have been imaginary, swirling into Cajetan's consciousness from a secret hankering to become important by building churches and founding orders? Perhaps. But it is a mark in his favor that the Church's investigation on Cajetan Errico has progressed to the point where "a life of heroic virtue worthy of veneration" (hence the title Venerable) has been established. Heroically virtuous people can imagine things. But considering how much doubt he had about his visions and how many people were counseling him, I think it improbable that Cajetan imagined St. Alphonse—whose appearance, after all, caused him, humanly speaking, nothing but trouble.

St. Clement Hofbauer (1751-1820) was the son of a very poor, very pious, half-Slovak (the surname was changed from its Slavonic equivalent, Dvorak) and half-German family living in the Austria of Maria Theresa and her son Joseph II. Apprenticed to a baker, the ninth of the Hofbauer's twelve children longed to be a priest. An enterprising fellow, he got himself employed at a monastery bakery, where the abbot permitted him to attend Latin classes. But the abbot soon died and it was back to a Vienna bakery.

Saving his money, the young baker managed two pilgrimages to Rome. On the second, he received permission to become a religious hermit near Tivoli. Then God made it clear that he was not to be a hermit, but labor in the world.

And this time, valuable lessons no doubt having been learned in those years of struggles, God smoothed the way. Clement was financed in his studies for the priesthood in Rome by two women whom he had met on a trip home to Vienna when he good-naturedly ran out into a downpour to grab them a carriage. Not only was he ordained in Rome, he joined the Redemptorist order founded by St. Alphonse there. Then he returned to Vienna.

The rest of his life is so extraordinary I can only hit a few highlights. Soon exiled from Vienna to Warsaw by laws against religious orders, Hofbauer's holiness made him known there as a preacher, confessor, convert-maker, and father to the poor. Once begging in a tavern for the orphanage he opened for Warsaw's homeless children, he was called over by a card player, who coolly spit in Hofbauer's face.

"Now that you've given to me personally, how about something for my poor children," the saint said with equal coolness. The anticleric dug red-facedly into his pocket—and became a follower of the dynamic saint.

After twenty year's work, Hofbauer was imprisoned by Napoleon's anti-clerical decree. In prison, Father Clement's influence only grew, crowds gathering outside the prison to listen to his hymns. Released but ordered to leave Warsaw, he finally made it back to Vienna where he became a magnet there, too, to all interested in the spiritual life.

At the 1815 Congress of Vienna, it is he who is credited, along with a spiritual son, Prince Ludwig of Bavaria, with defeating attempts to sever the German Catholic Church from the pope, as the English Church had been severed by Henry VIII. One statesman remarked he could name only three people with real energy: Napoleon, Goethe, and Clement Hofbauer.

"The apostle of Vienna," as he was called, needed every ounce. His role as a spiritual mentor to people like Prince Ludwig kept him in his confessional for stretches as long as eighteen hours. At the same time, he was at the center of Vienna's intellectual life. Besides promoting good literature, he founded a Catholic college in the city. And in a day when bigotry was the rule, he was known for his charity toward Protestants. Due to his holiness, the saint's twelve years there left Vienna at his death a city where Catholicism was a vital spiritual force. And he had done it in spite of the fact that the laws originally exiling him from Vienna were still on the books. The king had simply refused to permit his chancellor to enforce them against one all believed a saint.

Hofbauer died prophecying "scarcely shall I have breathed my last" than the Redemptorists would regain legal right to exist. This at once occurred.

Such a man can hardly be expected to sit quietly after death. God seemed to especially send Clement to those he had protected or mentored. Appearances include one in 1822 to intimate friend Father Zacharie Werner.

Father Zacharie had just finished his evening prayers ... when suddenly his cell was illuminated by a great light that surpassed the radiance of the sun. In the midst of this light he suddenly saw Clement....

He heard him say, "Zacharie, come. Come. Come soon." Then the figure disappeared. Zacharie Werner testified ... that he was not dreaming or hallucinating.

He answered the call, dying just a few weeks later.

Two other appearances were to a Sister Sebastiana of the Sisters of St. Ursula order. The first time he came to Sister Sebastiana, God's messenger told her that she was to become a saint. Embarrassed and bewildered because she was a very humble person, the nun could not answer at first. Finally she croaked, "I'm not worthy." What Clement answered she does not tell us. In fact, she goes blank about the rest of their conversation, except for one item: Clement assured her he would be present to assist her when she died.

When the day came that Sister Sebastiana lay dying, she exclaimed that Clement had kept his promise. And, quite unusual for such deathbed visions, suddenly the other nuns present also saw Clement Hofbauer. He disappeared just as Sister Sebastiana died.

In saints' after-death appearances to saints, a kind of spiritual compatibility can often be seen. This definitely seems the case in an 1869 apparition of Blessed Anna Maria Taigi. An impoverished housewife with a difficult husband and seven children, Anna Maria worked part-time to stretch her man's meager paycheck while carrying on all the time-consuming, early-nineteenth-century household chores. Pretty, she had been vain until Jesus began appearing to her. Then her life took a sharp turn God-ward. She died in 1837, revered as a holy mystic with great prophetic gifts and healing charisms. A member of a spiritual support group affiliated with the Trinitarian fathers, the Roman housewife's incorrupt body lies in a glass casket in one of the churches served by those priests.

Maria del Pinto was another Italian mystic, who—like Anna Maria—felt called to all sorts of sacrifices in the hope that Christ could use those gifts of love to help other souls. Such people (don't confuse them with masochists who *like* to suffer[1]) are wary of praying for relief when suffering comes their way, figuring God will weave some beneficial design into whatever happens, whether it was his direct will or only permitted by him. So when Maria del Pinto was reduced to a near-skeleton by an infection of her womb and its lining, she never prayed to be healed. Urged to pray for her life when the doctors' verdict became "hopeless," she still refused. Finally she accepted, making a novena to the Holy Spirit to ask if God *wanted* her to pray for healing. Maria later wrote:

> During the course of the novena, I seemed to see Our Lady Immaculate, shining with light, receiving a petition from the hands of a gracious old lady who was kneeling in front of her.
>
> "Beg for your cure, my daughter," said the Blessed Virgin; "you shall be perfectly cured of this disease. There will be plenty of other opportunities for you to suffer."

So finally Maria del Pinto began asking God to cure her. And now she had a second visit: Again the Virgin Mary was accompanied by the gracious old lady. "Behold your deliverer," said Jesus' mother, pointing to the old lady. Maria del Pinto understood that this person's prayers were to be responsible for her cure. Somehow it was also made clear to del Pinto that the gracious old lady was Anna Maria Taigi, then dead for thirty years. Anna Maria had a handkerchief in her hands, reports del Pinto, "as if to wipe away the tears that I shed in abundance because of the intensity of the pain."

Possibly. It's also true that during Anna Maria's lifetime, Jesus appeared and gave her the power to heal by touching someone with her hand. To keep notice from this gift, she always went to ill people with something in her hand, such as cotton soaked in oil. Carrying the handkerchief, then, was a further visual clue of the identify of this saint.

Del Pinto writes that no sooner had the Virgin Mary pointed to Anna Maria than:

> I felt a wrenching that made me cry out loud. People came to my assistance, but I was cured. I arose without difficulty to make a pilgrimage of thanks.

The "Miraculous Medal,"[2] often worn on a chain around the neck, is named "miraculous" because of the thousands of cures, rescues, and favors claimed by those for whom it is a visible reminder—like the cross or star of David others wear—to keep close to God. It was the Blessed Virgin Mary's appearances to St. Catherine Laboure (1806-76) that led to the making and distribution of millions of these medals. Long before those well-known apparitions, as an eighteen-year-old, Catherine was keeping house for her widowed father. At this time the young farm girl dreamed she was attending

> the Mass of an old priest, who was a stranger to her. At the end of Mass he turned and beckoned to her, but she fled in fright. Then, in her dream, Catherine went to visit a sick neighbor, only to encounter the same venerable priest.
>
> As she turned to flee from him a second time, he called after her, "You do well to visit the sick, my child. You flee from me now, but one day you will be glad to come to me. God has plans for you; do not forget it."

Four years later, her father having refused his permission for her to become a nun, Catherine was cutting a rather hopeless figure at the fashionable finishing school run by a sister-in-law who had rescued her from waitressing in a brother's cafe. On an outing with the schoolgirls, Catherine saw a portrait of St. Vincent de Paul (1580-1660), who had been dead over 165 years, and instantly recognized the old priest of her dream. Based on the interior understanding accompanying this moment, Catherine—who had known for years she was to become a nun—now saw God specifically desired she be a Daughter of Charity, the order St. Vincent founded to minister primarily to the sick and the poor. Daughter of Charity she did become, living a humble life in service to the aged poor for nearly half a century.

Young and beautiful, intelligent and charming, she who would one day be known as *Saint* Gemma Galgani (1878-1903) had lain in bed about a year in 1899, suffering nephritis, paralysis, and deafness. Even her lovely hair had fallen out. Worse was her spiritual turmoil: She who from childhood had always been so devout now wrestled with every spiritual temptation.

Then she was given a book, the life of a Passionist student for the priesthood who had died before he could be ordained only thirty-seven years earlier. Perhaps someone thought the story of Gabriel of the Sorrowful Mother (Passionist priests take such names) would comfort her for her own broken dream of becoming a nun.

Gemma read the book and felt a strong spiritual rapport with Gabriel. That night Gabriel Possenti (1838-62), who would be canonized in 1920, appeared to bedridden Gemma. "Go ahead," he instructed her, "and make your vow to be a nun, but add nothing further."

"Why not?" she countered, for she wanted desperately to know which religious order might even yet receive her if her health returned.

Gabriel, who in his pre-Passionist days had been nicknamed "the ladies' man" for his charm and good looks, only smiled.

"My sister!" he said warmly a few moments later. Dressed in the traditional black Passionist cassock with its heart-shaped badge on the breast, Gabriel unpinned this distinctive sign of the Passionists and wordlessly offered it to Gemma to kiss. A few moments later, he was gone.

Only later would his cautionary remark regarding her vocation make sense; for Gemma Galgani, saint, mystic, and stigmatic, would continue to knock in vain at the doors of religious orders:

"Too singular!"

"Apt to have a bad influence."

"Could prove divisive."

Those were some of the remarks accompanying the refusals. Although the investigation after her death that proved her sanctity would conclude that the pharmacist's beautiful young daughter had practiced poverty, chastity, and obedience *to a heroic degree*, Gemma would wear a nun's dress only in death. Then the Passionists (whom she had not known at the time of St. Gabriel Possenti's visit) would see that the young woman was dressed for her burial in the garb of one of their nuns, fulfilling Gabriel's gentle hint, "My sister!"

At the time of that first after-death appearance of Gabriel to Gemma, he said nothing about her health. But shortly thereafter the dead seminarian came again, chiding her for neglecting the novena for the prayers of Blessed (today Saint) Margaret Mary Alacoque for healing. Both a holy priest and nuns who had taught her were urging Gemma to make the novena, but Gemma kept forgetting. Let her be cured or not, as God willed, was her attitude. Now here was Gabriel, insisting God wanted to heal Gemma, and wanted to do it by utilizing the nine-day's prayer asking the intercession of Margaret Mary.

To see Gemma followed through, the cheerful, dead Passionist returned each evening to say the novena prayers with her. As the nine days drew to a close, Jesus appeared to Gemma, who was instantaneously and totally healed. (While everyone cheered her cure, Gemma was more delighted that Jesus said, "I choose you for my daughter.")

Although Jesus and his mother appeared to Gemma Galgani more frequently than did Gabriel, the visionary saw the young Passionist a number of other times during her brief life. Her Church, of course, in canonizing her makes only two assertions: She is with God, who worked miracles in her honor at the behest of her prayers after her death, and she practiced heroic virtue during her life. As to whether the visits Gemma received were in her head or "real," as with all saints, the Church makes no judgment.

But let me offer a few thoughts. That it was Gabriel Possenti—an individual who lived and died quietly, and who was neither beatified nor canonized during Gemma's lifetime—whom Gemma said she saw, I find interesting. One would be more apt to imagine an individual hallucinating visits by a recognized saint, not an obscure candidate for Church honors.

Bright and literate, Gemma had read many saints' lives and she was often ill. If she hallucinated a saint after reading about him when not well, this should have happened more than once. Yet Gemma never claimed any supernatural visits by saints (she did see Jesus, his mother, and angels) except one— Gabriel Possenti. He, she said, appeared to her at intervals after that first visit, the rest of her brief life. Before her death at age twenty-five, she predicted the date of her dead friend's future beatification, tying its occurrence to other events, all of which took place after her death in the order and time foretold. How did she know? She said Gabriel told her.

———————

Even canonized, most people regard St. Gemma—with her visions, ecstatic levitations, and stigmata—as a bit "flaky." St. Francesca Xavier Cabrini (1850–1917), on the other hand, is the quintessential well-balanced, equal-to-everything missionary—a "perfect" woman saint. Beloved teacher, foundress of an order of down-to-earth nurses, teachers, caretakers, and administrators, herself a master businesswoman who built hospitals, orphanages, schools, and other practical expressions of divine love all over the United States and other parts of the world, Mother Cabrini, on the surface, couldn't be less like Gemma. And yet, while she was much quieter about them, Francesca Cabrini, I believe, had as many dead visitors as St. Gemma. Throughout her life, the tiny, curly-blonde-haired north Italian was "shown [things] mystically in ... unusual dreams," as the nun who was her secretary puts it in her biography[3] of Mother Cabrini. These "dreams" were actually much more than the modest saint and her followers imply by that low-key word. Sister Frances Cairo testified to that.

For a brief time, Sister Frances shared a room with Mother Cabrini. Sister Frances woke one night to see the room flooded by a mysterious bright light and said aloud, "Mother, do you see it?"

Her bed was moved out the next day.

Whoever was appearing to Mother Cabrini—whether God himself, who often comes as warm, sweet, so-called Shekinah light, or one of the saints in an effulgence of glory, the very reticent Cabrini did not want it talked about.

While from childhood she yearned to do missionary work in China, Cabrini was asked to commit her fledgling order to work among Italian immigrants in the United States. Like all saints, she sought wise advice, trying not to get her own way but to discern the will of God, since she wanted that more than she wanted any dream—however cherished or holy—of her own.

During this time of interior struggle, Mother Cabrini worried because the bishop of New York had made her such a vague proposal. The saint wrote him from Rome, asking for the precise conditions he had in mind for her and her 145 spiritual daughters. At the same time in Rome, Monsignor Scalabrini, a saint himself, was pressuring her not to wait for the reply, but tell him immediately whether or not her nuns were going to the United States to work with the men's order he had founded. At this point

Mother [Cabrini] had recourse to the Venerable Antonia Belloni of Codogno ... in order that, through her intercession, she might obtain the desired answer [to Cabrini's letter]. After ten days ... the Venerable Antonia appeared in a dream in which she handed Mother a letter from New York that answered all her questions. In this dream Mother Cabrini also saw her own mother coming towards her. She asked her why she was hesitating and why she bore the name of "Missionary" if she was afraid of going to the foreign missions.

I omit the rest of the dream in which Mary and other saints appeared without speaking and in which Jesus showed up last of all, reassuring Francesca—whose motto was, "I can do all things through Christ who strengthens me"—that he would be with her.

The next day Mother Cabrini received the letter from New York.

While most of Mother Cabrini's other *known* (I've noted her extreme reticence) visits from the next world were by Jesus or Mary, it is certain other holy dead, too, came to her during those hours while her comrades slept and she received the guidance that let her run, with almost as much efficiency as love, what amounted to a missionary empire, with branches in North, Central, and South America, as well as in many European countries (but never China!).

She confided to her sisters that on one occasion when "she needed immediate help" in her prayers she asked one of the dead sisters, who had been very holy, to go to God and obtain the favor. Night came and Mother Cabrini heard a light knock on her unlocked door. Then the door opened and in walked the dead sister. She comforted her former boss, assuring Mother Cabrini that the problem of the moment would be solved happily. While she was there she also told her foundress where to find some important lost documents. The dead visitor's prophecy as to things turning out well proved as correct as her directions to the missing papers.

With Saint Faustina Kowalska (1905-38), we return to the type of saint who can arouse suspicion because her holy work is not tangible, like Mother Cabrini's, but purely mystical. That is, it does not build hospitals and orphanages for humanity but a new spiritual understanding or directive. Not that, as an uneducated, lay nun in pre-WWII Poland, Faustina did not do plenty of cooking, baking, gardening, and other work in her convent. Still, her claim to fame is based on the mystical, rather than the material.

Faustina's mission was to spread the word about the immense Mercy of God. So it is somehow fitting that souls undergoing purification after death came to her, as they did to Padre Pio, to request her prayers. Like Padre Pio and Adrienne von Speyr, Sister Faustina also bilocated, invisibly at times, to the bedsides of the dying to assist them with her prayers. Often Faustina saw Mary but Jesus was the humble nun's most frequent visitor. Saints were also sent to Faustina Kowalska.

On July 30, 1935, Sister Faustina, in fervent prayer, reproached St. Ignatius, the patron of her congregation, whose feast day it was, for not coming to her aid in carrying out a very difficult project God was asking of her. Quoting from her diary:

Then I saw Saint Ignatius at the left side of the altar, with a large book in his hand. And he spoke these words to me, "My daughter, I am not indifferent to your project. This rule can be adapted and it can be adapted to this Congregation." And gesturing with his hand toward the big book, he disappeared. I rejoiced greatly at the fact of how much the saints think of us and of how closely we are united with them. Oh, the goodness of God! How beautiful is the supernatural world, that already here on earth we commune with the saints! All day long, I could feel the presence of this dear Patron Saint (Diary, 448).

Again quoting Sister Faustina's own account:

I want to write down a dream that I had about Saint Therese of the Child Jesus. I was still a novice at the time and was going through some difficulties that I did not know how to overcome. They were interior difficulties connected with exterior ones. I made novenas to various saints, but the situation grew more and more difficult. The sufferings it caused me were so great that I did not know how to go on living, but suddenly the thought occurred to me that I should pray to Saint Therese ... (and) I started a novena.... (Diary, 150).

On the fifth day of the novena, I dreamed of Saint Therese but it was as if she were still living on earth. She hid from me the fact that she was a saint and began to comfort me, saying that I should not be worried about this matter, but should trust more in God. She said, "I suffered greatly too," but I did not believe her and said, "It seems to me that you have not suffered at all." But Saint Therese answered me in a convincing manner that she had suffered very much indeed and said to me, "Sister, know that in three days the difficulty will come to a happy conclusion." When I was not very willing to believe her, she revealed to me that she was a saint. At that moment, a great joy filled my soul, and I said to her, "You are a saint?" "Yes," she answered, "I am a saint. Trust that this matter will be resolved in three days." And I said, "Dear sweet Therese, tell me, shall I go to heaven?" And she answered, "Yes, you will go to heaven, Sister." "And will I be a saint?" To which she replied, "Yes, you will be a saint." "But, little Therese, shall I be a saint as you are, raised to the altar?" And she answered, "Yes, you will be a saint just as I am, but you must trust in the Lord Jesus." [Faustina then asks the state of soul of various relatives. Some are fine, Therese responds; others need "much prayer."]

In her diary Faustina concludes:

This was a dream. And as the proverb goes, dreams are phantoms: God is faith. Nevertheless three days later the difficulty was solved very easily, just as she had said. And everything ... turned out exactly as she said it would. It was a dream, but it had its significance (Diary, 150).

Although Faustina was dismissed as a nut or false mystic during one period after her death, her Cause was ultimately opened and successful: She is now "on the altars" as a canonized saint.

———— ••• ————

Therese (in German pronounced THER ez) Neumann, the Bavarian mystic and stigmatic, is known to the world for living many years on what the world called "nothing" and she corrected to: "I don't live on nothing; I live on the Savior," meaning the Eucharistic wafer, the Body and Blood of Christ.[4]

Thick books have been written about Therese and her visions, most principally again of Jesus. In a later chapter I will detail some of Therese Neumann's physical cures accompanied by visits from St. Therese of Lisieux. During those cures, Therese of Lisieux also gave Therese Neumann much spiritual guidance. But Therese Neumann saw noncanonized holy dead, too. Here is one instance:

When Adolf Hitler's Nazis seized power in Germany, some serious Christians fought the Nazis, not out of personal hatred, but out of hatred for evil doctrines that advocated eliminating from the earth whole segments of our human family: Jews, gypsies, Slavic races, the physically or mentally disabled—in short, anyone who did not conform to the perfect Aryan standard fantasized in one little dark-haired Bavarian's twisted brain.

Among those beaten to death, hounded to death, or executed by the Nazis were a number of Therese Neumann's closest male friends, including newspaperman Fritz Gerlich and two brothers, priests Adalbert and Karl Vogl. I have spoken to Albert Vogl, nephew of the Vogls, who fled for his own life. Albert recalls Therese telling him about his uncles. The dead priest brothers had appeared to Therese, she said, chuckling delightedly that the two balding men—one a Catholic editor hounded to death and the other formally executed for anti-Nazi work—came "in their prime," each sporting a full head of hair! Therese did not share their message but, whatever their guidance, the fine appearance of the brothers showed Therese that Hitler's horrors could inflict only passing, not eternal, damage on those who love God.

———◆———

Those who aspire to holiness at times receive guidance from very good or holy parents, even after their deaths.[5] Besides Mother Cabrini and Don Bosco in the nineteenth century, I think of Catherine de Hueck Doherty (1896–1985) in the twentieth.

Catherine's parents—her half-Polish, half-Russian, Catholic father and her mother of English and French descent, both bred and raised in Czarist

Russia—were extraordinary people. When Catherine's father, Theodore de Kolyschkine, died, it was found this great bear of a man had helped 250 young people through college, while financing a host of other secret charities. Catherine's mother, Emma Thompson Kolyschkine, a gifted pianist, rejected a concert career in favor of a menial job as a telephone operator so she could teach the catechism to workers, who would accept it from one of themselves.

Tiny and seemingly fragile, Emma even toiled as a domestic on farms, helping the aged with their crops and the young with their lessons. She survived the Russian Revolution and spent hard years in exile, including living through the Nazi occupation of Brussels, keeping herself and others fed while her daughter was off in the United States and Canada, carrying on Emma and Theodore's ingrained outreach to the poor and needy. Finally Emma died, a son telling a close associate of Catherine's, "my mother was a saint."

In October 1976, Catherine de Kolyschkine de Hueck Doherty was eighty years old[6] and very concerned about her health, as her doctor had just told her she had a severely diseased heart. At that time she dreamed her mother came to her. But Emma's visit was not to ready her for death or take her to the next life. Instead Emma told her daughter that God still had lots of things for Catherine to do. Laughing, Catherine told her confidant, Father Emile Briere, that they weren't even the things she herself had in mind: No, her mother said God wanted Catherine to write.

Shortly after that, doctors at the Mayo Clinic unexpectedly found Catherine's heart fine and she went on to a new, active, five-year period that included writing four books in a year!

Another person who experienced his mother's visits frequently was Blessed Andre Bessette (1845-1937), the frail yet indomitable little French-Canadian Holy Cross Brother in Montreal to whom God gave one of the twentieth-century's most tremendous gifts of healing. Blessed Andre's widowed mother had lived a life of tremendous hardship, yet never lost her trust in God even when her impoverished family had to be split up, kids sent to this and that relative who could handle an extra mouth or two.

Andre said, "I never saw my mother when she was not smiling—and what a lovely smile! Since her death she often smiles at me. She comes and, without speaking, looks lovingly at me." Andre added he *often* asked her to pray for him. We can only imagine the spiritual consolation and encouragement these wordless visits gave the humble little Brother.

Endnotes

1. Sometimes called victim souls, such individuals must be very carefully sorted out by experienced spiritual mentors from masochists. The true reparatory sufferer, agrees with one of their number, Therese Neumann, that "suffering is something one cannot want." Yet Therese also said when it comes, "I say, 'Savior, it's all right with me.'"

2. The medal commemorates God's creating Mary free from original sin, in order to make her a fitting vessel to bear Jesus. If original sin is a new idea, think of it as the innate human tendency to "screw up."

3. *Mother Frances Xavier Cabrini* by Mother Saverio De Maria.

4. See a chapter on her inedia in my book *The Sanctified Body*.

5. This does not imply that only people with good mothers become saints; Adrienne von Speyr, for instance, was rejected from birth by her mother and Caryll Houselander's very neurotic mother caused her daughter much suffering.

6. There is some confusion about her birth date but this is probably correct.

Chapter Nine

THERESE VISITS HER NEAREST AND DEAREST— AND A FELLOW NUN

No dead saint in the twentieth century has been seen by more people aspiring to holiness than St. Therese of Lisieux. During her life this great messenger of God received three known after-death visitations from holy people.

The first when, as a very ill ten-year-old, she was cured instantaneously by a "visit" of the smiling Virgin Mary, is outside the scope of this book.

The second was a numinous dream after Therese, by special dispensation, entered the Lisieux Carmel at the age of fifteen. The aged foundress of this Carmel, Mother Genevieve, who at age eighty-three was sixty-eight years Therese's senior, confirmed the young girl's call to serve God peacefully and joyfully with total confidence in his goodness. When Mother Genevieve died, Therese captured a tear that lay on the dead woman's cheek with a scrap of linen and kept it as a precious relic in the locket that held her own vows.

A few nights later, the youngest Carmelite dreamed about the aged one. In this dream Mother Genevieve was making her will. She had something to give each nun until she came to Therese. Then, with apparently nothing left, she said three times, "To you, I leave my heart."

The third instance, also in the form of a dream, came as a great consolation during a period when Therese was in spiritual turmoil. In her autobiography, *Story of a Soul,* Therese describes how in her dream she was walking in a corridor of the Carmel. Suddenly also there were three Carmelites from heaven, wearing long veils over their faces.

Immediately, Therese thought how happy she would be if she could see the face of one of the heavenly visitors. As if in reply to her thought, the tallest of the three came over to Therese. As Therese instinctively knelt at her feet, the other Carmelite lifted her veil so that it covered Therese, too. Therese recognized—her face "lit by a gentle glow"—Anne of Jesus, the long-dead Carmelite who had brought the order from Spain to France. (At that time titled *Venerable,* Anne since has been beatified.)

Anne caressed Therese, who felt moved by this gesture of love to say, "I implore you, Mother, to tell me if God is going to leave me on earth for long. Will He come for me soon?"

In response Therese received a tender smile and the murmured words, "Yes, soon ... soon. I promise you."

Boldly, Therese begged, "Tell me, Mother, if God is pleased with me. Does he want anything more from me beyond my poor little deeds and my longings?"

Therese noted that Anne's face "shone with a new splendor" and "her gaze grew even more tender" as she replied that God was pleased, very pleased, with Therese and asked nothing more of her.

The visitor then took Therese's head between her hands with an indescribable love that set her, Therese says, "aflame with joy."

She wanted to ask Venerable Anne to obtain some spiritual favors from God for her beloved blood sisters Pauline, Marie, Leonie, and Celine but at that moment she woke up.

Therese—bless her—adds to her account of all this at least some of its after-effects:

When I woke ... I knew that heaven exists and that souls dwell there who love me and look upon me as their child. The realization of this never left me, and it was all the sweeter because until then I had been quite indifferent to the Venerable Mother Anne of Jesus. I never thought of her.... But now I know and really understand that she is far from indifferent about me. This knowledge deepens my love both for her and for all the blessed ones in heaven.

In her turn, Therese after death returned to give spiritual direction to those aspiring to sanctity. Those seeking the heights of wholeness included some in her own Lisieux Carmel. A later chapter details how God used Therese to raise the Carmel as a whole to a higher level of love for God and each other. Spotlighted here is Therese as a God-sent guide to that elite group whose lives set a direct course to heaven, represented primarily by interventions in the lives of her four blood sisters—all nuns.

Like Therese, the four other Martin girls did not enter convents to become "good little nuns," but saints. Three of them lived in the Lisieux Carmel; the family's "ugly duckling," Leonie—not strong enough for the taxing physical demands of Carmelite life—found her path in the less rigorous cloistered convent of Visitation nuns in the nearby city of Caen. Undoubtedly, Therese carried God-given favors to her sisters, which will forever be unknown, particularly in the years after the investigative tribunal finished its questioning about such things, but here is a sampling (in the sisters' birth order).

Marie, the oldest Martin child and Therese's godmother, as Carmelite nun Marie of the Sacred Heart, shared a large-visioned way of thinking with her littlest sister that made them, in a sense, kindred souls. Marie early grasped the depths of sanctity hidden in her youngest sister's quiet life. Original and frank, Marie's disdain for much that passes for "pious" masked her own holiness; but Therese saw and reverenced in her a heart given totally to God.

The day after Therese's death, Marie later testified under oath before the tribunal investigating Therese's possible holiness, "after I did a charitable act, I felt her soul approach mine with an expression of joy that I can't [adequately] express."

In her private notes, Marie wrote:

The dominant grace, since my dear little sister went to Heaven, is that I sense her near me. I know that she is not dead, that she has only put off for a time her garment of flesh, but that her life is not extinguished, rather she is in the fullness of life.

Marie goes on to say that she feels Therese explaining to her the path Marie should follow to become a saint and details her dead sister's recommendations at length.

God guides Marie without miracles or apparitions for most of the remaining forty-two years of her life, since Therese's sisters want to follow her in living heroically by faith, rather than in the easy euphoria of "consolations." Still, perhaps a dozen times at the very moment when Marie—suspicious of "phenomena" by temperament anyway—would least expect such manifestations, showers of perfumes mysteriously envelope her. Like the very first grace the day after Therese's death, these signs of her dead sister's presence always sanction some act of charity or humility of Marie's, as if applauding, "That's the way!" Such events caused this thirteen-years-older sister, who had helped rear Therese (then four) after their mother's early death, to now humbly ask Therese to mother her in God, instructing Marie in his ways and helping her practice virtue.

The last eleven years of Marie's life, the independence-loving, free spirit was confined to bed or wheelchair with crippling rheumatism. If Therese did not come to cure her, Marie wrote to Leonie, "It's surely because there are some great graces hidden in all this." And Therese did show up a couple times. Marie writes, again to Leonie:

It was the night of January 29 [1939] that I was suffering a lot from rheumatism in my knees and my devoted nurse, who sleeps in a cell near mine in order to be able to look out for me, saw that I could feel my legs and knees all twisted—which happens sometimes. Being unable to help me after trying a lot, she said to me: "I'm going to ask our saint to come to your rescue." Then she left sad but confident. Just a few moments later, I felt as if someone was very gently straightening out my legs without any trouble, and I had no doubt of a supernatural intervention. The prayer of my nurse had been heard and my little Therese truly came to my aid. I had no more suffering and was able to sleep the entire night.

On a second occasion, Marie had a piercing pain in her shoulder, found herself as if paralyzed and unable to re-cover herself when her blankets slipped off. The account has the fuzziness of the true saint's efforts to downplay such things. Thus it is not said that Therese was seen, but simply that she

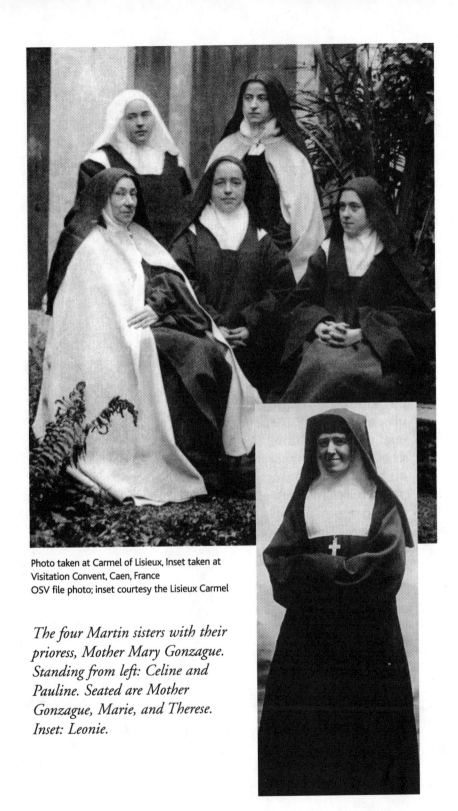

Photo taken at Carmel of Lisieux, Inset taken at
Visitation Convent, Caen, France
OSV file photo; inset courtesy the Lisieux Carmel

The four Martin sisters with their
prioress, Mother Mary Gonzague.
Standing from left: Celine and
Pauline. Seated are Mother
Gonzague, Marie, and Therese.
Inset: Leonie.

courtesy Sisters of the Blessed Sacrament

Blessed Katharine Drexel

courtesy Sheed & Ward

Caryll Houselander when young

Right, a typical statue of St. Therese as she appeared so some WWI soldiers, such as Roger Lefebvre. Below, a holy card representation of the saint.

(holy card from the author's collection).

courtesy the January, 1993, *Review Therese de Lisieux*

Sister Eusebia Palomino

Mother Frances Schervier

Father Maximilian Kolbe

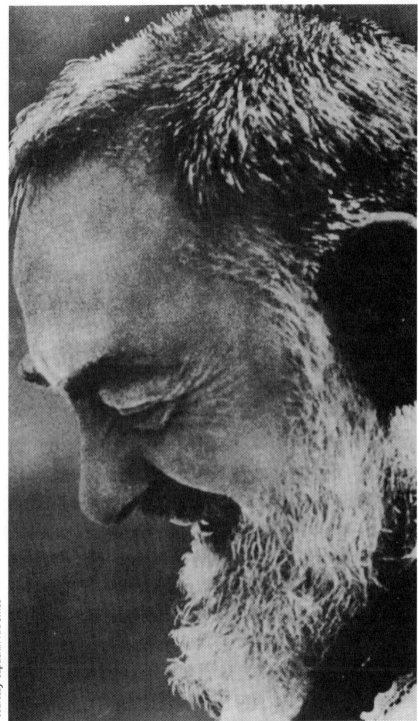

Padre Pio

Rochelle Freeman

St. Madeleine Sophie Barat

St. Henry de Osso

Father Aloysius Ellacuria

St. John Bosco

St. Gemma Galgani

Saint Gabriel Possenti / St. Gabriel of the Sorrowful Virgin

*Sister Therese took off her Carmelite habit to
portray St. Joan of Arc for a play staged
within the cloister in 1895.*

Blessed Philip Rinaldi

St. Gaspar del Bufalo

Bishop John Neumann

St. Pius X

Blessed John XXIII

*Black Elk holding
his rosary*

"descended" and, with her sisterly hand, pulled up Marie's covers and soothed her sufferings. But Marie *must* have seen her dead sister or been positive of her presence, for the account[1] from Lisieux says that after thanking her, the rheumatic said to Therese, "Go back to Heaven now."

Pauline (known in Carmel as Mother Agnes of Jesus), the second child of the Martins, was born the year after Marie and these two were always close. Pauline said, when questioned after Marie's quiet death at age eighty on January 19, 1940, that she felt neither Marie's nor Therese's "presence," but was certain of assistance nevertheless.

Pauline's winning, loving ways ("she sowed joy all her life," one source says) and her motherly style of leadership make her probably the closest to Therese of the sisters in personality. It was sixteen-year-old Pauline of whom their mother Zelie exclaimed as she lay dying, "I know you'll become a nun—and a saint."

As the prioress of Carmel for many years after Therese's death, saintly, capable Mother Agnes—so as not to lead her spiritual daughters into misplacing their energy from the quest for virtue to that for wonders—was very reticent about anything Therese did for her personally. We know from her sworn testimony that she, to whom four-year-old Therese had spontaneously turned when Zelie died with the cry, "Pauline, you will be my mother now," was not ignored by her dead "child." Pauline admits to the tribunal that at least ten times in the first decade or so after her little sister's death she has experienced "visits" from Therese through the odor of sanctity alone. But the bare fact is all we know. Not a single detail escaped those humble lips.

Diminutive Pauline, whom Therese always addressed as "petite mere," lived to be ninety, dying in 1951. In her old age, she did feel free to mention a humorous event she called a dream. Therese had come to her looking just as in life and said with a smile, "You're getting old, my little mother."

Eager to take off for heaven, Pauline said she replied to Therese, "Nothing could give me more pleasure than to hear that!"

Leonie became a Visitation nun only after Therese's death, having previously flunked out first at the Poor Clares and then twice at the Visitation cloister, physically and emotionally unable to take the demands of either lifestyle. As Therese lay dying, she promised she would see Leonie's dream fulfilled. Not long after Therese's death, the Caen Visitation got new leaders less severe in their demands: Thirty-six-year-old Leonie was permitted a fourth try and succeeded at last.

The rest of her life Leonie relied greatly on her dead little sister and often promised favors in Therese's name to those asking Leonie's prayers. During World War I, the families of soldiers she promised "Therese will bring them back" were not disappointed, even in one family where several sons fought four years in the front lines.

As with all her sisters, Therese's help was not so obvious that the Visitation nun lost the merit of living most of the time by "pure faith." But now and then a gesture reminded Leonie that Therese was looking out for her. Leonie testified during the official investigation of Therese:

Around 1900 one evening in winter, feeling a lot of ennui and revulsion, I was praying in slipshod fashion.... Suddenly a luminous form that dazzled me appeared on our Book of Hours. I wasn't afraid, quite the contrary. After an instant, I realized that this luminous form was a hand. I believe firmly that it was my little Therese; I was perfectly consoled and experienced a delicious peace. This has never happened again. But on September 30, the anniversary of Therese's death, I've felt, two or three times [during the day], the odor of roses; this has happened four or five years; other years it hasn't.

Not long after giving this testimony under oath, in 1912, Leonie writes her three Carmelite sisters about one of those visits:

On the thirtieth of September, Therese visited me in the evening by sweet, penetrating odors of roses. They only lasted several instants, long enough that, in my joy, I was able to say, "O my beloved little sister, you're here near me, I'm sure." Since [then] I feel myself more fervent [so that] this "little nothing" wants to become a saint too.

During her last years, Leonie was healed of pneumonia when someone at her bedside called on Therese, but her convalescence was long and painful. Several times in this difficult period the official account of her life from her Visitation convent[2] says, "a supernatural presence—that of her Therese—comforted her."

When Leonie died in 1941 at age seventy-eight, Cardinal Suhard of Paris spoke of her as one of the hidden saints who keep our world going. It was to her entire family's prayers and Therese's guidance that Leonie gave the credit for her change from a mentally slow, allergy-wracked, physically frail, psychologically damaged (a housekeeper secretly terrorized her in childhood[3]), melancholy person weighted down with a sense of inferiority into a woman buoyant with the joy that all her lacks and miseries were only so many more claims on God's mercy. To the minds of many, one of Therese's miracles, Leonie is a candidate for beatification.

Celine Martin—known in Carmel as Sister Genevieve of the Holy Face—was only four years older than Therese and the two youngest of this family were inseparable.

In October 1897, only two weeks after her death, Therese came to this artistically gifted,[4] independent-minded sister who had been depressed by certain spiritual difficulties for a long time. Fully awake—in fact, making the Way of the Cross (a holistic meditation on Jesus' Passion) outdoors in the Carmel cloister—Celine saw "a kind of flame coming from the depths of the sky." At the same moment she realized interiorly, "It's Therese." She told the tribunal she could not put into words "the interior grace I received then," claiming, "it is beyond my powers of expression." But years after seeing this "living flame" in the daytime sky, she insists it "was one of the greatest graces I have ever received." All sorts of groundless worries that had kept her occupied simply disappeared, questions were resolved, and she found herself securely on higher spiritual ground.

The following March, as Celine completed a retreat, she affectionately reproached Therese that her dead sister hadn't helped her, only to suddenly feel invaded by an intimate sweetness firing her with divine love.

Sometimes Celine experienced Therese's presence through the odor of sanctity. While often giving the "well done!" to acts of humility or charity, the perfumes also marked special occasions. Celine experienced these odors, for instance, on February 5, 1912, an anniversary of the day she entered Carmel—which was also the day that the diocese's investigation of Therese's sanctity was sent to Rome—and again on March 17, 1915, the anniversary of Celine's taking the veil and the opening of Rome's part of the Theresian investigation.

At other times Therese spoke to Celine. For example, on the Feast of the Transfiguration (August 6, 1939), Celine complained that she hadn't the strength to go on, only to hear Therese comforting her that "she had nothing to fear, that she would always have the strength found in having no strength...." (See instances of both speech and perfume visits to Celine in chapter 13.)

On the morning their oldest sister, Marie, died in 1940, Celine was inundated with those mysterious perfumes, which lasted for eight days and made her understand, she said, how precious the death of his true friends is to God. Were the perfumes an indication, as they can be, of the divine presence? Or did they signal the presence of Therese or Marie? Or of both sisters? Take your pick.

Celine herself would die February 25, 1959, just two months short of her ninety-first birthday, with the same reputation of holiness as her sisters. Her death replicated Therese's in many ways, such as its heavy suffering followed by something like ecstasy in the final moments. Did Celine's ecstatic gaze see Therese? Or the "good God" she longed for even more?

After little Therese lost her mother, her mother's brother Isidore Guerin and his wife Celine (Fournet) Guerin played important roles in their niece's life. Some of the last weakly scrawled or gasped-out verbal messages of the dying Therese were to gratefully tell Aunt Celine and Uncle Isidore how much she loved them and to promise her help once she reached heaven. Therese's Aunt Celine was easy to love, one of those "born-nice" people whose goodness deepened with the years. Two years after Therese's death, Aunt Celine—then in her fifties—experienced rapidly declining health. To a daughter after a sleepless night, she confided:

> I would suffer a lot, but my little Therese watches over me tenderly. All night I felt her near my bed. Several times, she caressed me, which gave me an extraordinary sense of courage.

Accepting death as sweetly as she had lived, Celine Fournet Guerin died smiling on February 13, 1900. The priest who brought her the last sacraments marveled that in twenty-five years ministering to the dying he had never encountered such "angelic piety."

Even before death, Therese had been a big help to her cousin Marie Guerin (one of Isidore and Celine's two daughters), curing her of scruples. A year after Therese died, Marie's spiritual life took a whole new direction—deep changes in her obvious to others—the day after she asked Therese to "take me in hand again and help me walk the way of pure love." Without seeing Therese or sensing her presence, while at prayer Marie suddenly saw clearly *how to* move toward her goal. She attributed to Therese her life-changing insight. In a letter written around this time, she writes: "It is certain that since the death of our little saint, I don't feel the same any longer and others notice too."

In her mid-thirties, Marie of the Eucharist, too, became tubercular. Near the end of her life, she wrote to her family that Therese was for her "a veritable Guardian Angel, guiding her every moment and proving her love" for Marie "by all sorts of little delicate attentions which could only come from Heaven." To our frustration, Marie leaves unspecified what forms the dead saint's guidance and little attentions took.

Instinctively repulsed at the thought of death, Marie turned that over to Therese, too, as her disease proved incurable. To Marie's astonishment and joy, all her fear and repugnance vanished. Sister Agnes of Jesus wrote to Leonie in Caen that their cousin Marie "died the death of a saint. It was absolutely celestial." Marie of the Eucharist's serenity, in fact, so struck even nonrelatives who witnessed her last days and death that nine years later, one witness, Mother Isabelle of the Sacred Heart, remarked, "When one has seen Sister Marie of the Eucharist die, one can no longer fear death."

That Therese played a major role, all were sure. But if any form of after-death appearances were involved, this again is hidden from view—perhaps a good reminder that all the appearances of Therese together add up to only a minuscule part of the works God has done through her.

Besides helping relatives, Therese has guided many men and women who want to give themselves completely to God. One of these is Sister Alphonsa, a Catholic candidate for official sainthood from the Malabar Syrian rite in India. Born Anna Muttathupandatu, when quite young this God-intoxicated girl had a dream in which "a young Carmelite" told her God was calling her to become a nun. Anna even burned herself—hoping to be less attractive—to get out of the marriage her family was arranging. After several close matrimonial calls, in her late teens she was allowed to become a Franciscan Clarist nun (not the same order as the Poor Clares, but sharing their name).

Sister Alphonsa had a lot of health problems. One day St. Therese appeared to her to talk about them. One of those "good news, bad news" conversations, God's messenger promised the young Indian nun would get no more contagious diseases, but said she would have other types of ailments until her death. Usually sent to heal people, Therese in this case confirmed a very unusual vocation. The invalid sister died in 1946 at only thirty-five.

Does Therese still show up to guide people striving for holiness? It appears so. In the Lisieux Archives I noted the letter from a Father Andre whose last name I withhold. He writes of how he saw Therese in 1979 while praying the rosary. She said nothing, according to his account, but definitely communicated, for her appearance left him "filled with joy."

Endnotes

1. I am working from the biography *Marie* published by the Carmel and authored by priest-Theresian authority Pere Stephane-Joseph Piat, O.F.M. As far as I know, it has never been translated into English.
2. Published by the Lisieux Carmel, however.
3. This abuse was uncovered by Marie twenty days after their mother's holy sister, a Visitation nun with a special love for Leonie, died, promising help for the difficult child from heaven.
4. Her painting based on the Shroud of Turin, for example, circulates in millions of copies and won an international prize for religious art in 1909.

Chapter Ten

AN ICON OF DIVINE COMPASSION

During World War I, an old man walked into the room of the friary where Padre Pio was absorbed in prayer. He said he was Pietro di Mauro, and that he had died on September 18, 1908, in the friary, when it was a home for the elderly. He died, he told the young friar, in room number four, having fallen asleep smoking a cigar that set the bed on fire. God, he said, had given him permission to come to Pio and ask his prayers, especially a Mass.

Padre Pio, who was still young at the time, found this hard to take. He confided in the friary Superior Padre Paolino, who had a few doubts of his own. Padre Paolino had the idea to go down to the town below the friary and check the death records, in which he discovered that this di Mauro, indeed, had died when and how he said. Padre Pio saw the old fellow again, when he had completed his spiritual growth and purification and was on his way to heaven.

In 1945, Brother Peter of the friary where Padre Pio lived went back to his room following the friary's usual midnight prayers.

To his great surprise and fear, he found seated at the desk a very young friar, his head covered by his hood and resting in the palms of his hands as if he were meditating. Even though he was scared, ... [Brother Peter] had the courage to ask in a loud voice, "Who are you?" But the only answer he received was the young friar's disappearance into thin air. Very scared, Brother Peter cried out and ran to Padre Pio....

Padre Pio, a dozen years Peter's senior and by now used to such things, put his arm about his fellow Franciscan's shoulder with reassuring words. Pio knew this spirit well; not yet purified enough to withstand the light of heaven, he needed prayer, but was no one to be afraid of.

While they did not upset Pio, the dead added to the "impossible" burden carried by the mystic, taken note of by publications like the *New York Times* as well as "those tabloids." An icon of divine compassion in a too often pitiless century, Pio tried—like a variant on the mythical St. Christopher—to carry the world to God on his spiritual back. In several other books, I have written of his own weaknesses, spiritual struggles, and physical disabilities—as well as his joy and sense of humor—as he struggled to bring others to God, while existing mysteriously on amounts of sleep, food, and rest unable to sustain human life, let alone a demanding, round-the-clock ministry.

After a lifetime given to the service of God and humanity, Padre Pio died September 23, 1968, in his armchair, a doctor present marveling at "the most peaceful and sweet [death] I have ever seen."

Barely had he slipped so quietly into the next dimension then the dead saint reappeared and conversed with his old friend, physician Andrea Cardone in Pietrelcina. It was only the start. Since his death, Padre Pio has been busier than ever. In *Nothing Short of a Miracle* I told in detail of Kelly Wilkinson from the village of Clogherhead in County Louth, born with such a serious heart defect she was baptized on the spot. By prayer, she lived to be three, but always frail, always expected to die. Then, at three, when her heart condition had reached the crisis point, the tyke saw dead Padre Pio in her bedroom and was completely healed.

A second chapter on Padre Pio will detail another great cure like Kelly's; here, I want to take the opposite tack and give short summations of many after-death appearances—concentrating on cures—to represent his work as God's messenger. All incidents are from the archives at the friary where Padre Pio lived and through the kindness of the late Father Joseph Pius Martin.[1] My point: like St. Therese before him, Padre Pio is a man who really gets around.

In fact, it can be said without exaggeration that the brown-robed Capuchin has appeared just about everywhere in the world since his death. Like Therese before him, God is using Padre Pio to cure, to redirect, to guide, to obtain great miracles, and to deliver everyday little favors, like the one to the elderly couple who told the dead saint they couldn't afford to replace their malfunctioning stove: they suddenly smelled "a beautiful perfume out of the blue" just at the hour a relative inquired of their son, "Did he know anyone who wanted a cooker?"

———◆◆◆———

Padre Pio's own family had been working-class—poor enough that gentle Papa Forgione did manual labor (in the United States) far from his loved ones for years, to send home the money that enabled little Francesco, who loved God so, to quit the field for priestly studies. Padre Alessio Parente quotes Padre Pio: "The immense pity I experience at the sight of a poor man gives rise deep down in my soul to a most vehement desire to help him...."

It is no wonder, then, that Padre Pio often carries God's blessings to poor working men. For example, on July 3, 1935, at his work site, Antonio Paladino was run over by a cart loaded with concrete. For *thirty-three years* he was pretty much immobilized as a result. In late September 1968, Padre Pio died. On the twelfth of December, the dead priest appeared to the invalid workman. Paladino felt Pio tap his left shoulder as the Capuchin—who could be seen clearly—told him to get up and walk without using his stick. Paladino obeyed. He found he could walk.

Similarly, on September 23, 1955, Antonio Di Pasquale of Pietranico, Pescara, Italy, was lifting a sheet of marble when he felt an acute pain in his spine. He was paralyzed for fifteen years. Frequent hospitalizations left him feeling helpless and hopeless, especially as his hearing and sight faded to almost nil as well.

His wife Lucia, upon Padre Pio's death, got hold of a handkerchief that had touched the dead saint. Very superstitious in some views. But the fact remains that God does not seem offended when people clutch at something belonging to his friends, the same way a desperate woman once grabbed Jesus' hem.[2] When Lucia begged Padre Pio's help, it appears he went to God and received a commission.

On June 7, 1970, Antonio Di Pasquale saw Padre Pio. In spite of his deafness, he heard Pio order, "Get up and walk." If he ignored that command, it was only because he had been, after all, completely paralyzed for fifteen years. But when Pio repeated the order, something broke loose in the former workman's soul, or body, or both. He felt strength surge through him. He stood up. In that motion he not only regained movement, his sight returned, too. After a pilgrimage of thanks to San Giovanni Rotondo, he pilgrimaged to the healing shrine at Lourdes. There, on August 6, his hearing came back.

Phyllis Capalbo's grandson Michael lost half his right toe when a thousand-pound cylinder fell on his foot. With his doctors not sure they could save the rest of the toe, Phyllis rushed to the hospital to give Michael a written novena requesting Padre Pio's prayers. As Michael read it, his father and sister arrived and, curious, looked on. Suddenly the room filled with the scent of flowers. No bouquets had been delivered or parked in the hall. Since the threesome knew nothing about Padre Pio, Michael's excited grandmother explained such perfumes often suggest the saint is making a visit. The toe was saved.

The cure may not always be physical: James Prior is also disabled in a work accident in March 1984, when in his mid-fifties. He dreams of Padre Pio five years later, and finds himself "more at ease with my disability." He begins saving money to visit San Giovanni Rotondo.

Of course, Padre Pio does not only turn up to help working men or those who are poor. The testimony of nurse Rita M. De Nitti:

In 1974 I was the recipient of what my husband and I consider a miracle from Padre Pio. I was told in July 1974 I would be opened for major cancer. Since I was also a nurse at the hospital I knew the score. The surgeon told me very bluntly, "We are opening you up for major cancer, with the expectation of finding it, and praying we don't." The night before surgery my husband awakened about 2:00 A.M. to the scent of roses (a miracle in itself, since he was just out of the hospital from nose surgery and could smell nothing at all). He followed the scent to the living room where on the mantle was a continuous candle burning in front of a statue of Padre Pio. Suddenly he heard a voice and it said, "Rudolph, don't worry; they won't find cancer: she'll be all right." My husband was stunned. The next morning I was in surgery six hours and the doctor came into my room smiling and said to me, "Do you know you had a miracle? There isn't a trace of cancer in your body anywhere. A large tumor was removed and it was benign."

The nurse made a thanksgiving pilgrimage to Padre Pio's grave.

———◦◦◦———

Rosario Mendoza suffered for nineteen years from a bad heart. At the time of her experience, her condition had deteriorated until she had to use oxygen monthly and felt "my health was failing very badly." A friend gave her a card soliciting Padre Pio's prayers.

On December 10, 1984, she fell asleep, weeping in great depression over her poor health and the lack of money for medical treatment. She dreamed "an old man" woke her up and asked her to get up and drink some water. He followed her and seemed to put medicine in the glass. The next morning she awoke feeling great. In a checkup, her doctor exclaimed, "with joy and amazement, 'a miracle! You are healed!'" Rosario's heart was perfectly normal. She was sure "the mysterious old man was Padre Pio."

———◦◦◦———

Ethna Smyth writes to the friars:

After two years of treatment I had lost the power of my right hand. I could use it very little and had to wear a support band as my wrist had dropped. I accepted the fact that I would be curtailed somewhat for the rest of my life. Then it happened. (I had been praying to Padre Pio. In fact, I brought a picture of him with me when attending doctors and hospitals, etc.) A friend of the family, a Holy Ghost brother, called at our house and just by chance had a relic of Padre Pio with him. I put the relic on my hand and we both said the prayer to Padre Pio [for his intercession]. I thought no more about it, but some hours later I thought I heard a voice in my own head saying, "You have not very much faith in me or you would not be wearing that old band." And I laughed and said, "Now Padre Pio, you know I cannot take it off." But the voice persisted and I felt Padre Pio was telling me I must have faith and take it off. After some more hours had lapsed the voice still kept on so I just pulled it off saying, "Now Padre Pio are you satisfied, but you know I cannot leave it off." But I did and I have never used it since that day over a year ago. I am writing this letter with my cured hand. I can also drive a car and do all my housework.

Teresita Fearon sends a picture of a lovely young bride, born Rosemary Johnson from Australia. The accompanying testimony goes back to 1965, when Teresita's friend, who had six daughters, found herself pregnant at age forty-four. Her doctor advised an abortion, but Mona Johnson, a staunch Catholic, said "no." Still, she worried.

Teresita gave her a scapular blessed by Padre Pio that Teresita had received from Father Alessio Parente, a Franciscan close to Padre Pio. Every day from then on, the pregnant woman asked Padre Pio's prayers. On October 13, 1965, Rosemary Johnson was born. It appeared all that praying had been worthless, for the parents were told, "the baby did not stand a chance." Teresita writes that Rosemary "was born with a heart that was upside down, back to front, on the wrong side and it had extra tubes and valves. In both the upper and lower chambers the heart also had holes." Surgery was impossible: her mother was told by the delivery nurse that the infant, a pathetic little thing, would just get weaker and weaker and be dead in a few hours.

"No, she won't," Mona replied. "She's going to be all right."

"How do you know that?" the nurse asked, humoring her.

"God told me so," Mona answered. If she didn't believe the medical verdict, she felt she had a very good reason: Immediately after the birth, everyone's attention diverted to the very blue newborn, Mona was left alone in the delivery room. As she lay there, Padre Pio appeared and told the worried mother, "Everything is going to be all right." Knowing the Australian medical people knew nothing of the Italian priest, she never mentioned him to them. But when the baby surprised the doctors by living long enough to go home, Mona pinned the scapular that Padre Pio had once blessed on her baby.

Teresita says, "She did look a very sick little baby. I remember seeing her so pale, so frail, with this lump on the right side where her heart is. I could see it beating very fast." Mona, however, kept faith that God had not sent Padre Pio to lie to her. Faith well placed, as the picture of the lovely, healthy-looking young bride shows.

———•◆•———

Marie Wallace's niece, in April 1987, was in such a serious traffic accident she almost lost her life. The doctors wished to amputate one leg, but her mother refused permission. Aunt and mother prayed hard and "a few nights later while staying in a house close by the hospital, I woke up," reports Marie, "and also woke up my sister with my shouting."

"Did you see him?"

"Who?"

"Padre Pio!"

"You're dreaming."

"I *wasn't*," Marie protested. In the end she half-convinced her sister she'd seen Padre Pio, who came with the message that Sharon would walk again.

What makes this testimony interesting is that, at the same hour, Sharon also woke, screaming, "Please stop pulling my leg."

"Who's pulling your leg, dear?" a nurse asked.

"The man in the brown habit. Don't you see him?" the injured girl cried.

The nurse was not surprised, Marie later discovered: The staff say Padre Pio appears a lot in that hospital, carrying God's healing. Sharon was a recipient.

When the testimony was added to the San Giovanni archives three years later in 1990, she walked without a limp and had 85 to 90 percent movement in the leg that should have been amputated.

Mary Ryan's brother returned to Ireland from Nigeria and became very ill with recurring malaria. Mary's mother sent a Padre Pio relic to the hospital. At 5:00 A.M. on November 14, 1989, a noise woke Mrs. Ryan, who found the room filled with "very strong perfume which lasted fifteen to twenty minutes." Her husband, *who had no sense of smell,* smelled the perfume, too. Meanwhile, at the same time—exactly 5 A.M.—Mary's brother awoke in the hospital and knew he was well. Amazed doctors ran more tests. No more malaria.

Georgina A. Lavandero wrote the friars in 1991 about a cure twelve years earlier:

> Back in 1979 my brother Carlos developed cancer in his larynx.... A widower ... (his wife had died of cancer), he had four children under his care aged five to twelve. He was immediately operated on. I started to pray to Padre Pio, asking him [to obtain] my brother's health. I was desperate. I considered this a very pathetic case.... One night while I was praying and weeping, asking Padre Pio for his intercession, a strong pleasant aroma of flowers surrounded my room. This perfume was too strong to be overlooked. Naturally I was frightened but I knew instantly that my prayers had been heard. I kept this secret to myself and waited for events to develop. And gracias Dios, after twelve years there is no sign of cancer....

Gil Gleeson had a moving—and somewhat comical—experience with his dying father. Born a Catholic, the elder Mr. Gleeson lost his faith and all connection to the Church in his youth. Gil, on the other hand, is greatly enamored of Jesus. A loving son, Gil found a Catholic priest and took him to his father. To his relief the dying man was glad. However, as Gil puts it,

Dad had some huge blocks to faith; one of them was that God, if he existed was far too holy to be approached and another was that he thought he'd committed sins that were too serious to be forgiven....

Gil turned to Padre Pio, specifically begging the dead Franciscan "to do something to persuade Dad of the reality of Christ, where I had failed miserably." Gil writes:

Next day I found Dad sitting up in bed looking so radiant that he reminded me of Moses after he'd been on the mountain. He told me that Jesus had come in the night and stood at the end of the bed. He'd opened his arms to Dad and said, "What are you afraid of?" They'd had a conversation in which his doubts had been resolved, his wrongs had been discussed and forgiven and he had developed a passionate attachment to Christ.

After awhile Gil's dad said to him, "This Jesus of yours—he's a funny looking bloke, isn't he?"

Gil wondered what he meant.

His dad described Jesus. As he listened to the description of the brown robe, the features, etc., the son realized it was Padre Pio who had appeared with open arms to Gil's father. He opted not to explain that to his dad, who died a few days later, reconciled to the Church, and assuring his son he'd give Jesus Gil's love.

A dying grandmother also found some relief—in her case not from spiritual problems, but plain old pain. Maeve Barry writes of her mother-in-law, who required larger and larger amounts of drugs to keep away the horrific pain. Until one day when she told the family that a man in a long brown dress had been there. Sitting on the end of her bed, he assured her "Your pain will soon be gone." Shown a picture of Padre Pio, she said her visitor looked like that. During the next several days of her life, she had no pain, "was in full command of herself," and died peacefully in her sleep.

———•◆•———

Mrs. D.A. Morley writes about the shock she suffered when her husband went to work "a comparatively healthy man and came back that evening close to death" from meningitis and encephalitis. The family "bombarded heaven," as she puts it, with prayer. When after four days her unconscious husband woke up, she writes:

> He tried to tell me about a man he had seen standing in the doorway of his room, wearing a long robe and tied with a cord. He had a beard and was wearing a skull cap....

When doctors discharged Morley fifteen days after he entered the hospital unconscious, they called him "the miracle man." For his part, he frequently spoke of the visitor in the robe. Morley's wife thought her husband was reliving some hallucination brought on by his illness.

Then someone gave this Catholic woman a video and written material on Padre Pio, of whom she had never heard. When she showed a photo from the book to her husband, a convert, he exclaimed, amazed, "*this is the man*" he'd seen in his hospital doorway. She was still uncertain, however: The bearded man in the brown habit her husband claimed to have seen he described as wearing a skullcap. In Padre Pio's picture, he was bareheaded. But when she saw the video—shot during Padre Pio's lifetime—she saw he did, indeed, sometimes sport a skullcap.

———•◆•———

On November 27, 1985, J.G. Hilton—who had angina problems—found himself having a bad night. The first dose of medication did nothing. The second let his pain subside enough that he slept for awhile. Then he woke and saw across the room "a priest dressed in his alb with his arms outstretched. In the background there were monks dressed in brown habits scrubbing and washing a refectory table."

A lapsed Catholic, Hilton hadn't been to Mass for over thirty-five years. At the same time he had this strange vision, he realized he was suffering a stroke. His left side paralyzed, he woke his wife, who wanted to call for medical help. "Wait a minute," Hilton said. Strangely, he could feel use returning to the paralyzed area.

Hilton confided in his Anglican wife about seeing the priest, expecting she would laugh. Instead she said, "It's Padre Pio." Running for a book he didn't know she had, she showed her husband a picture of the saint. Hilton recognized him at once as the friar he had just seen.

He decided to return to the Church. Would his wife agree to have their civil marriage blessed? She not only agreed, on June 24, 1986, she was received into the Catholic Church herself due to her great admiration for Padre Pio.

Shortly before this, as an aftereffect of his mild stroke, Hilton underwent a "risky" operation to clean out an artery leading to the brain. He says he felt no anxiety whatsoever—the implication being he felt God had Padre Pio on his case. And whether because he expected no trouble or because Padre Pio was indeed on the job, after surgery he made an "amazingly rapid" recovery.

———◆———

A nun, Sister Alberic, writes the friary to express her thanks. It has been a year, she says, since she fell and broke her ankle, hip, elbow, and shoulder. The ankle and hip caused her the most suffering. But the surgeon said he could not do any more for the foot. She'd "have to live with it." The nun did not throw in the towel, however: She attacked her problem both physically and spiritually, by going to physiotherapy and having another nun pray over her. A regular spiritual buddy of the dead Capuchin, she also daily asked his prayers.

One morning as, still in bed, she was in the middle of saying a rosary and praying her usual novena prayer to Padre Pio, she heard a "gruff voice saying, 'Alberic, move your foot.'" She writes:

For a moment I was shaken. I pulled back the covers and moved my foot in every direction and found I could freely do so. I walked all round the bedroom and found I could easily do so without pain in my foot or hip. I believe it was the voice of Padre Pio that spoke to me. I am very well now.

Endnotes

1. Most have appeared in various editions of the friary English-language publication *The Voice of Padre Pio*.
2. Similarly, others in need of healing sought handkerchiefs or any cloth that had touched the skin of the apostle Paul (see Acts 19:12) or tried to position themselves so even the shadow of Peter might fall on them!

Chapter Eleven

READY TO GO!

An old nun in the same Carmel as Therese of Lisieux, who habitually made biting remarks at Therese's expense, had even asked within her hearing as Therese lay dying, "what will we ever find to put in her obituary?"

Now God let Therese, only moments after her death, indulge herself in the revenge of the saints: Feeling a sudden change of heart, the spiteful sister placed her head on the young dead nun's feet, asking forgiveness and to be cured of a long-standing physical problem. The cure was immediate. Astounded, it was this aged nun—not Therese's blood sisters—who began to tell everyone of the dead twenty-four-year-old's sanctity.

All cures are God's doing, not any saint's. But since Therese's prayer inter- cession[1] had been specifically requested, it is reasonable to inquire how Therese could be at this work only moments removed from agonizing suffering?

One possible answer is that in God there is no time, only the eternal pres- ent. It also appears that saints are so ready to make the transition to the next world they often seem to need no "orientation" period. For some of them, of course—people like Adrienne von Speyr and Padre Pio—this is, at least in part, because they have been living with a foot in both worlds most of their lives anyway, relating to and communing with the dead almost as much as with the living.

Moreover, unlike the average soul, who usually has spiritual work to do after death to achieve the purity necessary for heaven, *all* saints have completed life's great task. They have achieved wholeness—or holiness, as we say from the spiritual perspective—by learning to love, to forgive, to trust God as a child trusts a good parent, to detach from one's particular idols, whether these be loved ones, projects, possessions, or whatever. They step into the next world "ready to go."

This, I theorize, may be why a dead saint can not only "pray" a miracle immediately after death, as Therese did, but even appear to someone so soon after death that news of the demise isn't even out yet. It is as if, as Daisy Dryden (p.23) put it, there is no river to cross between the two dimensions for those pure enough. Dead, as alive, the saint—at least in some cases—simply goes right on working in and for God without missing a perceptible beat.

Blessed Dominic Barberi is the little-known, delightfully good-humored Italian Passionist priest who, as a missionary to England, received Anglican John Henry Newman into the Catholic Church.[2] Father Dominic—a mystic who, even in great sufferings and persecutions, was so in love with God he "often felt like singing for joy"—suffered a fatal heart seizure in 1849 on an English train. Shortly after,

Dominic appeared to Father Vincent, the rector at Woodchester, and gave him certain vitally important information. The Superior (that is Father Vincent) was called away, and on his return Father Dominic was no longer there. It was later that day that the telegram giving news of Father Dominic's death at Reading was received. That afternoon three nuns, members of the Congregation of the Faithful Companions of Jesus, saw and spoke with Father Dominic as they were returning from school at St. Patrick's, Liverpool. Subsequently they learned that at the time he was already dead.

———◆◆———

St. Julie Billiart (d. 1816) once hid in a load of hay while maddened French Revolutionists screamed, "The saint! The saint!" as they searched the area frenziedly, hoping to parade her head on a pike. Yet her French countrymen rightly call her "*la sainte qui sourit,*" the smiling saint. Joy-filled, Mother Julie still could be firm when it was necessary for the welfare of a spiritual daughter:

On the very night of her [Julie's] death, one of her best-beloved daughters, Sister St. Jean, Superior of the convent of St. Hubert, heard the curtains of her bed drawn swiftly back and saw Mere Julie standing at her bedside.

"Daughter," she said in grave tones, "When did you do what I told you to do?"

Recollecting that she had neglected to fulfill a commission laid upon her by her General, and never dreaming but that the latter had arrived, as she sometimes did without sending word beforehand that she was coming, Sister St. Jean sprang from her bed exclaiming, "Oh, ma mere! I beg your pardon," but saw to her astonishment that she was alone in the room.

The next morning this sister mentioned the strange "flying visit" of Mother Julie—hardly the norm, even for saints, in that premotorized era. Two days later it was learned Mother Julie was dead at the time she chided Sister St. Jean.

⸻◆⸻

Some of these visits are in dreams. Here is the written testimony of a sister who lived in the same French convent of the Society of the Sacred Heart with Spanish-born visionary Josefa Menendez:

The night she died, not knowing that she was worse, I saw her in a dream. She was most lovely, and lay on a bed adorned with flowers. She made me a sign to come near and said to me: "Oh Sister, do not be afraid of suffering, and do not lose the smallest particle that God may send you. If you could but understand what a privilege it is to suffer for Him.... You must make a prayer of your work. Say to Him, as each occasion arises: 'For Thee, dear Jesus, I offer it to Thee'—so that He may see that you want to be with Him and to love Him. Oh if you only knew how much He wants to be loved!" She spoke impressively, so that I was very much moved. All the more so when on coming down to Mass that Sunday morning I heard that she had died in the night.

———•◦•———

St. Mary Mazzarello, a simple, Italian peasant woman who wanted to help young girls, founded the Daughters of Mary Help of Christians with St. John Bosco. Early in 1881 she was in Turin seeing a joint expedition of some of her nuns and Bosco's priests off to the missions. She was sleeping in a dormitory with two nuns when in the middle of the night she woke one of them.

"Sister Arecco is dead!" she whispered. Then she said that the dead woman had just been there. Sister Pacotto, the nun Mary woke up, just nodded and went back to sleep. She was sure Mary had just had a vivid dream. Maybe she did. But in the morning a telegram was delivered: Sister Arecco had died "precisely at the time" when Mary saw her.

A quiet personality of true holiness, Mary herself died a short time later on May 14, 1881. That evening, a priest in Sicily received a telegram with the news. His was the unpleasant duty of telling Mary's blood sister Felicina—stationed there as a nun in the same order—of her older sister's death. Knowing how much the two loved each other, the priest was nervous.

But when he arrived at Felicina's residence, before he could open his mouth she blurted out, "Father, last night I had the most wonderful dream. Yet, somehow *it wasn't a dream*. It was so real. I really saw my sister. She was clothed in a splendid white light. She was radiant. She smiled at me and said, 'Goodbye, Felicina! Goodbye!'"

Felicina ended her account by saying to her visitor, "I wonder what all this means?" The suddenly relaxed priest, sighing happily, prepared to tell her, sure that God had sent Mother Mazzarello herself to pave the way.

———•◦•———

St. Henry de Osso (1840-96) was canonized by Pope John Paul II in 1993. In his native Spain, the founder of the Society of Saint Teresa of Jesus[3] is recalled as "a remarkable organizer of religious classes," who also educated through retreats, preaching, writing books, and editing magazines, as well as teaching one-on-one by spiritual direction and hearing confessions. If Father Henry differs from the sixty-some priests who founded religious orders in the nine-teenth century, it is probably the importance the Spanish priest gave to working with women. Thus he founded an order of educators (today widespread, includ-ing to the United States) primarily to work with girls because he said, "educate a boy and you educate a man but educate a girl and you educate a family." It's fitting, then, that even after death Father Henry appears mostly to women.

He died at only fifty-six of a sudden cerebral hemorrhage. It may be that he had been crushed (although he said only "this is coming against us from good people") by the perfidy of some ungrateful cloistered nuns. After he had built them a convent free of charge, they immediately brought legal action against him in the Church's courts because they did not want him to use some of the open land next to their gift convent to build a school and a novitiate for his teaching nuns.

A person who dies in the middle of a big legal entanglement—especially an unjust attack on oneself—can be expected to die with unresolved issues of anger, bitterness, etc. In St. Henry's case, he died during a month of spiritual retreat in a Franciscan monastery where he went as a stranger of unknown his-tory. His spirit was so far above any bitterness or anger—he was certain God permitted everything only so a greater good should result in the end—that the friars raided his wastebasket for torn envelopes and even pencil shavings to save as relics, because it was obvious to them that an authentic saint had dropped into their midst.

Fray Francisco Domingo Paya, who heard Henry's confession on January 27, 1896, and venerated him as a saint, wrote that de Osso died that day sometime before midnight. That same night at just about that same time— "sometime after eleven"—one of the nuns of the order founded by de Osso was at work far away in a town called Taragona. This Sister Asuncion Mallol had the habit of staying up late to do certain work. Father Henry didn't like to see her missing her rest that way and had admonished her about it some-time before his death.

Glibly the sister promised she wouldn't stay up late anymore. Father Henry responded he had no confidence in her promise. It's hard, he explained, when one has such a habit, to give it up. Now she was proving him right, for she was up late working with two other sisters. Suddenly she noticed Father Henry in the room.

"Oh, our father!" she exclaimed with chagrin, caught in the act. He said nothing in reply but, perhaps having made his point just by his presence, turned and walked into the next room. The three sisters followed, but did not find him. The next day they learned that he had died about the time they saw him. Of course, due to the "around midnight" and "after eleven," it is impossible to say whether he appeared by bilocation minutes before his death or immediately after it. Either way shows a man, to borrow mystic Padre Pio's words, completely "attached to the thread of God's will."

Something interesting also happened in Toluca, Mexico, that same night. Young Concepcion Jimenez was one of the first boarders in the recently established school of the Teresian sisters, the order founded by Father Henry. At first she was terribly homesick, but gradually she was won over by one of the nuns who often talked a lot about Father Henry and the way he took such good care of his spiritual daughters, providing untiringly for their needs and giving them—in chaste fashion—the marks of affection women crave. Although she had never met this Father Henry, Concepcion began to feel he was her spiritual father, too, although she had no thought of becoming one of his nuns. Quoting directly the next part of her testimony:

On the night of January 27, 1896, I was sleeping soundly. In a dream I saw our Father dead and laid out on a table, poor and wrapped in a sheet or some white material. As I was familiar with his picture, I recognized him clearly. Frightened, I approached the table. With awe I saw him open his eyes. He looked at me with affection and extending his right hand, laid it on my brow, saying, "You will be one of mine."

At the touch of that cold hand my brow froze and I awoke frightened and screaming, "Our father founder is dead."

The sister ... who slept in our dormitory and the rest of the girls woke up in fright and, thinking that I was having a nightmare, tried to wake me up. But I continued screaming, "Our father founder is dead! My brow is still cold where he touched me!"

The next day ... the Superior ... reproved me seriously and admonished me neither to wake the girls up again nor to frighten them so. And to erase the impression that I still felt, she told me about the custom of laying priests out in ... vestments and not in a sheet as I assured them that I had seen our Father. I apologized for the scare that my dream had given them and promised sincerely not to perturb my companions' sleep again. The interview took place between eight and nine o'clock in the morning. On the afternoon of the same day a telegram arrived with the message, "Founder dead."

... Later it was confirmed that he had been laid out in the way that I had seen him and not in ... vestments. Three years later I became one of his.

Besides Spain and Mexico, Father Henry also showed up in Montevideo, Uruguay, according to a young maid named Carmen Gomez, employed in the Teresian sister's school there at the time Father Henry died. Later Carmen Gomez became a Teresian lay sister. As her testimony, formally written up some years later when she had become a member of the community, is long, I summarize it.

When word arrived that Father Henry had died in Spain, the Teresian sisters gathered to pray, their superior handing Carmen the keys to the front door.

That evening she opened the parlor door and saw "a venerable priest sitting on the sofa." She wrote, "I thought that it was someone come to see the sisters and in my timidity did not dare address him, for he filled me with a certain respect that even now, after so many years, I still feel." Silently, she shut the door and scurried away.

But soon the shy, young housemaid felt an irresistible urge to open the door a little bit and peek in at the priest again. This time she watched him walking back and forth. Again Carmen was filled with awe to the point that, years later, she writes, "I still seem to hear ... the noise of his footsteps as he paced the room." Again, she was unable to step in and ask whom he wished to see. Finally, she once more wordlessly shut the door.

As she went on with her work outside the parlor, she decided she really must ask his name and inform the superior of his being there. But when she opened the door the third time, the room was empty.

Remember ineffability, the certainty that something is real? Sister Carmen had that feeling. She had not imagined that the priest was there, she would swear. She knew that she had not let him in—remember, she had the keys to the locked convent door. And she knew for sure that she had not let him out. She says that the experience, "made such an impression on me that never again did I dare go into that room alone."

Nor did she tell a soul of the strange event. Two years later she joined the community and was sent to make her novitiate in Spain. There she saw a picture of Father Henry and "recognized," she says, "the venerable priest who visited us in Montevideo on the same day that he passed to a better life."

Endnotes

1. The prayer intercession of a saint gets its power from Christ who lives in the individual who loves him. The saint's lifetime of being and doing good at heroic levels (acquired "merits" Catholics and Jews, among others, would say) is also involved. The cure is attributed to God's response to a saint's prayers and is also a "yes" nod to the Church that God wants this person honored and held up as a model of following Jesus. Also true is that saints have no will but God's will and must not be seen, in that sense, as begging God to change Divine Providence. They, instead, are its instruments.
2. Newman became a cardinal and is a candidate for beatification.
3. Named for St. Teresa of Avila, not St. Therese of Lisieux.

Chapter Twelve

A CAJUN KID SAINT, A BASQUE MYSTIC, AND A SPANISH ARCHBISHOP

July 1959
Lourdes Hospital, Lafayette, Louisiana

A young, recently ordained priest, whose duties include patients here, makes another visit to the twelve-year-old Cajun girl dying in Room 411 of painful acute lymphatic leukemia.

To comfort the young Catholic, who has a deep devotion to Jesus' mother, he says, "Charlene, someday soon a beautiful lady is going to come and take you away with her."

For the rest of his life, Father Joseph Brennan will remember the simplicity and faith shining in Charlene Richard's (ree-SHARD) brown eyes as she answers with a smile, "When the Blessed Mother comes, Father, I'll tell her you say 'hello.'"

Charlene, Father Brennan will claim years later, was no ordinary twelve-year-old. An opinion strongly seconded even in 1959 by nurse Sister Theresita Crowley O.S.F., head of the hospital's pediatric ward, who spends as much time as she can with this patient.

The second of ten kids born to Mary Alice and Joseph Richard, the small-town girl played baseball, was popular with her schoolmates, and captained a tournament-winning basketball team. However, she also had the spiritual maturity of a very special kind of adult, the priest and nun believe.

"Her life was full in a short span," says Sister Theresita, adding humbly, "I learned a lot from Charlene, especially from her willingness to accept everything. She suffered a great deal but I remember her as a cheerful patient. She never complained." To Father Brennan, the Cajun child is a true saint.

The primary doctor who treated her, Dr. Daniel W. Voorhies, was interviewed by Louisiana Catholic press reporter Barbara Lenox Guiterrez. (It is to her series of articles in the Lafayette diocesan paper, combined with other material such as the book *Charlene,* that I owe most of this report.)

Ms. Guiterrez found that, predictably, the physician did not want to talk publicly about his former patient. However, the reporter noticed Charlene's framed photograph occupied a prominent position on the medical man's uncluttered desk.[1] Voorhies admitted that, of all his patients, hers was the only photograph he had.

Catholics believe that anyone may choose to "offer up" life's sufferings (joys, too) as prayers for oneself or others; for this reason, when suffering hits, instead of succumbing to the "helpless and hopeless" syndrome, there is always the possibility of turning frustrations, pains, and difficulties into prayer energy.

In Charlene's last weeks, Father Brennan talked to her about using what she was going through as prayer for others. Perhaps he sensed that Charlene—who asked her grandmother to teach her the rosary when she was five and confided several years later she wanted to be a saint like Therese of Lisieux—already did a lot of praying.

Charlene took readily to his suggestion. Thereafter she greeted the hospital chaplain each day with, "OK, Father, who am I to suffer for today?"

Perhaps this unusual girl, who Sister Theresita flatly calls "a holy child," felt a special mission even in eternity to pray for those in need. At least after her death on August 11, 1959, Sister Theresita—who claimed, "I felt she had gone into Life and ... was with me in a new way"—often found herself in Room 411, asking Charlene's prayers for others. She went there, the Franciscan nun said, because the room may have been "the last dwelling place of a saint," and because "I have great confidence in her [prayers]." More than fifteen years later, Sister Theresita still insists, "I feel her presence. I feel her smile."

Just a fancy of the sister's? Hardly. Every year thousands of people visit the grave of Charlene Richard to leave flowers, candles, photos, and notes, either thanking her for favors they believe they received through her prayers, or asking her to pray for them. In the book *Charlene,* several priests give instances of favors obtained, they believe, through this dead child, with whom they feel a bond reminiscent of the special feelings many priests have for St. Therese. Some of them know that Charlene offered some of her sufferings to have a brother who was a priest.

On August 11, 1989, when Harry J. Flynn, the local bishop, celebrated Mass at St. Edward's Church in Charlene's small hometown to commemorate the thirtieth anniversary of her death, five thousand people showed up, forcing the Mass to be held outside on the grounds of the little church. Bishop Flynn's diocesan archives hold hundreds of letters that testify to favors and cures granted through the young Cajun girl's prayers.

Among those who think a lot of Charlene Richard is the Price family of Morgan City, Louisiana. Parents and grandparents credit Charlene Richard with the cure of young Nicole Price from a rare cancer.

As a baby, Nicole was diagnosed in 1987 with neuroblastoma. Surgeons took as much of a cancerous mass out of her stomach as possible. Then she was put on chemotherapy. One day her working mother received a phone call from Nicole's baby-sitter. Nicole was begging her to talk to "Charlene."

"I have no idea who she's talking about. We don't know anybody named Charlene," Mrs. Price told the sitter. When the blonde, blue-eyed tyke continued to ask for Charlene, the adults concluded Charlene was an imaginary friend. Still, they noted something odd: Nicole didn't talk about doing things with Charlene, as is usual with imaginary playmates, but begged to *see* Charlene, as if speaking of someone she knew who was now absent.

Then the Price family had a phone call. A friend wanted them to know that she had made a special pilgrimage to pray for Nicole to the grave of a young girl—a girl named Charlene Richard.

Mrs. Price says her mouth dropped open. She questioned Nicole carefully, "Where is Charlene?"

"In heaven with baby Jesus," Nicole answered at once.

"Did she talk to you?"

"Uh-huh."

"What'd she say?"

"Told me to be good."

After that dialogue, Nicole's mother went to see Father Floyd Calais. Father Calais is one of the priests who feel that Charlene, like a spiritual little sister, is always there to help him out. Father Calais did not tell Mrs. Price that her little one was imagining things. Instead he suggested the Prices take Nicole to Charlene's grave. He would accompany them.

The trip was made on Easter Sunday, 1988. In the cemetery, a permanently displayed picture of Charlene was pointed out to Nicole, who exclaimed, "That's Charlene!"

Of course, the toddler may have heard something from her parents or grandparents that predisposed that answer. Mrs. Price says sensibly, "I can't say that Charlene appeared to Nicole. But from the first night we heard from our friend about her, we've been praying to Charlene."

In October 1991, a new tumor was found in Nicole's abdomen. Surgery was done immediately and the surgeon, while waiting for a preliminary biopsy before continuing the operation, came out to the waiting room to warn the Price family that lab tests would certainly show a malignancy. They did, and half Nicole's spleen was removed.

Between then and five days later when the full lab report came out, Father Calais got in his car and made another trip to Charlene's grave, asking her prayers for the toddler's new problem. And, of course, hundreds of other prayers—some invoking Charlene, others not—were going up for Nicole from other people. Only God can sort out the "credit" in such instances, but a funny thing happened: The full lab report found the tumor benign—no malignancy whatsoever.

As this is written, Father Calais tells me Nicole is a grammar school student who enjoys good health and "perfect medical reports."

Many people are alive who knew Basque-born Claretian Father Aloysius Ellacuria, who worked principally in Los Angeles but also in Chicago, Phoenix, and San Antonio. In my book *The Sanctified Body* are first-person accounts from people who swear to have seen this simple, kindly mystic levitate; others who smelled delicious perfumes emanating from his body; and some who found he read both their hearts and minds. Several other books report cases where Father Aloysius' prayers brought God's healing to people physically and spiritually.

The holy Claretian—whom Cardinal McIntyre of Los Angeles dubbed "the Padre Pio of the West" for his extraordinary gifts—had friends of every background. But two San Diego women, Melba Esparza and her daughter Lisa K., recall in a 1991 videotaped interview[2] that Father Aloysius and Lisa's dad had an extra bond because they were both Basques.

Once a month Father Aloysius traveled from Los Angeles to San Diego to visit a group of spiritual children, including the Esparza family. Lisa, who was a bridesmaid when her sister was married by Father Aloysius, also saw the priest at baptisms he conducted for her siblings' older children as well as at some of those monthly gatherings.

Around the first of September 1981, when she was twenty-four, Lisa got a call from her mom. "Rush to the hospital; your dad's taken a turn for the worse."

Lisa and her husband were soon standing on the far side from the hospital entrance of a crosswalk at Fifth and Washington Streets. Suddenly Lisa said, "That's Father Aloysius. He must have gone to see Daddy."

Only the length of the crosswalk from her, Father Aloysius had a slight smile, she recalls, while he "glowed" with a quality she stumbles trying to describe, searching her way from phrases like "emanating gentleness" to "peacefulness."

Peaceful or no, seeing the Basque priest was not wholly consoling for Lisa. She knew her father must be really bad if her mom had summoned Father Aloysius, now close to eighty years old, from Los Angeles.

As she stood there waiting for the light to change with her husband, who also saw Father but did not know him (later his description seemed "right" to a priest of the order Ellacuria founded), Father Aloysius walked away from the door. Because the hospital was under construction, there were the usual high board walls surrounding the site.

As he headed toward that construction wall, there were no doors, *no place for him to go,* Lisa emphasizes. Yet when she looked away for a second and then back, the elderly priest was gone. If she rushed into the hospital without focusing further on that peculiarity, it was only because of her anxiety over her father, whom she found unconscious in intensive care.

When she saw her mom, Lisa mentioned, "Father Aloysius has been here."

"Don't be ridiculous, Lisa. Father Aloysius is dead."

"No, Mom, he was just here," Lisa protested.

When Melba Esparza told her daughter that Father Aloysius had died almost five months ago, Lisa questioned herself. But her conclusion didn't change, even fifteen years later. "I knew who it was," she says simply.

When another priest said he didn't think Father Aloysius would smile in such a situation, Lisa didn't argue. As far as she is concerned, people may think what they like. She knows what she saw. She even has definite convictions on why she saw her father's dead friend. She was sure God sent Father Aloysius to guide his fellow Basque through a time of suffering and lead him to heaven.

Her sight of Father Aloysius, she feels, was a comforting reminder that there is a heaven and, in view of that, the family should not be afraid of the suffering and pain her greatly loved father was enduring for a brief time. Nor should they run from their own anguish at seeing him suffer. Lisa believes Father Aloysius, as God's messenger, helped the Esparzas surrender the situation to God, looking beyond it to eternal life.

In the light of the gathering legislative momentum and strong opinions among some Americans that the dying should be spared all suffering through euthanasia, Lisa's statements are neither the mood of the time nor politically correct. But they are, I hope, thought-provoking.

Joe Vorndran of West Los Angeles was a chief scientist at Hughes for thirty years before his death. Brilliant, handsome, life-loving Joe was married to vibrant Connie, a homemaker with cover-girl blonde beauty. They met Father Aloysius in November 1957. Their second child, Maureen, had been born that July, blind and with a hole in her heart, after Connie caught the measles from their firstborn.

Told about this very special priest, whose blessings almost always brought spiritual comfort and sometimes physical healing, the distraught but devout young couple took their infant to the Claretian residence the very next day.

A Sunday, as always there was a large crowd lined up waiting for Father Aloysius to finish praying with his Claretian community. When he left the chapel, however, he walked straight to the young couple sitting under a tree with their fussy baby (who would see through his prayers).

"Come, I've been waiting for you," he smiled.

At first they thought it a mistake. But no, this priest knew all about them before he ever saw them. Knew that they would become his spiritual children for the rest of his life.

Father Aloysius' Order, the Claretians, was founded by Spanish priest and later archbishop of Cuba, St. Anthony Maria Claret (1807–70). As would be expected, Father Aloysius was devoted to his fellow Spaniard. Not long after God gave the Vorndrans their third daughter—named Antonia Maria for this saint—Connie was enduring a horribly painful though not life-threatening ailment. So she stayed home when Joe and oldest daughter Terry went to visit Father Aloysius and receive his blessing on another Sunday afternoon. Those Sundays were exhausting for the priest due to the crowds seeking his prayers, but he insisted to Joe, "When you get home, I want you to put Connie on the phone." So that evening the priest she regarded as a saint blessed Connie repeatedly over the phone, asking each time, "Are you better now?" Honest Connie could only reply "no." There was no lessening of her pain. So much for the placebo effect in her case!

Finally Father Aloyisius told her to take the pain medication prescribed by her doctor and go to bed. He would continue to pray for her. Connie says: "I went to bed with a relic of St. Anthony Maria Claret in my hand. It was the first time I could sleep since my problem began. My first sleep in days. I woke in the night and sat up. There at the foot of my bed St. Anthony Maria was standing. I've never had a vision in my life before and I've never had one since. But I did see St. Anthony Maria Claret. He was standing there and he was smiling. He never said anything. Just smiled. I turned to wake Joe to tell him that St. Anthony Claret was there. When he woke and I turned back, St.

Anthony Claret was gone. I realized then that the pain was completely gone too. Normally with what I had the pain could have gone on for another week, certainly for several more days.

"When I told Father Aloysius about this, he just put his head down modestly and smiled. But he never said anything."

Around Christmas 1994 God apparently sent dead Father Aloysius to a Mexican nun. Foundress of a flourishing new order, this woman of great spiritual ardor and down-to-earth common sense had an experience she is willing to share for publication as an aid to others' faith in supernatural realities. She requested only that I withhold her name so there can be no question of someone seeking personal publicity.

"It was not a dream," she emphasizes in her excellent English. Beyond that she will tell me only that a "presence" made itself known—a priest from heaven who gave no name but said he would help her with the hard labor of creating the new community.

Then early in 1995, first-time visitors to her remote location, Americans Mary and Francis Levy, handed her a gift, a privately printed memoir by Francis of Father Aloysius. In it the new foundress read with awe exact words spoken to her by her dead visitor. She also learned that Father Aloysius founded the Missionaries of Perpetual Adoration, a men's order centered in Mexico with the same aims as her group—and discovered that only his death prevented his founding a companion women's order. She is now convinced it was Father Aloysius God sent with a pledge of heavenly help.

Endnotes

1. A nonpracticing Catholic, Voorhies returned to the Church and died in good standing—a change some credit to Charlene.
2. By Francis Levy, a close associate of Father Ellacuria.

Chapter Thirteen

LOWERING THE BOOM—GENTLY!

Guida (pronounced gUY dA) White was divorced, lonely, and depressed. Drinking helped to anesthetize her pain. One morning her kids were fighting and she was too blue to handle them. The stack of greasy dishes in the sink seemed equally insurmountable. She made a wine cooler.

Then another ... and a third.

But this day even wine coolers couldn't dull her misery. At some point, something snapped. Grabbing her car keys, she rushed unsteadily out of the house. Abandoning her children, she gunned the motor and roared down the street, heading down the south hill into the downtown area of Spokane, the Washington city where she lives.

As she tipsily navigated one of the swooping curves on the hill, Guida lost control of the car, which spun crazily like a top. She tried to grab the wheel, but it was moving too fast.

Then, suddenly, seated next to her in the car's passenger seat she saw her dead grandmother, who more than one person has called "a saint."

"Grandma, what are you doing here?" she choked.

"Go home to your children," was the only reply.

A few seconds later the car stopped, tipped precariously, one side higher than the other, on a roadside bank of earth. Her grandmother was gone, but Guida noted that even in the car's tilted position it pointed back up the hill toward her home. In her spin, she had barely missed various pedestrians. Now these and other people clustered around the car, not screaming at her but urging with concern that she extricate herself very carefully, lest the tipped car go all the way over.

Because of her grandmother's guardian-angel-like appearance, Guida knew she was in no danger. She did not even try to climb out of the car. Carefully, frequently using her brake, she eased the car onto a firm footing. Then, stone sober, she went home.

"I did the dishes," she told me. "I took care of my kids. And I didn't have anything to drink for a long time."

The Protestant Swedish-born daughter of a lay preacher, Frida Lindblad Sams, Guida's grandmother and my grandmother, too, is not an official saint. But the quiet one-liner spoken by this dead mother of nine exemplifies what this chapter is about: The appearance of God's good friends as his messengers to "straighten out" someone who needs a gentle hint, a nudge, or even a forthright scolding.

You will note Frida did not abuse Guida about her wine coolers. God's messengers don't encourage self-hate or despair. (Appearances that sow either, however radiant the visitor, have their source in darkness.) Whether given through the Holy Spirit or delivered by a dead saint, God's messages always leave the recipient's dignity intact.

The telltale mark of a godly experience of this type is the hovering sense of divine compassion, as when visionary Josefa Menendez, seeing Jesus after she had just disobeyed his explicit order, bewailed her failings, her miseries, and her fears, only to be told, "If you are an abyss of miseries, I am an abyss of mercy and goodness" while he stretched out his arms, inviting "my heart is your refuge...."

Often the recipient of this sort of "corrective" visitation is not even told directly what they are doing wrong; thus when French St. Julie Billiart appears to a spiritual daughter, she does not say, "You didn't do what I told you!" Instead she tactfully asks, "Daughter, when did you do what I told you to do?" And when St. Henry de Osso appears to someone who has broken a promise, his only reproach is—like Christ at Peter's denial—a wordless look.

To keep after-death appearances of saints in perspective, a reminder may be in order that when God wants to correct someone, dead saints are, by no means, the only divine resource. God speaks most often through the circumstances and people of our lives. Certainly the Lord speaks through Scripture and other books. And sometimes the Holy Spirit speaks directly (called locutions) through a word of counsel heard interiorly or audibly.

I believe I had an experience of that over a decade ago. I was engaged in some daily chore when an interior voice said very distinctly, "If you don't give up self-pity you're going to get cancer." My circumstances didn't immediately change. But my attitude sure did!

People may see Jesus or his mother. And, of course, God does not tap only saints who died in the modern era, to carry his messages. Two of these broader experiences will indicate the boundless horizon within which recent saints' appearances are situated.

Twentieth-century miracle-worker, Salesian Sister Eusebia Palomino y Yenes, became so holy among the pots and pans of her Spanish convent kitchen that she is a candidate for beatification. Not born some "spiritual genius," Sister Eusebia had to be nudged along like the rest of us. These nudges included visits from saints like sixteenth-century St. Teresa of Avila, who encouraged Eusebia to cultivate simplicity and humility.

Another experience of Eusebia's took place in 1923, on January 21—the feast of early Roman martyr, St. Agnes. In church that evening, Eusebia—then a novice nun—begged Jesus to tell her what about her was displeasing to him. She explained later to her friend Sister Carmen Moreno that she did this because "I wanted to correct myself and become a saint."

As she made her brave request, the church around Eusebia disappeared and she found herself in a lovely garden. St. Agnes was walking there, radiant, her hair like threads of gold. Jesus embraced Agnes and said, turning to Eusebia, "See how pure this soul is?" Then he indicated some of the garden blooms, "See how white these flowers are? Until my chosen ones reach this degree of purity, they cannot see me and speak intimately with me. Strive to acquire this virtue and you will be intimate with me, and I with you." At that moment, Eusebia saw herself clothed in a white garment that was spattered with mud.

In holy terror she asked if these spatters represented deadly sins. Gently Jesus replied, "Not even small sins. But imperfections that prevent your coming to me." He encouraged Eusebia to "have great purity of intention in all your actions," since this would permit him to "treat you as an intimate: 'you with me, I with you.'" From that day, Eusebia aspired to live this new directive.

Since, as with all Christian saints, it was with Jesus that Eusebia had her main relationship, as a reminder of this important reality, I summarize another guiding vision in which Jesus gently prodded Eusebia toward greater holiness. Around 1928-29 she dreamed she was lifted up so that she could see some supernatural things and vast groups of people below, who had no thought of supernatural realities but scurried to and fro "without any sense of direction." Many ran blindly into evil. While with sadness Eusebia observed this and three abandoned, broken crucifixes, she heard a voice say, "Ah, if you were better, if you prayed more, you could save and bring me all those souls.... Instead how little you love me."

Again, she immediately woke up. After that, offering her own daily chores, her prayers, her very self to bring others to God and wholeness became Eusebia's whole life. The devil, of course, loves to lay heavy guilt trips on people in any way possible, including, at times, with dreams or visions like this one of Eusebia's. That this was Jesus, not Lucifer, is clear because Eusebia became ever more content, loving, and joyfully alive.

———————

Epileptics were not ordained early in the nineteenth century. Studying for the priesthood in Paris, young Jacob Libermann—a German-born recent convert from Judaism—suffered a seizure reading a reproachful letter from his bitterly sorrowing rabbi father (who certainly loved God as much as his son did). When epilepsy was diagnosed, that was the end of Libermann's hopes to preside at a Catholic altar—but not the end of his movement toward sanctity. Kept on as a handyman out of pity at Saint Sulpice seminary, Libermann was recognized by the seminarians as "a saint."

Even in that wretched era of nonexistent Jewish-Christian understanding, Libermann—now known as Francis—burrowed into God's depths to that luminous place where the sad brokenness in our human family vanishes in a mysterious cloud of divine love. In these healing depths, epilepsy faded away. Libermann was ordained and went on to found the Holy Ghost Fathers, a group as notable for holiness as for missionary enterprises.

After his death in 1852, Francis appeared to the living a number of times, once with instant healing for a nun, another time spiritually benefiting a married woman.

And once he turned up to very gently correct someone. A "correction" more readily grasped if you know that for generations, Catholic men desiring to be celibate (in order to put themselves at the service of God and the human family) have turned to Jesus' virgin mother for help. For some, Mary's help involves, at times, a material object called a scapular. No magic token, the scapular reminds the individual to ask Mary's prayers and also acts as a visible sign of the individual's reliance on her motherly assistance. Bizarre-sounding, perhaps, but like a lot of things hard to explain, based on the experience that "it works."

I mentioned the impression Francis made on the seminarians at Saint Sulpice Seminary in Paris. One of these individuals, who lived beside him during the years 1829 and 1830, went on to become a Carthusian monk at France's Grande Chartreuse monastery. On December 21, 1860, eight years after Libermann's death, Dom Salier wrote [translated from the French volume 1 of Notes and Documents Relating to the Life of Father Libermann]:

My dear friend has served me not only when he was near, but also from afar. [That is, after death, according to Holy Ghost Father Michael Carroll] I recall ... [as a new novice] here at Grande Chartreuse, I lost my scapular of Our Lady of Carmel and I neglected to get another one. The following night,... I found myself suddenly so sexually tempted that I can't recall ever having been in such cruel agony. I resisted the temptation but was so hard-pressed I didn't think to pray. Thus the temptation grew ever stronger. In this state, quite despairing, I saw Libermann, wearing a garment as white as snow with great sleeves like those we had at Saint-Sulpice. He had a completely heavenly air about him as he appeared before me carrying in his hand a scapular of Carmel in a way that definitely called my attention to it. The sight of the scapular at once delivered me from every temptation. At that same moment I saw behind Libermann several other seminarians of Saint-Sulpice whom I didn't know, but who also appeared like him to be favored with an angelic purity. They were wearing the same garment and carrying in their hands the same scapular, like warriors returning from battle carrying their triumphal palms. They made a neat line behind Libermann. After I had taken my time contemplating them, they walked several steps off and all disappeared. The next day I made certain to procure a scapular and, thanks to God, I have never again given it up.

———•◆•———

St. Gemma Galgani's (p. 122) friend, dashing Passionist novice Gabriel Possenti, in life was a sharpshooter who in his black Passionist habit single-handedly subdued a troop of brigands who were attempting rape and pillage in the village near his monastery. Two years after his early death (this is fifty years before his canonization and long before his appearances to St. Gemma), the handsome young Italian returned to reprimand a blood brother. This Vincent had become addicted to card playing, with unpleasant consequences. "You have to give it up," the dead Passionist scolded. But since he knew that Vincent had true economic difficulties, God's messenger provided a way to clear up his debts and establish himself financially: the future St. Gabriel gave his brother three lottery numbers which won Vincent ten thousand lire!

———•◆•———

For the 1910-11 diocesan tribunal investigating Therese of Lisieux's possible sanctity, sixty-two-year-old Sister Aimee of Jesus of the Lisieux Carmel recalled that she once saw the young saint slightly ruffled. Something humiliating had been done to Therese's blood sister Celine [known in Carmel as Sister Genevieve] by the imperious, if loveable, superior, Mother Marie de Gonzague.

Perhaps because Sister Aimee—who liked Therese—was much less fond of Therese's three Carmelite blood sisters, she protested, "Surely Mother de Gonzague has a right to test Sister Genevieve!"

"There are some ways in which people should not be tested and this is one of them," Therese retorted.

Sister Aimee dismissed the comment as Therese just "sticking up for" her sister. Later Therese's critic felt the saint's criticism of Mother Marie had been a supernatural discernment that had nothing to do with family loyalty.

Mother Marie de Gonzague, their barely reelected superior, had her good qualities. And there is no doubt God used even her imperfections and honest mistakes to increase Therese's sanctity. Whether she always wielded her authority with discretion and benefit to the community or not, Mother Marie was treated with real respect and affection by Therese. The saint believed whatever happened to her—even the inadequate blankets or rancid food given to her because she didn't complain—was used for her good by God. But the fact remains that Mother Marie did not properly watch out for her young nuns, so that a number of them—not only Therese—became tubercular.

After Therese's death, it appears God sent her back to make sure such neglect would cease. Celine, the blood sister of Therese who had been humiliated by Mother de Gonzague, held no grudge. She testified under oath after the superior's death:

[Mother Marie] told me of a favor she had received before a portrait of Therese as a child. It must have been a very vivid experience, because our poor Mother could not look at this picture without crying.

I often saw her moved in this way, and she said to me: "Oh, the things she said to me!... How much she reproached me with! But how gently!"

The Carmelites found Mother de Gonzague much improved after God sent Therese to scold her. That Therese knew how to scold as well as how to encourage—and did it gently—came as no surprise to the small group of Carmelites for whom she had been novice mistress. Even one of the most difficult novices reported that Therese was "very sharp at seeing our defects and correcting us," but "she was kindness and charity itself...."

After her death, Sister Therese came to various of those novices, in one way or another, still urging—and if necessary scolding—them on to God. One novice, Therese's own blood sister Celine (Sister Genevieve) recounted a number of special "visits" under oath. One of these:

A sister took something from me that I needed, and I was just getting ready to recover it from her in a rather brusque manner when I distinctly heard the words "very humbly!" I recognized Therese's voice and my heart was immediately transformed and inclined toward humility.

For another novice nun, Therese worked a physical miracle. In the mildest possible way, it, too, is a reproach. From under-oath testimony by Sister Marie of the Trinity:

For the sake of convenience, I had made a large pleat in my habit so that I would not have to adjust it every morning when I [dressed]. It was firmly sewn with a lock stitch. I told the Servant of God about this a few days before she died, and she told me to unstitch it, that it was contrary to our [Carmelite] customs. I left it as it was, nevertheless, putting off the job of unstitching it till some other time. The day after her death I could not get this blessed pleat out of my mind. I said to myself: "She sees that I still have it, and maybe it grieves her." So I said this prayer to her: "Dear sister, if you find this pleat displeasing, undo it yourself, and I promise never to remake it." Imagine my amazement when on getting up the following morning, I found it was no longer there! My feelings were a mixture of terror and consolation. It was a warning to me to put all her counsels and recommendations into practice.

While few are so well-detailed as the one above, the under-oath testimonies of the roughly two dozen nuns of the Lisieux Carmel indicate that over the first twelve years after her death God apparently "deputized" Therese to raise that convent to a higher level of spirituality, through individual appearances, of one type or another, to almost every nun.

A number of these appearances, like those just mentioned, were to reproach or even scold, while in others Therese corrected or brought someone along by an encouraging word. In the majority of cases, in true Carmelite spirituality, the nun did not reveal the particulars of Therese's message in her testimony. We can claim, however, that the very fact that Therese came, a visitor from God, all by itself chided each individual that God and the afterlife exist and a Carmelite should shape her life accordingly.

In life Therese fancifully scattered rose petals around the statue of Jesus as a joyous visual representation of the love and sacrifices she offered him. In the language of the poems she wrote, she remarked, "after my death I will let fall a shower of roses," meaning special favors. In a sort of cosmic play on those prophecies, Therese's presence in the Lisieux Carmel was very often marked by odor—primarily the scent of roses. As mentioned in chapter two, such scents are called the odor of sanctity, a pleasant odor that speaks to someone's soul, has no possible human explanation, and leaves genuine spiritual after-effects.

Therese's sister Celine (Sister Genevieve) refers to the hidden spiritual component of the odors she received when she says they "always underscored some particular fact or were sent as a consolation in time of trouble." And Marie of the Trinity, whose pleat was undone for her, mentioned experiencing Therese's odor of sanctity "one day just after I made an act of humility" and "on certain occasions when I was about to perform some service in connection with her."

What did all these visits—by odor or otherwise—accomplish at the Lisieux Carmel? We know from the nuns' testimonies that some, if not all, nuns reached higher levels of spirituality. There was general improvement as well: One nun testified that since the young saint's death the Carmelite rule of life was better kept and everyone treated each other with more love.

Not even shaping up an entire Carmel kept Therese too busy to deliver God's gentle nudges or scoldings elsewhere. One last example.

A missionary priest of the order of Oblates of Mary Immaculate—who wanted his name withheld for reasons you will probably soon sympathize with, as I do—shared with the Carmel an experience he had in Asia early in 1920. He'd yawned his way through the autobiography of Sister Therese: very nice and all that, but not his cup of tea. Then he began hearing how powerful

Therese's prayers were from fellow missionaries and various publications that trickled into his distant outpost.

He began to feel like some teens I know, who heard that a new restaurant was serving complimentary hors d'ouevres on opening night. With no intention, because the place was out of their price range, of ever becoming customers, they threw on their best duds and rushed over for the free goodies. To the missionary, some similar kind of thought occurred. God seemed to be handing out favors right and left through this little dead nun. So just because he wasn't particularly one of her admirers, why shouldn't he get some, too?

One of his mission projects—"very useful to the glory of God," he underlines a trifle defensively—needed financing. To that end, he began "a fervent novena" for Therese's intercession. On the third day as he prayed, to his "surprise and emotion," he had barely made his "insistent request" for the desired funds when Therese suddenly appeared before him.

She said "in a tone of sweet reproach," as he puts it, "Ask me for spiritual favors." Then, tactfully—after all, he is facing her with spiritual egg on his face—she vanished.

That he wasn't really a spiritual slouch can be seen by the aftereffects: He went on with the novena—changing its purpose completely—and a few months later sent off a humble testimony of his experience for the Carmel archives. In this he comments that the nun whose prayers he turned to only for "free goodies," he now considers "his holy little sister," to whom he daily confides—I suppose he'd want it underlined—his "*spiritual* interests."

Over the years to come he must have heard many times of Therese helping other missionaries obtain needed funds. Probably he only smiled, knowing that God sends to each friend what he needs—whether it be cold cash or a gentle shaking up.

Chapter Fourteen

FATHER KELLEY MEETS FATHER NEUMANN

Genial Father Thomas Kelley quotes his father, "Don't ever let them drop the 'e' in Kelley, for we're descended from the Kings of Tipperary," adding his own view with a chuckle, "probably some guy who owned the Kings of Tipperary Pub."

Full of life and good health, the retired Navy chaplain exercises his priest-hood at the naval and civilian hospitals and nursing homes in Beaufort, South Carolina. That's when he isn't standing in for priests who need a break from their parishes.

And yet energetic Father Kelley, seventy-seven years old in 2001, should have died more than twenty-five years ago.

Back to 1975, the year the kindly mannered fifty-one-year-old celebrated twenty-five years as a priest of the Oblates of St. Francis de Sales. On leave before starting a new naval assignment in Taiwan, Father Kelley was at his brother Martin's in their hometown of Philadelphia.

The brothers, two of five siblings, hadn't had much time together for awhile, and were enjoying a good talk. But toward bedtime, Martin, an oral surgeon, remarked, "Tom, you don't look well."

The priest admitted he was awfully tired. He blamed the high humidity on Parris Island, his last post, coupled with long working days. But Martin's professional eye rested on him uneasily. The doctor persuaded his brother to come in the following day to Philadelphia's Holy Redeemer Hospital, where Martin was on staff. A quick checkup would make sure everything was OK.

Everything was not OK. The next day's blood analysis revealed one reason for fatigue that even a good night's sleep no longer mended: internal bleeding. Father Kelley admitted he did feel some "uncomfortableness" in the appendix area and agreed to stay in the hospital overnight so a lower GI series could be run.

Dr. Martin Kelley went home that night afraid for his brother. Barely two weeks past, the family had buried their aunt and the previous year her sister—the Kelley's mother—both dead of colon cancer.

Those fears proved warranted the next day, October 1. Clearly upset, Martin accompanied three other physicians into his brother's room to inform the naval chaplain that the GI series had revealed a mass in the appendix area. From the symptoms, family history, and the patient's age, it was undoubtedly colon cancer.

Eventually, the stunned priest was left alone, except for his roommate, a non-Christian colitis patient, who did not intrude. Perched on the side of the hospital bed, the devout Oblate quickly came to terms with his situation, although with his hospital-chaplain experience, he knew exactly how bad colon cancer can get. What troubled him was whether to have surgery. He had seen surgery deplete patients like himself, who didn't seem all that sick until operated on. Then they lingered in an unpleasant condition in hospital rooms for months until released by death.

As he pondered, his thirty-five-year-old roommate suddenly interrogated, "Didn't you hear what the doctors said? If that was me, I would have fainted."

Father Kelley shrugged matter-of-factly, "What can I do about it?" and went back to his thoughts, which turned to reviewing his life and searching his soul in the face of the final hour suddenly soon to come.

He was interrupted again by another priest walking into the room. It was not Holy Redeemer's chaplain, with whom gregarious Father Kelley was already on good terms. Whoever the priest was, it was clearly Father Kelley he was here to see, for the visitor walked straight to his fellow priest.

Dressed in the standard clerical black suit with vest and white collar, the visiting padre was slightly built, a short man who appeared to be in his late forties or early fifties. Gentle in manner, he seemed in no hurry, Father Kelley recalls.

Being experienced at visiting sick strangers, Father Kelley was struck that the priest didn't identify himself, something any priest making a hospital call of this type does right away.

But there was no time for queries, for the visitor started right in, "Father, I understand you have a tumor. I have a relic of Blessed John Neumann."

Father Kelley recalls, "Then he touched me around my appendix area and touched my lips with what I assumed was a relic of St. John Neumann." When Father Kelley says he "assumed" the visitor had a relic in his hand, it's because a Catholic chaplain with a saint's relic may offer it like this for a patient to kiss. Later Father Kelley would say thoughtfully, "When I look back on it, I could swear he had no relic because his fingers—nothing else—touched my lips." Since any part of the body of a saint is a first-class relic, perhaps both the Oblate priest's first and later impressions are right: If this priest was a dead saint, his finger was indeed a relic.

After blessing Father Kelley, the black-suited priest walked out. In spite of the fact that he did not act like a person in a hurry, he still had not identified himself.

Bothered by that, Father Kelley ran his visitor's description by all the nurses, since they knew all the local priests who dropped by the hospital to visit parishioners.

"Gee, Father, he doesn't sound like anyone we know," the nurses agreed. Nor had they seen anyone who fit the description.

He asked the chaplain, who also drew a blank.

And finally he asked his brother Martin, who had worked at Holy Redeemer for many years and could name any priest who regularly walked its halls. "I thought I knew everybody here," Martin said, shaking his head.

Still Father Kelley knew better than most people how a priest may be called to see someone at a hospital he usually doesn't visit, or drop in at an additional room while on such a call. Although he could discover no one who had sent the relic-bearing priest to bless him, nor who the guy might have been, he put the mystery out of his thoughts.

That a priest in Philadelphia would have a relic of Neumann was not odd. Since Father Kelley was born in Philadelphia (on Christmas Eve, 1923, to a couple named Mary and Joseph, he chuckles), he was familiar from boyhood with local regard for the city's nineteenth-century bishop.

If Neumann could help, great.

The ill chaplain went back to reviewing his life and thinking about what to do.

One decision was easy. Being in the Navy, he was obligated to transfer to Philadelphia Naval Hospital, which he did the next day. The Naval physicians were blunt: Surgery must be done immediately. On October 6, however reluctantly, he was on the operating table. The news after the operation was bad: What the doctors called a Dukes class B (A being better) tumor of the colon was in an advanced stage. It had eaten through the intestinal wall and erupted into his hip, releasing its deadly cells to create more tumors in other parts of the body.

Although the colon tumor was removed, the question was how to fight the cancer silently working in new areas. To try to trace the malignant enemy, his doctors used bone scans, liver scans, bone marrow biopsies, and other tests. Chemotherapy, they judged, would be no help. Instead, that December over a period of two weeks, 4,500 rads of radiation were pumped into the area around the chaplain's appendix purely as a precaution, since the tumor was removed and all efforts had failed to pinpoint new cancer sites.

The radiation made him deathly sick. Vomiting and unable to eat for months, his normal weight of 160 pounds dropped to 123 before he decided to stop weighing himself.

As he had feared, after the surgery he remained hospitalized, weeks stretching into months. Still, ill as he was—from medical procedures like radiation as much as disease—he had no pain. And instead of dying—perhaps because the couple hundred kids he'd taught religious education at his last assignment, their families, and many others were asking God to help him—he amazed everyone by getting better instead of worse. In fact, after five months of inactivity, frustrating for such an active person, Father Kelley felt pretty good.

So good that by March 1976 he was released from the hospital to undertake a limited assignment at the Chief of Navy Chaplain's Office in Washington, D.C. Certainly his new post was not as rigorous as his previous assignments: three tours of duty in Vietnam, two sea duties on navy vessels, assignments on Marine bases in San Diego and Parris Island, postings at naval bases and hospitals in Florida and New York, or even his prechaplain work as coach, teacher, and athletic director at Duffy High School in Niagara Falls, New York. Still, it was good to have work to do again—even if only until the new tumors doctors predicted showed up.

But at his frequent checkups, to his doctors' amazement, there were no new malignancies.

That May, however, as he moved—tumorless—toward once more resuming full duties, something hit the chaplain hard. Father Kelley still subscribed to Philadelphia's *Catholic Standard and Times* to keep up with the church in his hometown. When he picked up the paper one day, there was a picture of Bishop Neumann, who was to be canonized.

"Oh my Lord," he gasped, "it sure looks like that priest who came in to see me."

From that moment, he says, "I became very involved with Bishop Neumann." Struck once again by the oddity that the priest who had him kiss the "relic" hadn't identified himself, he began some personal research as to whether the unknown priest visitor could have been from one of the parishes around the hospital. He found no one who fit the bill.

Since then he carries a relic of the dead bishop, with which he blesses others in his hospital calls or when he occasionally gives talks on the saint. He also prays a novena in Neumann's honor daily, asking the saint's prayers for those he ministers to as well as for himself.

Father Kelley believes John Neumann helps him help others. For instance, in August 1991 he visited a longtime helper in the Parris Island Catholic educational programs who was in the hospital. As usual he had with him his first-class relic of St. John Neumann. Mary Oenbrink, wife of a military dentist, had been diagnosed with a Dukes class C cancer of the colon. In other words, her cancer was even more advanced than Father Kelley's had been. After surgery, her doctors wanted to do both chemo and radiation, but Mary elected, she says, "to pursue no other treatment."

Father says he did not know her diagnosis, for he did not ask. ("Ask a woman and she may tell you in great detail," he grins.) But he said a prayer for Mary and had her kiss the relic. Then he said a novena to St. John Neumann, asking the saint's prayers for her good health. Almost three-and-a-half years later—having taken no medication and having had none of the recommended treatments—Mary Oenbrink's tests all "register normal." Of course many people prayed for Mary's recovery, but Father Kelley thinks St. John Neumann's prayers are worth mentioning.

His brother, Martin, obviously can't say whether for over twenty-five years his sibling has had no new tumors because he once kissed the finger of a dead saint; but Martin does have a firm opinion that—given the medical diagnosis and prognosis of his brother's case—something "miraculous" occurred.

Retired since 1986 (the navy has mandatory retirement for chaplains at age sixty-two), Father Kelley is as busy as most working priests. However, Father Kelley still prudently makes time for checkups.

Recently he went in for his regular examination. The doctor looking him over was not a Catholic and knew nothing about Father Kelley's experience with the mysterious priest in his hospital room. Shaking his head, the physician said, "You should have had many tumor recurrences."

Then he told the Catholic priest, "You know, you're a miracle."

Chapter Fifteen

"I'LL FIND SOMEONE TO HELP MY GIRL"

Alice Topping, born February 10, 1932, was a much-loved only child in the north England household of her parents and grandmother. From an Anglican family, Alice attended Sunday school, church, and youth activities in the city of St. Helen's (northeast of Liverpool) where the Toppings lived. Attendance was not just for show, either. From a very early age, the child was especially aware that her grandmother—who frequently quoted the Bible—had a deep faith life.

Alice grew up, married registered nurse Frank Jones, had daughters Alison and Lesley, and by 1960, at age twenty-eight, was happily making a career change from personnel work to primary-school teacher. She and Frank were now living in the smaller town of Haycock in a large Victorian house, but she remained very close to her family in nearby St. Helen's.

In 1968 her father died suddenly on September 23, the same day the Catholic world mourned the death of Padre Pio. But Alice Jones, now a teacher at St. James Anglican school, knew nothing of Padre Pio. As the 1970s began—"always fit and well"—she loved her job, and in addition, recalls, "I was very active, looking after my family, and also my mother and grandmother."

As for church or a spiritual life, all that had sort of fallen to the side. Teaching at their school, she did attend services at St. James now and again, and saw that her daughters were confirmed there, but it was Frank, her husband, who was the more regular churchgoer. Alice felt no lack. In her view, life for the four generations of the Jones-Topping extended family simply flowed along, busy and good, until what began as an ordinary day in March 1973 suddenly changed everything forever. Let Alice tell it in her own words:

My classroom was being renovated, and I moved with my class of thirty seven-year-olds into the parish room of the church, which was used as a dinner room for the children. On March 27 at 2:35 P.M. I was instructed by the head teacher to stack the tables in readiness for a meeting that evening. I was then to take the pupils into school for the music lesson. As I began to move the heavy tables, two boys began to fight, and one of them ran into me. I swung away from his face but fell on the central heating pipe, still clutching the table. I could not get up. There did not seem to be any power in my legs. I had a severe pain in my back and a member of staff took me home.

Frank came off duty and immediately called in my own doctor, who ordered bed rest and drugs for the pain. After a month I was referred to Dr. Heron, the Consultant Orthopaedic Surgeon. I was put into a corset, and was then seen at monthly intervals. I did try to resume my career, but each time I was defeated by extreme pain. In March 1974, it was agreed that I should have surgery, and I was admitted to Broad Green Hospital in Liverpool. At the operation, the surgeons found debris in the spinal canal, but much more serious was the discovery of a neurofibroma [a benign connective tissue tumor of the nerve fiber] which had become trapped during my accident. They were unable to remove the tumor, so a hole was drilled in the base of the spine to allow a little more freedom within the canal.... I appeared to make a good recovery, although the pain was still there. I returned to my post in September, but found that I was unable to continue with my teaching career.

Whereas life had simply trundled along from one blessing to the next, suddenly troubles began to pile up with equal ease. Just when she needed their support, her ninety-three-year-old grandmother died and her mother, to whom she was very close, suffered a heart attack. Then in January 1975, Alice's trusted physician, Dr. Heron, died suddenly, a real blow to Alice, who relied on his medical judgments. Her new orthopedic man, she says, tried various treatments, epidural injections, and manipulations, but my condition continued to deteriorate. He suggested a spinal fusion operation to stabilize the spinal column. I was starting to fall, my left leg was very weak and there was no feeling in my foot. We talked it over with my family, and eventually I agreed to surgery.

In November 1976, I went into St. Helen's Hospital and had the operation. I was totally encased in plaster of paris for fourteen weeks. I spent Christmas and New Year's in hospital, but we all believed that the operation would be a benefit to me. I was turned every four hours by a crane, the plaster cast was very heavy, and very uncomfortable.

In February 1977, I came home, still in pain. Any movement in my left leg had gone. I was totally devastated and began to lose hope. Five other patients also had the same spinal fusion and, like me, they all had problems.

In November 1977, I had to be readmitted to hospital, with an infected donor area, where they had removed the bone from my right hip to transfer into my spine. Another operation followed, and the infected site was drained. The pain now was very acute and I had to rely on more powerful drugs. I used crutches to walk and wore a spinal brace.

I was readmitted to hospital for traction in January 1978. It was from this time that I began to experience spinal spasms in the muscles, which used to contract, and I felt unable to breathe. I was sent home and felt totally useless.

In order to walk, she needed a metal contraption called a caliper on her left leg. This was a kind of support that went down one side of the leg, under the foot, and up the other. Springs around the ankle and knee lifted the foot as she moved, but the whole device was heavy and cumbersome. She writes:

I tripped easily and found that the safest place was on the floor. I developed a deep ulcer [from the caliper] in my left heel, which Frank dressed daily. I was embarrassed by the smell that accompanied the discharge. In a last attempt to regain some mobility, we paid for a consultation with a

Neuro-Surgeon in Liverpool. He said that I had had too much surgery, and there was nothing he could do. He could only suggest further drugs. I gave up hope, and sank into despair. At this point, I really wanted to die. It was only the love of my family that really kept me going....

The heavy drugs that eased her awful pain at times created dreadful mental confusion. As if all this was not enough, something else happened that seemed the last straw. Alice says:

The first of April 1979 is a day that I will never forget. My mother, who was ill, came to visit. I was lying on the floor as usual. She said, "Alice, I feel that I have boarded the train for Heaven. I am only waiting for the Master to take me out of the station." I was angry and shouted, "You can't die," but she smiled at me and said, "I will find someone to help my girl."

We spoke no more about this, but the following Friday, April 6, Frank found my mother dead in bed. She was clutching a religious card. It said, "Jesus Himself drew near and went with them."

Today, Alice sees significance in this final message of her mother's—a woman who, like Alice's grandmother, had a deep love of God. But at the time, believing the bond between them snapped, Alice was devastated. "I cannot begin even now," she says, "to tell anyone how I felt: it was like a deep wound." She put no stock whatsoever in her mother's selfless promise to find and send help. On the contrary, she felt abandoned. Alice says:

I went downhill rapidly. I was angry and turned against God, blaming him for all our misfortunes. I refused to attend church, and even refused Holy Communion on several occasions.

The birth of a grandson was "a spark of light," but basically, she says, the next year—the seventh since her 1973 accident—"passed in bitterness." Not that she cared, but 1980 was the centennial of the Anglican Diocese of

Liverpool, within which the Jones family lives. Every church made plans to celebrate, including St. James, the family's parish, where she had once taught in what now seemed to be a never-to-be-recaptured life. Alice recalls:

> In May ... two priests were invited to speak to the congregation. One was Father Gabriel, from the Community of the Resurrection at Mirfield, Yorkshire, and the other was Father Eric Fisher, from Buxton in Derbyshire. The latter was reputed to be a healer. Friends begged me to see Father Eric but I was adamant. I was bitterly opposed to any thought of faith healing.
>
> On the evening of May 18, our parish priest phoned to say that Father Eric would visit the following morning. Frank accepted the offer, but I became quite angry, vowing not to see him. However, the following morning, he arrived on my doorstep, and I told him "no sermons" and raised my crutch to emphasize that I had no time for him. We began to talk and I was able to pour out my bitterness and pent-up emotions, laying the whole blame on God's shoulders.

Father Eric accepted her anger, she recalls today, "with great gentleness." At the end of the bitter invalid's tirade, the Anglican healer gave her his blessing. That she had released so much anger was, of course, all to the good. While anger can help in illness when it motivates someone to struggle against a disability, the anger of despair can block healing. Not because God rejects the angry, but because those filled with despair's anger reject God and God's blessings. With all those festering feelings lanced, as it were, Alice remembers that the visiting priest:

> placed his hands on my back, and I felt heat and a radiating warmth. He left but the pain was still there and the disability. I treated the whole episode as a waste of time. The next morning I was surprised to find Father Eric on my doorstep again. He told me that during [his prayer for the sick] ... he had been told to come back to me. He then told me to remove my caliper, which I promptly refused to do, so he knelt down

and began to undo the straps. I undid the strap at the top of my leg. Then he began to pray. And there was a sharp pain running the whole length of my leg and my foot felt like fire. I shouted for him to stop and, as I looked down, he seemed to change. There was an older face, almost like a negative photograph in front of the priest's face. I looked away. Then I was aware of another man [wearing a brown robe] in the room, standing by me. I presumed it was the other visiting priest, Father Gabriel.

The man in the brown robe blessed me three times, saying "Jesu Maria!" Then he took my arm, and said, "In the name of Jesus, walk!" I left my chair and walked across the room. Looking round, I noticed that my "visitor" had gone, but Father Fisher was still kneeling [in prayer]. I was so overcome with emotion that I passed no comment. I wept with joy and strangely I could only think that I had no shoes to put on. My shoe with the caliper would no longer fit my foot. So when Frank phoned me, I told him that I was walking and intended to go into town for shoes. He was very alarmed [fearing a drug-induced hallucination] and begged me not to go out alone. When he came home later, I ran down the drive to meet him, and he almost passed me by. He did not recognize me until I called out to him.

Later that evening we went to a Healing Service at church. All the congregation were absolutely amazed. It was a time of great emotion. I looked around for my visitor, and then it gradually dawned on me that I had had some kind of mystic experience. When we arrived home, I told Frank that I had seen Moses!! He advised me to go to bed. I think he believed that I was hallucinating.

The next morning, Frank was going to dress my heel. I raised my leg and there was nothing. My ulcer had gone. The skin was completely clear. We both looked in astonishment. It was the first time that Frank used the word "miracle." We both wept.

Besides the completed physical cure, Alice Jones was still in the midst of receiving a cure of heart and spirit as well. She continues:

At 9:30 I went to church to receive Holy Communion. Everything looked different. Colors were clearer. And for the first time, I became aware of the true meaning of the Eucharist. I "saw" in my mind Christ's Suffering on Calvary. It was like being a witness to the Crucifixion. Heaven and earth became united in that moment. I stood in awe of the tremendous sacrifice for me.

How did this all happen to her—a bitter woman who had lost any faith she ever had in God's mercy or healing power? Today she feels that her mother when in heaven ran to the Savior, as she promised, to get help for her girl. And he sent a trusted friend. Alice writes:

On leaving church, Father Eric gave me a prayer card. And I instantly recognized my visitor—Padre Pio. I was content. I realized that he was a person and not someone I had dreamed up in my mind. I went home rejoicing.

Since one can—especially when taking heavy medication—as Alice feared, "dream up" things in the mind, I asked Alice what her previous experiences were with Padre Pio. She answered, "None." She had never heard of him until he appeared in her home to tell her, in Christ's name, to walk.

She didn't know about after-death appearances of saints, either. For when she learned the same day she received the prayer card that Padre Pio was dead, she got very upset. She says, "I truly believed I had become involved in Spiritualism and ran all the way back to church." Father Eric had gone back to his church in Buxton. But Canon Wilson, the St. James' priest, "a wise old man," she says, explained she had just had a vision in her moment of extreme joy—something that can happen, he soothed—and encouraged her not to worry about it.

The newly alive woman went home, determined to put that part of her cure "out of my mind." But "Padre Pio had other ideas," Alice says now. She found herself more and more curious about the dead mystic. Finally she and Frank went to visit Father Eric in Buxton, seeking information on one she today calls "my heavenly friend."

That November, on the advice of the Anglican priest, Alice and Frank journeyed to San Giovanni Rotondo. There a number of things took place: She found the answers to many spiritual questions. Her case became part of the archival material on Padre Pio. And the Anglican Englishwoman was enrolled as a spiritual child of the dead Italian Catholic who, she now believes, was sent by God to her at her mother's prompting.

What about medical verification of her cure? Her English doctors preferred not to go on record about "faith cures." Then, before her trip to San Giovanni Rotondo, she met Dr. Francis Mooney, "a highly respected forensic pathologist" from St. Helen's who was interested in taking an objective look at Alice's claim of having received a miracle. Dr. Mooney took her to Providence Hospital in 1980 for X rays and other tests on her spine; then he prudently had all the test results—and Alice—examined by another physician, a Dr. McCarthy. The results, Alice says, left both men "dumbfounded."

The open-minded medical men concluded, Alice jubilantly quoted to me, "that there had been supernatural intervention in the disease." They said this because with their own eyes, they saw two things: First, the X rays reveal a badly deformed spinal column that made it clear the patient could only walk with the help of devices like crutches and calipers; second, the physicians saw Alice not only walk unaided, but bend, stretch, run, and hop—things her X rays "prove" she can't do.

Things she smilingly says, "I do, thanks to God and Padre Pio."

As for the neurofibroma, something interesting has happened there, too. Discovered in her first surgery and deemed impossible to remove surgically, the tumor has not been mentioned in any X rays since she saw Padre Pio.

Since her cure, the Anglican lady has an active spiritual life. Devoted to "making Padre Pio known in England," she talks to groups but prefers, Padre Pio relic in hand, to quietly visit the sick, especially "those with no hope." To such people and their families, she finds Padre Pio brings God's peace. And no one knows better than Alice what that means.

Chapter Sixteen

THE PRIEST OF THE GENTLE SMILE

"Be sure the Lord gets the credit," Jolene Gil of Eunice, Louisiana, begs me anxiously at the start of our interview, a plea she repeats before we say good-bye. Not that she feels the prayers of Father Seelos and others for her fourteen-year-old son, Brian Gil, are of no value—she herself has a prayer ministry—but because she wants to make certain no one becomes overfocused on those who pray and forgets the One prayed to.

God heals *all kinds* of people, I have learned in my research. If I thought he cared only for "the devout," I could trot out the Gils as an example. As it is, I find their story a wonderful reminder that God is so responsive to those who steadfastly call on him that sorting out who deserves "credit" for a healing often becomes a reminder of how varied and many are the ways God showers his love and mercy on people—whether the person prayed for is to be healed or called home to God.

Brian's story starts when Jolene and Nicholas Gil were considering adopting the little thirteen-month-old, the first of their four "chosen children." The baby was pitifully sick at the time, suffering from bronchitis and pneumonia. Worse, the local doctor they asked to look him over heard ominous sounds in the baby's heart, which was beating way too fast.

The physician shook his head ruefully. "Don't take this baby," he told the young couple. "You'll just end up with a lot of medical bills."

But Jolene said to God, "Even if it's only for a few years and then we lose him, I still want him."

And the Gils adopted the sick baby anyway.

Only after the adoption went through did they take Brian to a heart specialist, who confirmed the first doctor's discouraging words: Brian did not have a healthy heart. In fact, he had aortic stenosis, that is, a narrowing of the heart's aortic valve.

Surgery was not advised. Instead the Gils were urged to let their new son grow for as long as he could. At some point, probably as he entered his teens, the heart would demand medical attention. By then, hopefully the boy would be more able to withstand the arduous surgery. But not unless he stopped suffering seizures so severe they often lasted forty-five minutes. To Jolene's joy, when he passed his fourth birthday, these ceased.

What he lacked in health, Brian made up for in personality. Bouts of ill health made him neither bad-tempered nor self-centered. Cheerful and very loving, the Gils' husky, brown-eyed, brown-haired child was easy to care for, although he could tease his siblings like any normal child.

By the time he was twelve, surgery could no longer be put off. Not only suffering a lot of chest pain, Brian was so short of breath he could take no more than four steps at a time. Doctors Terry Dean King and Myles Schiller, who saw the boy regularly in Opelousa, Louisiana, scheduled an operation at West Jefferson Medical Center in New Orleans to try to open his narrow heart valve.

Just before the Gils made the three-and-a-half-hour drive east to New Orleans, Jolene's mother, who lives in Opelousa, had a home Mass. Jolene was there, as was a friend known through the Cursillo movement. The friend took a relic of Father Francis Xavier Seelos (a Bavarian-born, Redemptorist candidate for beatification) off her own scapular and told Jolene to put it on Brian's. "Ask God to let Father Seelos pray for Brian's healing," the woman urged. And she gave them the phone number of the Seelos Center, next to St. Mary's Assumption Church in New Orleans, where Father Seelos was once stationed and where he is buried.

Jolene was asking *everyone* for prayer and already had Brian's name on prayer lists stretching from Texas to Florida—from those of Carmelite nuns and the local Catholic charismatic group to "The 700 Club" and evangelist Benny Hinn's healing ministry. She laughed to her son that every time God turned around some angel must be telling him, "Here's some more prayers for Brian Gil." She gladly took the number and phoned the Seelos Center when they arrived in New Orleans.

The Center added a petition for Brian's healing to those in the basket kept on Father Seelos' grave in front of St. Mary's altar. Besides seeking Father Seelos' prayers in this fashion, the Center sent a volunteer, carrying the dead priest's mission cross, to the hospital to pray for Brian. Jolene found Mrs. Gerry Heigle a very sweet lady who really cared. Besides coming twice to pray for Brian, the Seelos Center volunteer kept in touch by phone to see how things were going.

They were going well. Jolene was amazed at how "the Lord took care of everything." She and Nickey arrived in New Orleans to find the free accommodations they'd been promised had fallen through and they didn't have the money for a hotel. But immediately they were called to the phone. Nickey's boss—who had no idea of any of this—was on the line: "I'd like to pay for your motel for five nights." During the next days, whenever money ran short for meals, someone would come along and press a fifty-dollar bill on Jolene. Even her clothes were taken home by a kind soul, washed, and returned. And when they left the hospital, money from friends and family had come in to the exact amount of Brian's entire bill, which they gratefully took away marked "paid."

The actual operation and its aftermath were less smooth. After surgery opened the aortic valve—which was only the size of a pen-point—Brian began hemorrhaging. It turns out he is a "free bleeder," as Jolene puts it; that is, he has a blood disorder that makes surgery very life-threatening. His doctors had to reopen their young patient's chest and pour scalding hot water inside him to try to stop the hemorrhage.

During that emergency, Jolene recalls being half-crazed in the waiting room, where many members from both Jolene's and her husband's extended families had joined them. Suddenly she saw a flash of light that she felt was supernatural. Angry at that moment, she groused at God interiorly, "I've done everything you wanted me to do. Don't come here. It's my child who needs you." Immediately the light disappeared.

Moments later, a relieved doctor came out and announced the bleeding had stopped.

The hospital priest, Father Prescott, also proved to be a great support during such times. "He even helped us to laugh," Jolene recalls with gratitude. But Father Prescott did get a little upset about one thing. Hospitals don't allow just anyone, even in a Roman collar, to disturb their patients. In charge of such matters, Father Prescott permitted other priests to visit if they were closely connected to a patient, such as someone's parish priest. Two priests the Gils knew hoped to get over to New Orleans to see them. Neither made it.

But a smiling priest did come striding into the intensive care unit where Brian, as he recuperated from surgery, was enjoying a game of Nintendo with another kid. This priest carried a crucifix that Brian noticed looked just like the one Mrs. Gerry had blessed him with, only bigger. The visitor asked the boys if they wanted to receive Jesus in Communion. They said "yes," so he fed them the wafer that Catholics believe is truly Jesus present. Then he prayed for both boys, touching the cross, Brian remembers, to the young heart patient's head. Having finished the prayer—of which Brian can't recall a single word—the smiling priest turned and strode out again. He had not given his name.

The Gils thought Father Prescott had sent an assistant. But Father not only has no assistant, he was unhappy about this incident. It was the sort of thing that shouldn't happen in a well-run hospital.

Driving home in their van after the hospital released him, Brian, who was wide awake, became frightened because he saw the Virgin Mary. "Mama, am I dying? Has she come to get me?" he asked Jolene.

His mom, who has visions herself, reassured him. Later when they were at home and Jolene had to insist, to Brian's disappointment, that he follow his doctors' instructions to rest when he wanted to play, he saw Mary again, this time splendidly crowned.

They did not know that while they faced the dangerous surgery in New Orleans, Father Joe Alexander back in Eunice, was asking the Virgin's intercession, promising if Brian came back alive the priest would consecrate this boy—who from his earliest years has spoken of being a priest—to Jesus' Mother. Father Joe did this shortly after Brian's return home. But at that time, Jolene had a shock. For while they were in the church, Brian saw a picture of a priest and said, "Mama, that's the priest who prayed for me in the hospital."

"Why, Brian," Jolene sputtered, "that's Father Seelos."

His mother knew Brian to be an innocent, honest child. Age fourteen when this is written, he remains firm about what he saw.

With so many prayers and so much supernatural support, one would think that Brian's heart would be strong as an ox. But God's ways are not always so simple. Not long after the surgery, in December 1992, Dr. Schiller gave the Gils bad news: Brian's valve had closed again. More surgery would have to be attempted—even with the bleeding problem that could kill him—because with the valve's tiny opening, his oversized heart muscles, severely thickened from having to pump so hard, were creating new problems. This time there could be no simple effort to open the valve. It would have to be completely replaced—an undertaking with more possibilities for complications.

"I'd like to operate in January," the doctor said.

"If it won't be bad for Brian, could you wait until February?" Jolene asked. The doctor thought he could.

In her testimony submitted to the Seelos Center, Jolene wrote:

We came back home and I told my family that I was tired of trusting the doctors, that I was putting my trust in God.

She and the family had sometimes watched Protestant evangelist Benny Hinn's healing crusades on television. When Jolene saw people apparently healed of physical problems by God through this man's prayers, she'd say to her oldest child, "See, Brian, it's possible." Then she read Hinn's book *Good Morning, Holy Spirit* with profit. "It opened my eyes," she says, "to the presence of the Holy Spirit I felt in and around me but which, until then, I couldn't identify." While she didn't agree with everything the evangelist had to say, and she worried that people would put their faith in Hinn rather than God, she was still happy to learn the healer was to come to Houston, Texas, in January 1993. She would take Brian, Jolene decided, to Hinn's healing crusade.

While the decision brought criticism from some of her Catholic friends, it turned out to be a growth experience for Jolene. The Lord revealed to this cradle Catholic, she says, that she did not have to be either prejudiced toward Protestants or afraid of mixing with them lest "they pull me into something cultish." God loves all people, she realized, no matter which religion they belong to.

Jolene worried that Brian needed faith to be healed (actually, infants too young for faith, people in deep comas, and atheists have been healed when others prayed for them). But how, she asked herself, do you give a young boy who has just been through a harrowing experience that almost killed him this kind of faith? His mother tried varied ways. One was home prayer: The family prayed over their oldest child each night after saying the rosary and Brian often felt heat—many times a sign of healing—around his heart. One night Jolene recalls, "I asked the Blessed Mother to come in and carry God's healing to Brian. 'Touch his foot, please,' I said to her—not out loud but inside. Although we all had our eyes closed, Brian and I both saw a flash of light just after that. Then Brian said, 'I feel somebody touching my foot and the warmth is going up to my heart.'"

Besides continuing to ask the Blessed Virgin Mary, Father Seelos, and "all the saints" to pray for Brian's healing—in order to build faith that healing miracles were *possible*—Jolene nightly read aloud to the family Bible passages on Jesus' healings. The four children, who are stairsteps, each only a year apart—at this time, nine, ten, eleven, and Brian just turned thirteen—sometimes protested mildly, "Oh, Mama!" But Jolene was adamant, "sit down, hush up, and listen." Nickey Gil is a man of serious faith but even he—a *cursillista*[1]— wondered if his wife was pushing things too hard.

Jolene was putting God on the line. She knew, she says, you shouldn't put him to the test. But on the other hand, Scripture says that faith can achieve healing. "I'm either going to look like a fool or your promises are going to come true," she goaded God.

In this, Jolene was acting in one genuine Catholic tradition. Twentieth-century beatification candidate Father Solanus Casey, for a recent example, used to encourage people to feel free to put God "on the spot" so long as they got out of his way by giving up worry and anxiety. "How wonderful are all God's designs for all who have confidence in Him," Solanus encouraged—

and the American healer-saint meant this equally whether one was to be healed or enter the next life.

Similarly, Franciscan James McCurry counsels it is always right to pray for healing, with the understanding that leaving this life for heaven can be a healing, too. Of course equally holy people may decide to simply pray, "Thy will be done."

During this intense period, one of Jolene's close friends mentioned a book she had just borrowed called *Nothing Short of a Miracle*. Jolene says "the minute she mentioned the book to me, I could feel the Holy Spirit's anointing all over me; I knew the Lord wanted me to see something in this book." She asked to borrow it, but the friend was reluctant to loan something she had borrowed herself.

"Well, just bring it over before the crusade," Jolene asked.

About 5:00 P.M. the day before they were to leave for Houston to attend Hinn's healing service, Jolene was feeling the stress; if a miracle didn't occur, more surgery could not be postponed. Suddenly she had that same sense of the Holy Spirit. She looked out the window and saw a familiar car pulling into the driveway.

Her friend rushed in just long enough to hand Jolene the book and say, "I'll leave it with you until after the crusade."

"Let's go in the living room and see what the Lord wants to tell us," Jolene said to her kids.

"Gosh, the Holy Spirit's so strong," she exclaimed.

"I feel him," Brian agreed. From the stress she felt and her great need, Jolene began to weep. She began flipping through the pages, reading a word here and there. Then she came to a chapter about a miracle.

She slapped her leg. "That's us! That's what we need!"

Brian grabbed her arm.

"I think you're going to be healed, baby," she crowed.

"I'm starting to believe you," her son replied.

Jolene began to read the story. Suddenly Father Seelos—whom she recognized from his picture on the relic given them—appeared to her, giving the homemaker his characteristic gentle little smile. A second later he was gone.

Shocked, she looked down at the book and realized the chapter was on cures given through the prayers of Father Seelos.

While they had asked God to permit Father Seelos to pray for Brian, and Brian believed Father Seelos had come himself to pray for him in West Jefferson Hospital, Jolene still was not particularly focused on Father Seelos. Given a prayer card asking this saint's intercession while they'd been in New Orleans, she had prayed that prayer no more than twice. But she could see now that it was Father Seelos the book was meant to remind her of.

That night about midnight, she woke suddenly, as often happens to her, feeling the familiar presence of the Holy Spirit. At the foot of her bed, again with "a soft smile," stood Father Seelos. "He didn't say anything," she recalls. "He just looked at me with that gentle smile and then disappeared. I knew the Lord was trying to let me know that Father Seelos was praying for us."

The next day they took off for Houston and were among many at Benny Hinn's service. Jolene writes:

> During the Our Father (we were singing) I had my arm around my son with my hand resting on his chest. His heart started beating very rapidly. It felt like it was going to jump out of his chest. And then all of a sudden his valve popped open. I felt it hit against my hand. And Brian felt it open up in his chest.

God had put some money down on those biblical promises of his.

When they returned to Eunice and prepared for the trip to New Orleans, Jolene stuck her spiritual neck further out. She told everybody that, yes, Brian was going to the hospital but he would not need surgery. They'd only be there three days, in fact.

"They all thought I had lost it," she laughs. Let her tell it:

> We went to the hospital and the doctor ran the tube up Brian's leg and into his valve to check it. Then he came out white like a ghost. He kept telling us he was sorry—that he must have misread Brian's X rays. That the valve was open now. On the third day we came home with no surgery. Everyone was in shock. No one believes in miracles anymore.

She phoned the Seelos Center and left a thank-you message on their machine. Then she promptly forgot about Father Seelos again, until a day when she was on the phone with her cousin. Father Seelos' name came up and Jolene said, "If I mention Father Seelos, I get chills all over me and I feel the Holy Spirit." Her cousin said, "I'm getting the same thing." They began trying to figure out what God wanted to get through to Jolene.

Suddenly she saw Father Seelos for a third time. Standing before her in the long, black cassock the genial Redemptorist wore during his missionary endeavors until his 1867 death caring for yellow fever victims, the dead priest gave the Louisiana mother his usual gentle smile. As before, he said nothing.

After that, Jolene felt she should contact Mrs. Gerry Heigle for a little cross touched to Father Seelos' relic that the volunteer had spoken about bringing Brian, then forgotten. The Seelos Center volunteer sent it at once. Today the cross—a smaller version, Brian says, of the one the priest he believes was Father Seelos blessed him with in the hospital—is kept in Brian's room, but Jolene takes it with her many times when, her kids in tow, she makes hospital calls to pray for the sick.

She also felt she should let the Seelos Center know in writing the role that the dead priest's prayers had played in Brian's heart valve reopening. Her seven-page letter appeared in the Seelos Center bulletin in May 1994. Since then the warm, compassionate Father Seelos has been beatified.

The reopening of his heart valve at Benny Hinn's service gave Brian a several year reprieve from surgery. Then in April 1997, now sixteen, Brian received a new heart valve in Rochester, Minnesota. Not only did Brian not hemorrhage during this successful operation, doctors could find no evidence of the bleeding disorder that in his previous surgery almost killed the Louisiana boy.

Endnote

1. One who has attended a Cursillo, an intense, life-changing encounter with God.

Chapter Seventeen

"THAT LITTLE MAN PUT HIS HAND ON MY FOREHEAD"

The same issue of the *Father Seelos and Sanctity* bulletin that featured Jolene Gil's letter asked prayers for two-year-old Rochelle Freeman, who had "an inoperable tumor." Rochelle, the daughter of David and Elaine (Abadie) Freeman of Marrero, Louisiana, would soon after apparently also see Father Seelos.

In the summer of 1993, Elaine—barely home from delivering her third child—took Rochelle to the doctor, concerned that her middle child was lethargic—wanting just to lie around, without appetite, and losing weight. What Rochelle's doctor found made the tiny girl a patient in Children's Hospital of New Orleans just two weeks later—that is, in August 1993.

Children's Hospital doctors were attempting to treat a firm malignant tumor called a neuroblastoma, the size of a grapefruit, that had wrapped itself around the two-year-old's aorta. Pressing against it, in fact, so hard that the aorta was pushed out of its rightful position. Smaller tumors, common side-kicks to this sort of major mass, lurked in the child's bone marrow and behind her eyes, so that one eye slightly protruded. Staging cancer by how far it has progressed from a "stage one, a mild situation, to the final stage four," Rochelle's tumor was a four. Her hospital physician, Dr. Schorin was blunt. "She will die of this."

But he assured her parents chemotherapy could buy time.

To start the particular chemo recommended by the hospital's tumor board, Rochelle was admitted for three weeks. Her little sister Kyla was just eight weeks old, and her mom, who also had seven-year-old Jeffrey at home, was a working mother.

So Elaine's mother-in-law, Mabel Freeman, spent a lot of time sitting with Rochelle at the hospital. When she stepped inside the bathroom attached to the child's room one day, Mabel could still hear clearly if someone came into the room or if anyone was talking to her granddaughter. She heard nothing in the few minutes she could not actually see the child.

But when she came out, Rochelle told her, "That little man put his hand on my forehead. He told me I was sweating. Then he put his hand on my belly."

Perplexed, the grandmother stuck her head out in the hall. She saw some nurses at their station, but no men. The doctors making rounds had been by long before and none were visible on the floor.

Yet Rochelle was adamant.

Later, when Mabel Freeman told her daughter-in-law about it, Elaine wondered if it could have been one of the saints they were praying to. These were principally Father Seelos, St. Jude, and St. Peregrine, the patron saint for cancer.

She decided to show Rochelle some pictures of different saints and ask, "Did any of these look like the man who visited you?"

Rochelle pointed to the picture of Father Seelos. Elaine had some other pictures of Father Seelos, different enough that a two-year-old might not recognize them as the same man. She mixed these in. Unerringly, Rochelle picked out every Seelos representation.

Maybe I just led her in some way, Elaine began thinking. Chagrined at the thought and tired after a long day at her job, she said, "You didn't really see anyone, did you?"

Rochelle was also weary—and she was getting tired of being pestered by her mother with all these pictures. "Mama," she said indignantly, "*this* is the man I saw." Then she went through the array of sacramentals pinned to her hospital gown, little relics and scapulars that had been put there by Elaine with no explanation to the child whatsoever, until she found a tiny relic of Father Seelos with his picture on it.

"*This* is the man," and again she whipped through the sacramentals until she found another Seelos relic. The two-year-old continued until she had pointed out each of the Father Seelos items and no others.

Elaine was moved, for she knew that no one had named these tiny pictures to Rochelle. That same evening the doctor making rounds—a young resident—came in. He put his hand on the little girl's abdomen where the very firm, grapefruit-sized tumor was easily felt. He frowned. "I don't feel anything here. It is on the right side, isn't it?" he questioned Elaine, checking his chart.

The next scan showed the tumor was indeed still there. But from the time Rochelle insisted that Father Seelos had visited her, the hard mass had turned very soft. This, said Dr. Schorin, meant that the chemo was changing a thriving tumor into a sick one, whose cells were now "on the run."

Elaine did credit the chemo. But she also credited prayer.

Among the many seeking Father Seelos' intercession with God for Rochelle was Seelos' fellow Redemptorist, Elaine's great-uncle, Father Alphonse Abadie. Father Alphonse, who died in 1994 after a long period of suffering, including kidney failure, confided to the young priest who gave him the last rites that he was offering all his suffering for this little niece's cure through Father Seelos. Elaine is sure Rochelle now has two Redemptorists praying for her in heaven.

By February 1994, the main tumor had shrunk by a third, to the size of a large orange. The tumors behind her eyes were gone. However, the malignancy in the bone marrow which had been gone was now coming back. As this signaled that the bone marrow cancer was growing resistant to the combination of drugs, these were changed.

That August, after a year's chemotherapy, the main tumor was reduced to the size of a large egg while the smaller tumors were all gone. The aorta was also back in its normal position.

The doctor reiterated that the chemo was doing its work.

"I believe it's prayers and chemo," Elaine said boldly.

In December Rochelle's doctors decided they could try to remove at least part of the shrunken tumor CAT scans had repeatedly shown wound about the child's aorta. During surgery the doctors were cheered—a minor miracle?—to discover the tumor and aorta were no longer attached. It was "child's play" to remove a malignancy that floated on abdominal viscera instead of melding into the aorta. They "got it all," although they could not guarantee no malignant cell was left behind.

To deal with that possibility, several severe measures were taken, even though Rochelle was "in remission" following the surgery. In late January 1995, small doses of radiation were given to Rochelle's eye and abdominal areas, where tumors had once been. Then as February came to a close, the child was hospitalized anew for chemo so intense it endangered every organ in her body. Other intravenous medications attempted to shield the nonmalignant parts of her body, while deadly chemicals coursed through her on a search-and-destroy mission for hidden neuroblastoma cells.

Because there had also been cancer in Rochelle's bone marrow, some marrow was harvested before it was completely killed off by radiation and the intense chemo. From previous treatment, what was harvested was only 1 percent malignant. That 1 percent was purged, then the marrow frozen. On March 1, 1995, Rochelle underwent a marrow transplant, receiving back her own, once-more healthy bone marrow.

Surviving the critical one hundred days following these radical treatments, as summer arrived Rochelle smilingly took off the mask she had to wear against germs and took up a normal child's life. If she survived past the one-year anniversary of this transplant, her doctors agreed she might be cured. But the medical men did not expect that outcome. Considering she was in its "final stage" when her illness revealed itself, her doctors looked for the neuroblastoma to return. Then there would be nothing more they could do.

A woman of spiritual depth, Rochelle's mother accepted that "God is in charge," and he may know it best for a family that a child goes to heaven as a little innocent. Elaine Freeman also notes, "God uses these things to teach people." She had seen Rochelle's illness change a lot of people. Still, like any loving mother, Elaine prayed ardently for her child's healing. No longer accepting the prognosis that Rochelle must die, she followed the counsel of those like healer Sister Briege McKenna (who had prayed over Rochelle) to trust God and persevere in prayer.

Five years later when Father Seelos was beatified on April 9, 2000, in Rome, a number of Rochelle's relatives were there rejoicing because Rochelle was still healthy. Now not only her mother but many others believe that God sent the dead Redemptorist to put a cure in motion when he dropped in, Rochelle insists, to soothe her brow and give a reassuring pat to her sick tummy.

Chapter Eighteen

DIVINE LOVE

Some saints so frequently see those from the next life that when they themselves turn up as God's messengers after death, it only continues a life lived in both worlds. However, there are equally genuine saints of a different ilk, ones I imagine saying to God, "You're kidding, right?" if asked to make an after-death appearance.

Take St. Madeleine Sophie Barat (1779-1865), for instance. In Burgundy, where Sophie Barat was born, people traditionally distrust imagination or fantasy. The very look of the area's ordered rows of staked vines marching in perfect conformity across their land—less than a hundred miles yet, in lifestyle, worlds away from Paris—is earthy, antimystical. So was the Barats' financially comfortable lifestyle—the father a barrel maker, that most down-to-earth, essential trade in wine-making country. Sophie, the youngest of three children, inherited her father's practicality and steady good nature as much as her mother's fine intelligence and capacity for love. No Barat was prone to visions or supernatural experiences.

Had vivacious Sophie shown any mystical tendencies, they would have been squelched at once by her severe, humorless eleven-years-older brother. Louis, a Jesuit educator, took charge of Sophie from the time she was seven, giving her an education so broad it was rare even for boys and unheard of for girls: from geometry to Greek, theology to physics, Bible history to Latin literature.

Perhaps because of the excellent mothering she received in her first years and the break she got from his rigors while her brother was imprisoned during the French Revolution, Sophie maintained her equilibrium under Louis' thumb. She learned to laugh both at herself and—without unkindness—at his severity.

211

Somehow Sophie grasped that God was not like Louis: God is not severe, does not carp on our imperfections and sins; instead he reaches out to us with love and forgiveness. This way of divine love became the superbly educated young woman's official spiritual path in 1800, when she was inducted into a new post-Revolutionary religious order, The Society of the Sacred Heart. As a foundress and administrator for the order, over the next sixty-three years Sophie used her intellectual and spiritual training to educate and spiritually form upper-class girls.[1] She hoped that by molding these young women into upright souls, they would one day do the same for their sons and daughters, to the benefit of their societies.

Sophie also was a spiritual mother to the order's nuns, including the 1,368 preceding her in death and the 3,500 alive at her passing. Some of those dead nuns had been very holy. At one's death, for instance, miracles began. Sophie asked God to "knock it off." God obliged. But God—whose sense of humor is well-known to his friends—had his revenge: When Sophie died on the Feast of the Ascension in 1865 at age eighty-six, he started working miracles through *her*. Due to the miracle cures atop her Church-verified heroic virture, the dead Burgundian became a canonized saint in 1925.

Some four years earlier the Lord had begun sending down-to-earth "don't-give-me-any-of-this-miracle-nonsense!" Sophie to Josefa Menendez (1890-1923), a humble, much less educated woman so mystical she could hardly keep *one* foot in this world. This celestial "odd couple" met many times, primarily at *Les Feuillants* monastery at Poitiers, France. Visits that helped Josefa—who didn't *want* supernatural experiences that made her "different" but had no way to turn them off—keep her equilibrium. And which, through dead Sophie's counsels recorded in the diary Josefa was ordered to keep, help the rest of us to grasp divine mercy.

The diary order came from leaders in Sophie's Society of the Sacred Heart, in which Josefa, a former Madrid seamstress, was a lay sister. Because of this diary, which helped her Superiors determine that she was a true mystic rather than a fraud or a nut, I report Mother Barat's visits in Josefa's own words (translated into English):

Today, the feast of [then Blessed, today St. Sophie], I went into her cell many times to whisper a little prayer to her, and once (I was in my blue working apron) I just stood for a moment and said, "O Mother, once more I ask you to make me very humble, that I may be your true daughter."

There was no one in the room and this little invocation escaped me out loud. Suddenly I became aware of the presence of an unknown nun. She took my head in her two hands, and pressed it lovingly, saying, "My child, commit all your frailties to the Heart of Jesus and be faithful to the Heart of Jesus."

I took her hand to kiss it, then with two fingers she made the sign of the Cross in blessing on my forehead, and disappeared.

This first meeting, on May 25, 1921, was followed by many others up and down the cloisters of the old Cistercian monastery whose monks, driven out at the Revolution, had been replaced years later by Barat's nuns. Dead Sophie Barat acted as a spiritual mother to Josefa, counseling her just as her living superiors did. Had this sort of thing happened to Sophie during *her* life, she would have found it very hard to deal with. Josefa, who had trouble accepting that Jesus Christ should take note of her, accepted her dead foundress' visits gratefully.

On March 14, 1922, alone in her cell, Josefa fretted that she had been less than generous with Jesus, who both passionately attracted and terrified her because she had to report every one of his frequent appearances to superiors, who were not looking for "visionaries," but simple, devout nuns. As she was torturing herself that due to her latest "misdeed" based on this terror, she'd never see Jesus again, Mother Barat came to comfort her.

"Remember, daughter," she said, "that nothing happens unless it is in God's designs."[2] Josefa moaned that there was no way she could repair the consequences created by her weaknesses, most specifically that fervent desire to be safely ordinary while the Lord toyed with her in extraordinary ways.

"But my child, you can repair your fault[s]," Sophie insisted, "if from your fall you draw great humility and generosity."

Josefa writes, "I asked her whether Jesus would ever return again...."

"But you must expect his return, my child," interrupted her visitor. "The longing and expectation of the bride are the glory of the Bridegroom."

Only a couple of Poitiers' superiors knew of Josefa's visions. They observed that the mystical phenomena in the Spanish nun's life took much of her psychic energy, but—a sign of the genuinely supernatural—never interfered with fulfilling her chores or spiritual obligations. Convinced in part by the lay sister's mistrust of her own experiences that Josefa was a true mystic, they transferred her temporarily in May 1923, to Marmoutier Monastery so the superiors there could observe her as well. Jesus assured the anxious mystic he would go with her.

At the new, strange monastery, Josefa asked Blessed Madeleine Sophie to help, "and suddenly she came herself."

"So my child, you are here!" Sophie said, her face warm with love and concern. Josefa poured out all her anxieties to the dead woman as easily as a child to its mother. And recorded later in her diary Sophie's advice:

> I have but one word to say to you, and you must turn it over all day, my child: "Love meets with no difficulties that it does not change into food for the flame of love." Later I will explain this to you, but while you are here just love—love—love....

That year Mother Barat's feast was moved to May 28. When that day came, the Spanish nun was naturally thinking of her French foundress. Blessed with loving parents, Josefa was basically a well-balanced person; but the closer she came to God's radiant perfection, the more her human imperfections loomed forbiddingly, marring the total gift of self she longed to make. As Josefa begged the dead saint's intercession for her "unworthiness and wretchedness," Mother Barat appeared to guide her in how to use even personal inadequacies to make spiritual progress—including Josefa's tendencies to anxiety, lack of confidence, imperfect humility, and wavering trust.

"My own dear child!" Sophie exclaimed with her usual vivaciousness, making the sign of the Cross on Josefa's forehead. "I love you just as you are, little and miserable.... I too was just the same and as little as you, but I found means to utilize my nothingness by giving it totally to Jesus who is so great! I abandoned myself to His holy will and sought the glory of His Heart only. I tried to live in the knowledge of my lowliness and nothingness, and He took charge of everything. So, child, live in peace and confidence. Be very humble, ... deliver[ing] yourself over wholly to the Heart that is all love."

About seven o'clock that July 16, the first anniversary of Josefa's vows in the society, Josefa went into the little cell that had once been Mother Barat's and was now a little prayer room. In the diary she notes:

Suddenly I saw her there, simple and humble as ever.... She said to me: "So, my child, it is already a year since you made ... [your vows]."

Josefa's diary records her joy at having vowed herself to Jesus forever, but that she was also worried, as usual, over what she saw as "my ingratitude." Sophie reproached her:

But my child, surely you know that His Heart is a blazing furnace, and its fire exists only to consume our miseries. As soon as you have owned them to Jesus, He remembers them no more. And if, in exchange, He has already granted you so many graces, He is prepared to grant you others greater still. His Heart is an inexhaustible Fountain: the more He gives, the more He desires to give. The more He forgives, the more He wants to pardon.

Josefa told Sophie of her promise to be faithful to whatever Jesus asked until her death, a death she knew was near. Mother Barat encouraged her:

Believe me, child, Jesus has forgiven and forgotten all your failings and all your strivings against His will, but He never forgets your good resolutions and He takes pleasure in them. His Heart is an abyss of mercy, and it will never fail you. It is, too, an abyss of riches which will never diminish, however largely distributed. Love Him as much as you can. He cares for nothing else....

There is more, including a reminder not to fall into pride—which is always a temptation of those led on extraordinary paths like Josefa's. Finally, Josefa writes, Sophie "gave me her blessing, I kissed her hand, and she was gone."

That fall Josefa went to Rome, ostensibly accompanying the mother superior of the Poitier Monastery to help with the extra housework at a gathering of the order's superiors. In fact, she was being given the once-over by the head of the society herself. During Josefa's days in Rome, Jesus asked the lowly lay sister to deliver a message to this woman who, however kind, was formidable in Josefa's eyes. Quite happy to do housework, Josefa experienced terror at the thought of saying to the head of her order, "Jesus Christ told me to tell you...."

Some days after the message was delivered, on October 15, passing a little prayer room where Sophie had once stayed, Josefa heard the well-known voice of the dead saint call her.

During this day's conversation, Sophie confided, "During my life I sought nothing but the glory of the Divine Heart. And now that I live in Him and by Him, my only desire is to see His Kingdom come."

At Sophie's next visit that same month, just before Josefa left Rome, the dead saint comforted her:

> You must not be afraid or worried when light is not granted you [regarding what to do], as Jesus will give it to you when you need it and will do everything to bring about the full accomplishment of His wishes. Your part is to obey and surrender your will to His. True, there are moments when all is dark; the Cross rises stark before us and prevents our seeing Jesus Himself. But then it is that He says to us, "Fear not, it is I." Yes indeed it is His very self and He will guide and finish the work He has begun. Have no fear, be faithful and remain in peace.

That December was the last month and the last Advent of Josefa's life. Sophie appeared to her several times, once humbly announcing herself as "your mother, the poor creature whom God chose to be the foundation stone of this little Society." She urged Josefa to pass on to other members of the Society not only Jesus' special love for them, but to urge these women—who by the nature of their mission associate with the rich and powerful—to never lose their humility.

On December 20, as thirty-three-year-old Josefa lay in her final illness, she was attacked by terrible pain; alone, she felt herself dying, but had no voice to call for the last rites. Suddenly St. Madeleine Sophie was there and, taking her spiritual daughter in her arms, comforted and supported her until the crisis passed. Two days later as Josefa received the last rites, she saw—others did not—Sophie there with Jesus and his mother (both of whom had appeared many more times to Josefa than had her foundress).

The Church has not yet completed its investigation of the heroic sanctity of Josefa Menendez. But the Society of the Sacred Heart believes time will prove that sanctity genuine. They point to various signs, including one on the night of Josefa's death. The nuns went to clothe the corpse in its religious habit and discovered something strange: Their monastery is not open to the public; still someone had been there ahead of them.

Under the blankets which were tucked in to the very top ... Josefa was lying, her arms by her sides, clothed in her gray petticoat which was carefully tied at the waist and covered her down to her feet. When? How? Who had done it? No one had entered the room since her death, as her next-door neighbor in the infirmary testified, and the little sister [Josefa], who had been incapable of the slightest movement, could not have done it, nor did she even know where the petticoat had been put away.

Jesus had told Josefa that she would die alone. She had, expiring during a sliver of time when, at the sick woman's urging, her nun attendant rushed down to community prayers and the sister infirmarian dashed away for a few minutes. But his mother and Sophie had promised Josefa they would be there to lead her to paradise. They knew, too, the little Spaniard's extreme modesty.

The schoolmistresses of the Sacred Heart, who have taught the children of prime ministers, royalty, and even an American president, are well-educated women not given to credulity. But they suggest the hands that clothed Josefa, who so dreaded "being handled after death," were those of one—or maybe two—who were long finished with this life.

Endnotes

1. Mother Barat also tried to open day schools for poorer girls when possible.
2. That is either desired by God or permitted by him in deference to free will.

Chapter Nineteen

"MY MOTHER FELT A HAND ..."

No saint has turned up more often in the past hundred years to bring God's healing to ordinary people than St. Therese of Lisieux. And that says nothing of the even larger number of cures through her intercession that take place with no visible sign of her presence. Healings in mission lands having had their own chapter, here is a sampling of cures from nonmission countries where Therese, in some way or another, "shows up."

For immediacy I have sprinkled events from recent years throughout this chapter. Some reader may wonder why I give far more from the prebeatification period. It is not, I assure you, that no one ever writes Carmel these days saying they have seen Therese, although with Europe a post-Christian society, there are certainly fewer letters. In my files are at least fifty names and addresses of people I could contact regarding recent "favors" from Therese, some including appearances. But I would have to try to authenticate these myself, for the cloistered Carmelites no longer feel the need to require testimonies come with corroboration. The investigation into her sanctity is over. There is no longer any need to "prove" anything. If someone today sends a letter of testimony, the nuns simply add it to the archives without any judgment as to its authenticity. In a sense, letters today are almost surely sincere, for there is absolutely nothing to gain from sending a testimony. But, as you know, sincere can be sincerely wrong!

It is the older cures, then, with their statements of corroborating witnesses and testimonials from competent sources as to the reliability of the person making the claim that I primarily rely on. Most of these individuals now dead, they can no longer be pestered by TV or tabloid emissaries, so I can generally give their names. On the other hand, to protect the recent recipients of Therese's attentions, while I assure you I have held the original letters in my own hands in those chilly archives, I will use no names. While I realize this may cause some reader to conclude St. Therese never helped anyone after 1915 and, in my shame over that, I am inventing "new" cures, let me simply refer doubters to the Lisieux Carmel, where every letter quoted or summarized (usually in my translation) may readily be found.

You may have read of one important early cure in John Beever's excellent, authenticated biography of Therese, *Storm of Glory.* Fortunately, at the Carmel archives in an old publication of the nuns I found the full medical statements by the original, attending Protestant doctor; other Protestant medical men who treated the patient; and the doctor brought in by the Church to investigate the cure, who also called in his own medical experts. Due to all this, I can offer you more details of this well-authenticated cure, which took place in Glasgow, Scotland, in 1909, before Therese was an official saint.

A Scotch Catholic widow in her early fifties, Mrs. Dorans of 9 Stanley Street, entered the Western Infirmary in Glasgow for the third time on April 28. Suffering for years from various nasty symptoms centered on the left side of her abdomen, her medical chart shows that, when admitted this time, she complained of great pain in that area, sickness, and vomiting. Her doctor of eight years, Daniel George Carmichael, who had sent her to the hospital, notes in his formal testimony that she was extremely weak and emaciated with a distended abdomen, dropsical legs—especially the left—and a tumor about the size of an orange that was very easy to feel. His hope in admitting her was that surgery could be done.

But the conclusion of the hospital surgeons was that her tumor, which they diagnosed as *carcinoma of the sigmoid flexure of the colon* (that is, a cancer of the intestines) was inoperable. Because she preferred to die at home, she was released on May 8, having had as treatment only some enemas (which found the area nearly blocked), pain medication, and a "careful diet" in hopes of the patient's keeping some nourishment down.

For ten weeks at home, still nauseous and vomiting, the Glasgow woman grew weaker and weaker, able to take only a few liquids. Finally even liquids were not retained. All this in spite of the fact that her family, friends, and various priests were making novenas of varied kinds, including directly to Jesus, begging God's cure of the cancer. By August 22, conscientious Dr. Carmichael making a Sunday house call, warned her children that she could not live much longer.

That same day, a Sister of Mercy visited, too, and, aware of the dying woman's great faith and desire to live, suggested a novena to "this young French nun people say is so holy." With no time to lose, they began the novena on the spot. For four days it seemed any healing granted through the prayer intercession of this Sister Therese was going to be the final one of entrance into the next life, for Mrs. Dorans' decline simply accelerated.

Thursday, Dr. Carmichael said she would die that night.

At eleven o'clock the widow sucked on a little ice to moisten her dry mouth. Even those few drops of water made her retch violently. Exhausted from pain and vomiting, finally she slept. According to the experienced doctor's expectations she should have slipped into a coma, followed by death before dawn. Instead, about 5:30 the next morning the Scotswoman wakened from "the best sleep she had had in years." What made her eyes open was a gentle pressure on each shoulder as if someone were leaning solicitously over her. She looked up. Her daughter slept soundly in a chair across the way. Otherwise the room was empty. Yet surely someone had just bent over the bed and gently touched her.

With a sudden start, she realized another oddity: Her constant pain was gone. Her hand moved at once to her abdomen. Her searching fingers could detect no trace of the orange-sized mass, not even a little bulge. The formerly distended abdomen, in fact, was flat.

Waking her daughter, she asked for something to drink. While just sucking a chip of ice had brought on violent vomiting six hours earlier, now she relished a glass of soda water, then moved on to tea and a roll for breakfast. When Dr. Carmichael dropped by to sign the death certificate, he found a healthy, if emaciated, woman who had only a marble-sized lump where an inoperable tumor had been the night before. (The "lump" was no tumor either, as the church's medical experts later verified by X rays, which showed only perfectly normal abdominal contents.) Mrs. Dorans' Protestant doctor, in his formal testimony, says what was most impressive to him was the suddenness of his patient's change from the final stage of terminal illness to health.

Mrs. Dorans was an honest woman. She said she hadn't seen Therese. She hadn't heard her say anything. She didn't dream of her. But she remained certain nonetheless that early that Friday morning God sent the young French saint to touch her and make her whole.

Why didn't Jesus respond to the earlier prayers to him? Apparently, as in Galilee where he could have healed everyone in the whole country, but preferred to send out seventy-two disciples to cure in his name, he wanted this healing to come through his later disciple, Therese.

July 9, 1913, is the date on a testimony from Le Champ near Thouarce in France, signed by both parents, their parish priest, Abbe Gustav Hautreaux, and a "bystander," that is, a person with no connections to church or family. The foursome certifies the cure of Bazile Horeau Jr. in the preantibiotic era when many children died of childhood diseases or simple infections. Quoting my translation:

In March four-year-old Bazile became gravely ill. He had a high fever and suffered from a terrible headache. The doctor, who was coming daily, declared he had meningitis in a tubercular form and was frank with the parents that there was no hope for their child.

Having learned this sad news, Louise Gazeau loaned the parents a relic of Sister Therese of the Child Jesus. They placed it near the head of the little one and commenced a novena. During the novena he improved visibly. They made a second [novena] and from that time their child was in great shape. *In fact he was stronger than he had been before he fell ill* [italics mine].

He had no convalescent period at all, only a little weakness in his legs the first few days after his recovery. As to his intellectual faculties, there was no brain damage—he showed simply no trace of the terrible malady but was simply a very intelligent, very nice child.

One morning after his cure, while his mother was dressing him, he said, "See, Mama, she passed her hand like this on my head and then I was cured and [after that] I've never been sick!"

The mother, very surprised, replied, "But who do you mean passed her hand on your head?"

"Why Sister Therese. I was in my bed. Papa was there. He saw her!"

How to judge this naive tale from a child of four? The adults, that is parents and the friend who loaned the relic, decided that Sister Therese *had* come and caressed the child, because when his mother questioned him about it, he always said, "Papa knows all about it: he saw *her.*" The father no doubt had been keeping watch by the sickbed when the child saw Therese [so the child assumes his father saw whatever he did].

Another day, more recently, Madame Horeau was talking to little Bazile of his guardian angel and the child had a bunch of questions. "Oh, so do you have a guardian angel, too? Where is he then? When we sleep is it around us?" Then, raising his short arms up as high as he could, the little boy questioned, "Is it like that—like Sister Therese was?" indicating that Therese showed herself raised up before him.

———◦•◦———

Born April 17, 1903, another little French girl—whose family wanted names withheld—was only a year old when she became ill with deadly influenza, with such a high fever she went into convulsions. The toddler lived, but was "stone deaf." Obviously this made learning to talk very difficult. Mostly the child made her wants known by signs while saying a few more or less unintelligible words.

Her parents had sadly decided to send her to what at the time was called a "deaf and dumb school" where she could hopefully get some sort of education. Then the warmhearted mother of a family the parents were very friendly with learned of their decision. She urged they let her first make a novena to Sister Therese of the Child Jesus, begging the child's cure.

The friend, identified only as Madame C., must have been a woman of great faith, for she did not make this novena quietly. Instead she began the audacious undertaking with the totally deaf little girl kneeling with her for the prayer each day, as if saying, "See this youngster they plan to send away. I've told her you can help. You certainly aren't going to disappoint her now, are you?" And she applied further pressure on the heavenly throne by beginning the novena on September 30, the anniversary of Therese's death.

They say God just can't resist people with faith like that—especially when it is expended so unselfishly for someone else. The child remained deaf as a stone on days one, two, and three of the novena—but on the fourth day, the child's mother suddenly noticed her little girl could hear.

When her hearing returned, the little girl's speech was at the level of the one-year-old she had been when she became deaf: she used only the simplest, usually single, words. Madame C. at once began working with her, teaching her short prayers and new words. The child seemed quite intellectually gifted, the family's motherly friend noted happily, and made good progress.

Although the deafness was gone, Madame C. joyously continued the novena in thanksgiving and had the healed child kiss a relic of the Carmelite nun each day.

On October 6, the seventh day of the novena, the little girl became frustrated with her limited vocabulary and reverted to some pantomime to try to explain that the day before, she first received a lovely odor from the relic, and then, going to bed, saw Sister Therese "very beautiful and surrounded by a heavenly light." The saint, the child managed to communicate, extended her hands as if to bless the little girl, then disappeared.

As a test of whether this was perhaps a case of an overexcited imagination, Madame C. gave the child a piece of brown material of the color worn by Carmelites. Immediately she ran to a picture of the saint and placed the piece of brown cloth against the robe that Therese wore. This was verification to Madame C. If only the account said the picture was not in color, it could be equally important to us!

But Madame C. offered other "evidence," as well. She pointed out that over a period of many months, whenever the little girl saw a picture of Sister Therese, "her face brightens" with obvious joy. Madame C. also noted that "when she sees the sun shining on anything bright, she says joyously ... pointing to its rays, 'Little Therese.'" A mother herself, Madame C. observed "to my mind the best proof of the vision is the enthusiasm she shows after so many months have elapsed; for as a rule, children forget so easily and tire so quickly of any one thing." Eight years old when the formal report was made in January 1912, the little girl often happily prayed near the saint's relic.

The report sent to Carmel contained not only statements from members of the child's and Madame C.'s families, but also the medical reports and references as to these people's stability, all in the form of legal documents, certified at the Town Hall and the respective parishes of the two families.

There are many cures from the late twentieth century as well, some with apparitions of Therese, such as the tiny French boy cured in 1984 when he sees her. Since they can be nebulous, I report few nonphysical cures. But most people can relate to the fear of death or grief over a death. In the archives I read a touching letter sent to the nuns in 1980 by a woman whose nineteen-year-old daughter had died. A few days after this devastating event, the woman went to her daughter's grave to pray. As she knelt there, she looked up and saw in the sky the Virgin Mary and St. Therese *with her daughter*, who used to say, "St. Therese is the one I love best of all the saints."

Remember the old fellow cared for by the Little Sisters of the Poor for whom Therese got a new tongue? I want to spotlight here another aged man with a terrible fear of death. Members of the same order of Sisters gave him a picture of Sister Therese, asking her to reconcile him to dying. Shortly thereafter, according to the Sisters' report:

Therese appeared to him in a dream, in which he saw himself all laid out and ready for burial.... Taking him by the hand, she assured him that the moment of death had not yet come. From that time onward, he became very fervent.

During his final hours, he asked, "Don't you see that beautiful lady?" Was it Therese? Or someone else giving him comfort and support? In any case, all his fear was gone: The report closes, "he died like a saint."

That cure occurred around 1910. In 1992, at "The Hermitage" in Trosly-Breuil, France (one of the "Arks"[1] scattered around the world, where families are formed by mingling mentally handicapped and so-called normal folks), a sixty-two-year-old retarded man suffered from advanced Alzheimer's. Rene no longer responded to things such as photographs, could not eat or drink without help, and was only a month away from his December 18 death. But two individuals who lived at the Hermitage reported to Carmel[2] that on November 14, when they brought Rene into the kitchen, where one of the two had hung above the stove a photograph of Therese costumed not as a nun but as Joan of Arc, something quite "impossible" took place. I translate a portion of their long account:

> to our great stupefaction, we heard him say "There! There! Look! Look! Look! ... and we saw him completely radiant, all "illumined" pointing his finger toward the photograph. His whole body was stretched upwards and his eyes raised....
>
> One has to understand that in such an advanced state of Alzheimer's for him to take such an attitude and speak like this was, for us, a true "miracle."
>
> It was visible that something was taking place between him and her.... We were bowled over.... We felt that Therese manifested her presence and said to us, "I am here and I am going to help you."
>
> ... And that day on his own initiative Rene ate and drank on his own, something that had not happened for a long time, and which never happened again.

The writer of this long testimony reports other ways he personally witnessed by which Therese kept manifesting her relationship with the mentally disabled old man. These include the frequent experience that if Rene suffered a coughing spell or had trouble breathing, showing him a picture of Therese brought obvious physical relief. Rene also intelligibly said, "Come! Come!" several times when shown this picture. And yet this was a prayer-card likeness of the saint, a stylized interpretation of her in nun's garb, not anything like the photograph of Therese he had reacted to in the kitchen.

Just two nights before his death, unable to move, not only did looking at this picture stop a coughing spell, but the advanced-Alzheimer's patient stared fixedly at the photo, indicating mental attention, and tried to kiss it. By his grimace when it was withdrawn, he made clear he wanted it back.

When Rene died very peacefully, the witness, who was rubbing his feet at the time, says one could feel a "presence"—the implication is that this was Therese—near him.

———•———

Lest someone worry God reserves Therese's visits for old men, here is a January 11, 1913, letter from Havana, Cuba, signed by E. Daura:

My mother who is sixty-five years old, was bedridden, suffering from great problems [paralyzed] which made it impossible for her to move; her mind was also affected: she could hardly articulate a few words.

A friend, who felt for us in this trial, sent us *The Story of a Soul.* Full of hope after reading it, I proposed to my mother that we make a novena to the Child Jesus in order to ask her cure through the intercession of Sister Therese.

During the novena, nothing changed: but the day after it ended, at dawn, we suddenly saw our dear patient get up, walk, and go out of the house.

We were stupefied. My mother said simply, "I saw Sister Therese. She put her hands on my shoulders and she's the one who helped me get up and walk."

There is a postscript that after six months of walking, the mother fell and had to take to her bed again. Still, the aged mind, cleared by Therese's visit, "remained perfect."

Another cure was received by an aged Dutch nun, Sister St. Peter of Limbourg, Holland, whose rheumatism-riddled hands became more and more crippled the older she grew. As aged nuns, St. Therese's blood sisters Marie and Celine suffered similarly. When the pain of her hands got so bad that sleep became a problem, Sister St. Peter turned to "little Therese," as she called her, wrapping the worst hand with a picture of the then-unbeatified dead Carmelite in the wrapping. One night when the infirmarian had been unable to massage Sister St. Peter's hands to lessen the pain before bedtime, Sister St. Peter called with greater earnestness than ever on Therese.

In the depths of that night she felt someone take her swollen, crippled hand and gently rub it. Without seeing Therese, the old nun was sure the young one was at her bedside. Eventually Sister St. Peter sensed that Therese slowly withdrew. From what the testimony writer calls "that happy night" the rheumatism was gone. Sister St. Peter could do any work, even things like laundering in cold water, without discomfort. The Dutch nuns end their testimony, "May God be praised for the favors bestowed through the intercession of Sister Therese of the Child Jesus!"

From Scotland, dated April 13, 1913, a packet came to the Lisieux Carmel containing the testimony of Charles Campbell of Glasgow; medical photographs; an accompanying attestation by the family's confessor, Jesuit Bernard Blake; and a long, detailed testimony by nuns of a Glasgow convent who visited Charles Campbell's mother for several years while she endured great sufferings.

While Charles' statement is clear, the nuns' more detailed contribution shows that the situation was even more serious, and the cure more wonderful, than the son's testimony indicates. This is a good reminder that many times the full extent of a miracle never is known—or known only by a few. Rather than giving these long testimonies separately, I combine pertinent details from each to report what took place.

In 1913, it had been almost twenty-one years since Charles' mother injured her leg as she entered a horse-drawn tram. The wound had never healed, causing her, now more, now less suffering. Eight years after the accident, much of the leg was affected. She had by this time consulted several doctors, but the only recommendation they had for her was to try three months of bed rest, something impossible for this busy mother. Still at times the pain became so acute she did have to take to her bed until it eased up. Various salves and other healing remedies all proved ineffectual.

By the winter of 1912-13, the pain was nearly unbearable. Sores covered her leg from ankle to the knee, with two deep, large wounds above the ankle and another gross swelling above the knee.

In January 1913, that is, over twenty years since the original injury, she had just spent a month in bed, her leg swollen to double its normal size and full of open sores that in places had eaten away the flesh to the bone. With abundant matter oozing out, the doctor the family summoned believed blood poisoning was setting in. He ordered an ambulance to transport Mrs. Campbell to the hospital. Her son's and the nuns' accounts agree that death seemed inevitable (remember, this is before antibiotics could challenge such an infection) and the son believed it only a matter of "hours."

When the ambulance arrived, the Scotswoman stubbornly refused to get in it. Her daughter-in-law had obtained a relic of this "little French flower," as some Scots called Therese. Feeling that two decades of medical help had been decidedly ineffectual, Mrs. Campbell insisted her family join her in praying for a cure.

Giving up all medical remedies—never a recommended thing to do, of course—they began a novena for Therese's prayer intercession. Somehow the dying woman hung onto life for the nine days. Then the final night of the novena, she heard a voice say, "your leg is cured."

The next morning when it was time to change the bandages, they were full of corrupt flesh, as if it had all suddenly sloughed off. As for the leg, it had new, perfect, and healthy flesh. Where the wounds had once been there were well-healed scars.

This woman, too, only heard a voice. But her family and the nuns agreed with the healed woman's opinion that words accompanied by a cure like this could only come from one of God's messengers. To them that messenger was obviously the young French saint.

Seventy-one-year-old Mrs. Campbell resumed an active life—even traveling a lot—without ever having another problem with her leg. A year later, as the formal testimony was put together, she said her more than twenty years of sufferings seemed hardly real—more like some barely recalled nightmare.

In 1979 a woman writes the Carmelites about her husband's two open-heart surgeries. A blood clot from the first surgery formed a thrombosis in the body's largest vein, near his kidneys. During the second surgery the clot, which was the length of a cigar, got away and went through the heart to a lung, causing a pulmonary embolism. In the middle of it all, she remained calm, the wife says, because before the surgeries, St. Therese had "manifested herself" through a strong, unaccountable odor of roses, giving the woman the certainty that her prayers for her husband would be heard.

She concludes the account saying that her husband not only survived, although he was still under medical treatment for his kidneys damaged by the thrombosis, but his state keeps improving. "At the hospital," she happily tells the nuns, "my husband is surnamed 'the miracle.'"

From Ireland, Sister Mary John of the Convent of Our Lady of Mercy at St. Michaels in Athy wrote on behalf of a man who apparently didn't want to deal with this "supernatural stuff" himself. Sister Mary John had sent her account to a French priest, Pere A. Roche, stationed in Liverpool, who sent it on to Carmel, vouching for the nun's integrity and sanity. I translate from a 1913 French Carmel publication what is probably a Carmelite's translation of original English!

A man from Kilkenny was attacked by a leg problem, which rapidly got worse. It was a wound of a very nasty aspect.... Soon he had to give up all work and take to his bed, which desolated him, especially since his chances of cure were doubtful.

One of our sisters having spoken to him of Sister Therese of the Child Jesus, he got the idea to start a novena, persuaded somehow that only through her [prayers] would a cure come to him.

The second night of the novena, he woke suddenly, feeling several strokes by a mysterious hand on his bad leg. He looked all around and saw no one....

The cure didn't happen at that second; but the morning of the last day [of the novena] to the astonishment of the poor man when his bandages were lifted off, the leg was perfectly cured to the point that the wound had disappeared without leaving a scar or a trace of any sort.

In 1982, an Englishwoman suffered a brain hemorrhage and was in a semiconscious state for an entire month. She had no particular devotion to St. Therese, she says frankly, when she later recovered and wrote the Lisieux Carmelites. But she wanted them to know that at the point she felt she was dying, "into my line of vision came a pair of praying hands and then St. Therese followed. She came across and put her hand on my head." The woman put her own hand up and felt the crisp mantle of a Carmelite, which seemed for that moment to be on her own head. An illness-induced hallucination? Or a saint's presence? The woman feels a need to write the nuns ...

———◆◆◆———

In 1916, after three years of illness from an ulcer so severe she once received the last rites, a Sister Louise began her second novena to Sister Therese. On September 10, 1916, Therese appeared to tell her: "Be generous with God; I promise you'll soon be cured." The next morning when Louise climbed out of bed, she gasped: the floor all around her bed was sprinkled with rose petals. No human explanation for their presence was ever found. She actually grew worse after this visitation but on the morning of September 26, she woke healed. X rays proved the ulcer gone. This cure was one of Therese's three beatification miracles.

———◆◆◆———

No one is more sophisticated, they say, than a resident of Paris, so one hardly expects testimonies from Parisians about a saint known for advocating simple, childlike confidence in God. But in 1985, the Carmelites receive a letter from a woman in Paris who wants to tell them what happened to her on April 15, 1938. A little slow with the report, perhaps, the family has still never forgotten what St. Therese did for them.

On that spring day in 1938, the writer's mother was trying to eat her lamb chop while her young son and daughter—proving even in Paris children are the same—were driving their mother literally to distraction by their squabbling. In her agitation, she swallowed a bone. Lodged in her throat, it would neither come up nor go down. The doctor, immediately summoned (this is long before the Heimlich maneuver), said the sufferer was going to die from asphyxiation. That they had been tormenting her, of course, in no way meant the children didn't love their mother. Seeing her menaced, the girl immediately began to talk to St. Therese of Lisieux on her parent's behalf. Wanting to cut a deal, the child promised to donate her First Communion outfit to a little girl who couldn't afford a new dress for that important occasion, if only Therese would ask God to let Therese come help her mother.

Years later, one can still sense the joy of that moment when, she writes, "the miracle took place. My mother felt a hand turn the bone so that she was able to get it out. She was saved." To the family, there is no question that the hand was Therese's.

Endnotes

1. More often spelled L'Arche, the French for ark.
2. Their witness is in the periodical *Therese of Lisieux,* June 1993.

Chapter Twenty

CURES OF THE HOLY

Mother Madeleine Sophie Barat (1779-1865), whose life sings of divine mercy, has returned to guide and to deliver God's healing even though the miraculous was definitely not the Frenchwoman's style in life. While she would, no doubt, modestly have preferred God send someone else, it was dauntless Sophie whom the Lord chose as his associate for a first-class miracle to one of her spiritual daughters—a cure accepted for Sophie's canonization.

This spiritual daughter was Marie de Salm-Salm, born at Anholt in Westphalia (Germany), February 20, 1874. Marie was a healthy child until age eleven. Then her spinal column began to twist. Doctors put her in a so-called orthopedic appliance, which—like the baby boards of some Indians or the foot bindings of the Chinese—was supposed to force a body part into the desired shape. The youngster also spent several periods in an institution where specialists labor to unkink backs like hers. None of this straightened the child's spine. While not the sort to talk of her own sufferings, no doubt the young girl also had her share of the cruelties afflicted children face from other kids.

Suffering can make or break. In Marie's case, it drove her to God. At the age of twenty-one, just thirty years after Mother Barat's death, on July 2, 1895, the young Westphalian entered the Society of the Sacred Heart Sophie founded. As you recall, this is an order devoted to education. Although following the tightly scheduled life of a teaching nun was harder for Marie than for her fellow aspirants, she did not flunk out. In fact, her order recalls Marie steadfastly carrying on her work assignments "with great courage," in spite of constant suffering from terrible headaches and pain in her deformed bones. Admitted to first vows in 1897, in February 1903 she was allowed to make permanent ones. She was in Austria by then, teaching at Riedenburg.

Sister Marie did not complain about her physical problems, even on those days when healthy teachers would feel overwhelmed. What caused this holy soul suffering was having to be dispensed from fully keeping the Society's relatively mild rules due to her rotten health.

In 1912, during the summer vacation, she was sent to her order's place in Jette, Belgium, for some rest. In Jette also rested the "exiled," incorrupt body of Mother Barat—spirited out of France during one of those anti-Church uprisings that periodically sent these influential and intelligent nuns fleeing Sophie Barat's homeland.

Marie began a novena by the tomb of the dead saint. She was not asking to be cured. No, Marie's modest—some might say foolish—request was simply to be strong enough to "keep the rule." Particularly she wanted to be able to function with less sleep and get up at 5:00 A.M. daily to join her community in prayer.

Those who think God very strict warn that you must be careful in prayer: you will receive no more than you ask, they insist. But one of the special gifts of Sophie Barat was to grasp how lavish God can be, how readily—even "wastefully"—he showers goodness and blessings on those who approach him with confidence or love. Undoubtedly when she took the request to God then, Sophie plumped it up a bit.

Making her daily prayer by the tomb, Marie felt inspired one day to help herself to some of the oil from the lamp that burned before the reliquary holding the foundress' intact body. She dabbed this on her forehead and at once her dreadful headache stopped. Given heart by this wonderful event, the next day she took some of this oil back to her room and smeared it on her chest before she slept.

When she awoke, her pain and suffering had vanished. Much more incredibly, while she slept God had untwisted her spine. Her back was suddenly so strong the German nun could kneel and adore God with her arms extended sideways, shaping her very body into a symbol of her faith. Apparently that is what she was doing in ecstatic thanksgiving when Mother Barat appeared to her.

We must forgive Marie that she doesn't say what they talked about, only that they conversed for a short while. Her reticence only shows we're once again dealing with the genuinely holy. Was the deformity that vanished overnight very small? I think not. Once her spine became straight, the official account says Marie's clothes had to be lengthened because she was "much taller."

X rays, taken as part of the formal investigation of the miracle, showed a beautifully normal spine. Mother Marie served the rest of her long life in Austria, except for a period as superior of the society's members in Rome. She died, straight-spined, at the age of ninety-two on August 18, 1966, at Riedenburg—the spot where sixty-three years earlier as a determined young nun she ignored constant pain to dedicate herself to loving and serving God in others.

———◆◆———

During her lifetime Mother Barat, as head of nuns working with the "upper class," had to graciously interact with the cream of European society, while on her frequent business journeys making friends with coachmen and people of every class. She took it all in stride, although she would have preferred to live a hidden, contemplative life. St. Therese of Lisieux lived that hidden life, but exploded into action after death. While Sophie probably blissfully enjoyed the hidden prayer chambers of heaven, Therese was joyously flitting all over the world on God's errands, including carrying healing to those aspiring to holiness.

Among these was an Ohio woman named Rhoda Wise. In 1932, at the age of forty-four, the Canton housewife had a thirty-nine-pound tumor removed without any complications. Four years later, in December 1936, while walking down a dark street she was less lucky: Stepping off the curb, she plunged into a drain opening whose iron cover had broken. One leg and foot were seriously injured. After medical treatment had done its best with plaster casts and other techniques, the foot remained bent inward, and putting her weight on it caused pain so severe that she could walk only with crutches. A number of doctors advised the problem was permanent.

Determined to seek health whatever some doctors said, in June 1938 she returned to Mercy Hospital in Canton to get still another cast. A nurse noticed an abscess on her six-year-old abdominal incision. Doctors found the abscess was caused by adhesions formed on the bowel underneath the surgical incision, where the big tumor had been removed. To try to deal with the adhesions and cure the abscess, Rhoda endured surgeries in July and August that year and again in January of 1939. Far from mending matters, the last incision from these surgeries refused to heal. Shortly after the third surgery the bowel underneath the wound perforated and intestinal contents began to come through the unhealed incision.

During her various stays in the Catholic hospital, Rhoda became interested in Catholic prayer. By 1938, she was saying the rosary and making novenas to St. Therese of Lisieux. About the time the bowel perforated she was received into the Church by Monsignor G.N. Habig of Canton's St. Peter's Church. With her medical problems she was unable to attend Mass, however, and was even confirmed in bed at the hospital.

February 12, 1939, her doctor told her there was no hope of curing the abdominal wound. Still they kept her in the hospital where it could be dressed daily until May 8, when she was discharged as "incurable."

To her relatives the doctor explained that Rhoda was now suffering from cancer, something that sometimes occurs in old surgical scars or adhesions. From that time, a visiting nurse came daily to her home to dress the middle-aged woman's wound. There was little to be done for the state of the patient's abdomen, which was raw-skinned and terribly sore.

Then on May 28, 1939, at 2:45 A.M, her bedroom suddenly became bright and Jesus appeared to Rhoda. He sat on a chair by her bed, robed in gold and gloriously beautiful, with the marks on his forehead where thorns had once pierced his brow.

"Have you come to get me?" Rhoda asked, thinking she was dying. But the Lord told her it was not yet her time. They discussed some things, including Jesus assuring Rhoda that her dead mother was in heaven, then he disappeared, telling Rhoda he would be back in thirty-one days.

On June 28, 1939, at the same time of the night, he returned in an effulgence of light clothed in white. With him was St. Therese. Therese walked over to the invalid's bed and motioned to her to pull back the coverings and remove the dressing from the wound. The saint placed her hand on that malignant ugliness and said, "I'm the Little Flower [Rhoda's usual way of referring to Therese]. You've been tried in the fire and not found wanting. Faith cures all things."

Rhoda made a movement to replace the dressing. Therese forestalled her. The saint then walked back to Jesus' side. He said he would come again, then both vanished.

As so often occurs after such apparitions, Rhoda immediately fell into a deep, healing sleep. She awoke at 5:00 A.M. to find the wound closed. The raw skin extending over her whole abdomen was also gone, healthy, apparently new skin in its place.

With this cure, Rhoda found new impetus to deal with her inability to walk. On July 14 she returned to Mercy Hospital for a new cast on her leg. When this fairly light cast did not keep the foot from turning inward, on August 11 the frustrated doctor decided to go all out. He encased her leg in the-cast-to-end-all-casts, which he intended to leave on for three months.

The only problem with this (pardon the pun) heavy-handed approach: because it was so heavy and tight, the new cast was very painful. On the night of August 15, Rhoda was sitting up in bed awake, weeping from the pain. Suddenly the room lit up and St. Therese was there again, standing by the Ohio housewife's bed.

"That's a very little thing," the saint smiled. "Stand up and walk."

Obediently Rhoda placed her feet on the floor and stood up. As she did this, the cast, which was over a foot long, split open from top to bottom. (Having once watched a doctor struggle to remove a similar cast, I regard this as at least slight evidence that Rhoda was not imagining or making up this visit.)

"Go to church now," Therese said and disappeared.

Rhoda looked down at her foot. It was straight. She could place her weight on it without pain for the first time in two-and-a-half years. Joyfully, she walked freely around the house until 6:00 A.M., when she went to Mass at the chapel of Mercy Hospital.

Rhoda Wise was to see Jesus and St. Therese on a number of other occasions, and herself become, Monsignor Habig believed, a genuine mystic and stigmatic before her death in Canton on July 7, 1948.

God's sense of humor is the only reason I find for why the "straightest" dead saints are often sent as messengers to the "flakiest." Thus learned, practical Sophie Barat was sent to visionary Josefa Menendez, while simple, uncomplicated Therese appeared to stigmatic visionaries like Rhoda Wise and Therese Neumann, whose Cause is under way in spite of her many Catholic critics.

In March 1918, twenty-year-old Bavarian Therese Neumann was a strong young woman who planned to become a missionary nun. For the moment, with her village's men away fighting WWI, she was taking the place of a male laborer on a local farm. Hoisting heavy buckets of water above her head while clinging to a ladder that March 10 in order to put out a barn fire, she seriously injured her spine. With repeated serious falls—down cellar stairs, for instance—as she tried to keep going until the men returned, she eventually lost movement and sight—the blindness from repeated head injuries and consequent hemorrhages, both affecting the optic nerves. The last straw was a hemorrhage at the base of the skull when she slipped out of a wheelchair.

As often happens with those who are paralyzed, in spite of her parents and younger sibling's efforts to give her devoted care, Therese Neumann suffered from terrible ulcerated bedsores. She, too, is one of those whose sufferings carried her deeper into prayer and compassion for others. After several years in this state, God cured her completely—but not all at once. Instead her healing took place over a couple years, each incident related to Therese of Lisieux.

While this book is only about after-death appearances, Therese Neumann's cure from all the accident-caused disabilities is one healing, in stages, it seems to me, so I am going to give a few details of even those portions of the cure where St. Therese made no discernible appearance.

The resurrection of the extremely devout invalid began on April 25, 1923, when a relic of Sister Therese of Lisieux was touched—with a prayer—to a stomach abscess on Therese Neumann, which immediately broke up and healed.

Four days later Therese was beatified in Rome. That day blind Therese Neumann received her sight back after four years in the dark. In May that year, when Therese Neumann's left foot was to be amputated due to "unceasing festering" of terrible sores that laid the foot open from ankle to toes, a relic of Blessed Therese, wrapped in the bandage with prayer for the saint's help, healed everything overnight.

Two years later, on May 17, 1925, Blessed Therese of Lisieux was to be canonized. As Therese Neumann was saying her rosary, she witnesses:

> Suddenly there was a light before me. At first I was frightened at it. The light was before my eyes over the bed. It was good for my eyes. In the first excitement, I let out a cry that my parents heard downstairs.

Therese Neumann—whose family called her Resl—did not see anyone, just the light. But an unknown woman's voice talked with her familiarly in German, as follows:

Voice:	Resl, do you wish to be cured?
Resl:	It's all the same to me. To be cured, to be sick, to die—whatever the Good Lord wants.
Voice:	Resl, would it not please you if you had a lessening of your suffering, if you could at least sit up and walk?
Resl:	Whatever the good God sends pleases me.
Voice:	You'll still have plenty to suffer; but don't be afraid. I've helped you up to now and I'll help you in the future.... It is precisely through suffering that many souls will be saved.... I wrote before that through suffering more souls will be saved than through the most brilliant sermons.[1]

"You can have a little joy," the voice urged the paralyzed woman. "You can sit up; go on, try it: I'll help you." To the mother and father of Therese Neumann, who had run upstairs at their daughter's cry, she now seemed to reach her arm up to air. Therese Neumann herself experienced being pulled up in her bed.

The voice gave Therese Neumann more guidance as to how she was to serve God—and then added, "You can walk, too." At the most painful spot of her spine, Therese Neumann felt pain and a click, as if something snapped into place. The seconds-before paralyzed woman got up and walked around the room with the help of her father. In those same moments all the remaining terrible bedsores—some open to the bone—disappeared as well.

How does anyone know the unseen "visitor" was St. Therese? Setting aside that it was her canonization day—a day when God often works miracles out of joy, it appears, at the honor to one of his friends—the voice referred, not only to having helped Therese Neumann before, but to the visitor's writing a specific phrase.

Carefully Therese Neumann—who jumped to no conclusion that it was Therese—repeated that phrase to her pastor. Therese Neumann had no writings of the new saint. Nor did the pastor. But he borrowed some and, sure enough, found the precise words written (in a letter, one source says) years earlier by Therese.

That September 30, the cure was completed. The same voice—again no one seen—told Resl that she would now be able to walk without any help and that problems she still had with her eyes "would be lessened." The rest of this "visit" was devoted to spiritual guidance.

As October began, Therese Neumann was once again a well young woman. However, she received another cure from God carried by Therese that year. Early in November, a doctor who specialized in appendicitis was summoned to the Neumann home, where Resl had suffered horrible pain for three days. He said surgery must be done immediately and raced off to prepare the operating facilities in Waldsassen, five miles away from the Neumann's village of Konnersreuth. As this Dr. Seidl sped away, Therese Neumann, with her pastor's concurrence, asked St. Therese of the Child Jesus to "help me." She heard once again the same voice, saying, "So that the world may know there is a higher intervention [than surgical], you will not have to be operated on now," and was cured again. Again, the voice also offered spiritual guidance.

The acutely infected appendix harmlessly emptied itself, Dr. Seidl noted with awe. He explained later to Therese and her pastor that this does occur spontaneously in rare instances. But in such cases, the patient takes longer to recuperate than if surgery were done. Therese Neumann had no convalescent period.

Even before she was canonized, Therese of Lisieux helped many who aspired to holiness who would never be candidates for beatification, as is Therese Neumann. And perhaps because the young Carmelite herself had died after so much suffering from her lungs, God used her often as the agent of divine healing to illnesses centered in the lungs.

In Holland in 1922, a young German nun, a schoolteacher, wrote up her experience from four years earlier for one Father Caenen, a Jesuit, who sent it to the Lisieux Carmel archivist with a letter and addendum of his own. As it is very long, I sum up some of the less important statements (indicating this by brackets) as I translate:

It was in April 1915 (I was twenty-three) that I came down with tuberculosis in my lungs. I began to bring up blood, then to cough, and I got weaker and weaker. The doctor judged my situation a grave one: already both lungs were affected and from that winter, I was bedridden.

In spite of all the cares my superiors surrounded me with, this bad state just kept getting worse until August 1917 when, having tried without any success all possible treatments, the physicians had to declare they could do nothing for me.

My hemorrhages were frequent and my feebleness extreme: I was given the Last Sacraments. I had made the sacrifice of my life yet I could not think I was going to die: at the bottom of my heart I conserved an unbreakable confidence in Sister Therese of the Child Jesus. From the day, when studying with the Ursulines in Holland, I had read the *Story of a Soul,* Therese was my celestial friend who helped me in every circumstance. From the beginning of this illness, I had charged her with asking God to cure me if it was His wish; I carried her relic and I kept her picture near my bed, pleasing myself by repeating a prayer I had taught sometimes to my little students. Here it is....

Little Therese, soul so pure

Remember me at the side of the Child Jesus

And help me become like you.

However my fever kept going up. In the first months of 1918 it was 40 Celsius in the morning. [She tells how her superior also was seeking Therese's prayers, having all the Sisters and students make novenas and promising God that if the young Sister were cured, the mother superior would see to it that everyone under her knew and loved Therese.] Yet during two novenas the danger to my life just increased.

Holy Thursday I could no longer take nourishment. My neck was edemous, my tongue had turned black, and so swollen that it adhered to my palate. By Monday April 8, my life seemed to have run its course. My chaplain told me the end was near, which was also the doctors' opinion. I could no longer recognize and hardly hear the Sisters who prayed by my bed. [She gives details of their prayers].... Having brought up more blood, I rested so spent that I couldn't even open my mouth.

I heard Sister Superior affirm that I would die either in the evening or during the night. [After that the dying nun lost her ability to follow the conversation between the infirmarian and superior over the next six hours or so while they prayed and vigiled at her bedside but she gathered that the superior was very disappointed that Therese hadn't helped them. She did understand when the mother superior said to her directly,] "Therese could have saved you, but she undoubtedly didn't want to because she's French and you're German and there's a war on between us."

As she said these words, my eyes wandered to the image of Therese which I could see clearly and I heard at that moment this word: "Don't fear anything; you'll be cured."

Sister Superior had barely left when I felt suddenly so happy, oh so happy with a happiness unknown. Then the same mysterious voice of which I can't find words for its sweetness said, "You're cured." And all my illness disappeared: I could see, hear, speak, get up—I was truly well. Impossible to express the sentiment I experienced in that unforgettable hour.

The Sister watching over me was stupefied. She couldn't believe her eyes.

Later I learned my superior had left me to hurry to the chapel. There on her knees before the tabernacle, she begged God to prove that the prayers of St. Therese were powerful before Him. His response was immediate. In curing me, the Lord glorified Therese. I never suffered any more: my neck, tongue and lips all were normal again and I was very hungry. At 10 P.M. that night I was eating a rich tart.

There is another page of aftereffects, which I sum up: The next day the "dying" teacher was up. The doctor, of course, was flabbergasted, but in spite of being a non-Catholic materialist, was willing to declare that her lungs were completely healthy. She went back to teaching and four years later, as she writes in her testimony, enjoys good health. Her readers will understand, she is certain, that she likes to tell children about her very powerful heavenly friend!

The Jesuit's addendum is interesting, too. He points out that the funeral Mass was all arranged and the nuns' chaplain had deferred a trip to attend; there was no doubt of imminent death because the doctor, the day before the inexplicable cure, found one lung destroyed—"eaten away"—and the other so far gone that it had no more than a day or two left.

The Lisieux Carmel received a testimony in June 1913, from a group of Notre-Dame nuns in Torokbalint, Hungary:

Around the month of April 1912 one of our postulants became gravely ill with pneumonia. Her fever was 41.3 and she was gasping for breath. Her cough was tearing and she expectorated dark-red, rusty-colored matter. All of this augured as badly as could be. The evening of the 3rd day of this the doctor left us very concerned, fearing some complication [was developing]. The night began badly.

Then our Reverend Mother gave the sick one a relic of the dear saint of Lisieux, as well as her picture, telling her to have confidence and Therese would obtain her cure. At once the postulant began to pray [for Therese's help]. A Sister stayed by her side.

Toward one o'clock in the morning, the sick girl sat up a bit in her bed and exclaimed in low tones, "How beautiful you are. I beg you to cure me!"

The Sister on duty was very moved and said. "You see the little Therese?"

"But of course. There—above my bed. Don't you see her? Her clothes are so marvelously white and there are beautiful angels all around her."

The Sister, although she did not have the happiness of contemplating this apparition, still felt herself penetrated by the supernatural to the point that she shed sweet tears.

An instant after she had seen Therese, the postulant fell asleep.

When she woke up, she told everyone joyfully that "the little saint" had come to cure her. And in effect the fever while it had never been lower than 40 degrees in the preceding days was 37. All the danger was past and a few days later, the privileged one was back at work.

Seeing Therese, of course, could have been some sort of fever-driven hallucination. But the nuns, who were on the spot, thought not, because of the sudden cure. The report is signed by the superior, the two Sisters in charge of the infirmary, and a fourth Sister who acts as assistant to the nuns' physician.

Not every appearance meant a cure. Here is the last portion of the report of a mother superior, who requested anonymity:

We made several novenas to our Seraph [Sister Therese] but Sister Teresa of Saint Augustine only laughed saying, "She will not cure me; she is coming to fetch me."

..."Little Therese," I cried sadly, "you work miracles everywhere, and yet in spite of all my supplications, you do not cure our daughter."

All that evening I was heartbroken.... Sleep came to me and with it this beautiful dream: The bells sounded loudly and the community intoned the *Latatus sum*. Soon the harmonium in the Church sent forth the most beautiful music and a multitude of voices were heard singing; one voice louder and more distinct than the others brought these words to me, which I believe awakened me. "She has always desired heaven. The gates are opened and I will lead her there without delay."

On awakening my soul was filled with mixed feelings of joy and sadness. I was unable to account for the supernatural atmosphere with which I was surrounded.

When I related this dream to Sister Teresa of St. Augustine she cried joyfully, "It is I, Mother; little Therese is coming to fetch me."

On the eve of her death, being with the invalid and wishing to give her a drink, I suddenly found the room filled with an exquisite perfume that gave me a sweet consolation.

Assuring myself that there was nothing in the Infirmary that could give such an odor, I said to myself: "It is Sister Therese who is near the bed of our sick daughter." On August 30th, our dear Sister asked all those near her to look at the beautiful roses strewn upon her sheet. She alone saw the beautiful heavenly flowers that Sister Therese had doubtless caused to rain on her.

Holy Viaticum was then brought to her. Immediately after receiving it, she opened her eyes, which were of a heavenly brightness. She seemed for some time to be beholding something of ineffable beauty and, in this ecstasy of love, she expired.

All these holy women thinking they see Therese and being cured—or carried off to heaven in ecstasy—may seem just too nebulous and otherworldly to some. Let me end the chapter then with a cure testimony that arrived at the Lisieux Carmel in August 1913, from the Sisters of St. Joseph in Chambery at the Savoy region of France, because this time Therese left physical evidence of her visit behind her. Once again, translating from the original French:

One of their postulants named Delphine Miege on August 15th met one of the Sisters in a narrow corridor. Trying to draw back so the other could pass, Delphine hit her elbow against the door of a wall cupboard with unusual force.

For the next quarter of an hour, the poor young thing endured indescribable pain. But not wanting to say anything, she carried on. It did not pass away, however. The next day toward the end of the morning, she had to reveal her condition. The night was very painful and the following morning she could not dress herself nor even make the sign of the cross.

All the usual measures for such an injury were taken but in vain. Everything tried only aggravated her sufferings and increased the swelling.

Sunday, the 17th of August, the Superiors asked the infirmarian to take Delphine to a surgeon, who also proved unable to help her.

That same evening, moved by the pain the poor thing was enduring and her concern that due to this health problem she would be sent away (not being yet a formal part of the community, since as a postulant she had yet to take any vows), the Sisters commenced a novena to Sister Therese to ask Delphine's cure. At the same time a relic of Therese was placed over the painful area.

That night and the next day the suffering only augmented. However the evening of August 18th, around 9 o'clock the postulant fell asleep, weeping. As she slept during that night—she could not tell at what hour—she saw a religious who touched her injured arm, which was completely bandaged even to the hand.

Deeply asleep, because for several nights she hadn't slept, she believed it was the infirmarian and just let her do what she would without coming out of her drowsy state.

The next morning, when she woke up, she realized she felt no more pain. Astonished, she moved her arm. It was perfectly supple. Then she looked at it. The bandage had been removed and the arm no longer was the least bit swollen—all trace of any injury was gone.

She noticed next that the bandage had been carefully rolled up and placed on the chair by her bed. This didn't surprise her in itself because she still thought the Sister infirmarian had visited her in the night. What seemed strange to her was just the so sudden [and] so radical cure.

[She went to] the Mistress of Novices who was also astonished and who sent her to find the infirmarian.

The infirmarian was stupefied. And she said she had *not* returned to the injured girl since the previous evening. Then they asked all the Sisters: none had touched Delphine's arm nor the bandage.

After all these undertakings, the Sisters were obliged to conclude that Sister Therese of Jesus had "descended," as they put it, "on our humble convent to save a vocation and give us a sign of her heavenly protection."

The testimony was signed by the cured girl, the mistress of novices, and the superior.

Endnote

1. This diologue will be found in many English-language biographies. One which also gives the precise German words Therese Neumann heard is Adelbert Albert Vogl's *Therese Neumann: Mystic and Stigmatic*, Tan, 1987.

Chapter Twenty-one

OF BLACK ELK—HOLY CATHOLIC CATECHIST

Under the term "shamanism" are hundreds of belief systems, ranging from sophisticated to extremely simple, from benign to horrific. But all shamanistic peoples are open to the other world and its inhabitants as they conceive them—often as positive spirits, which may take human, animal, or other forms, or "demons," which also take varied forms.

Some shamanistic peoples have been dominated by dark spirits—often seen as dead ancestors—who are feared and placated; but that is not our topic. Other shamanistic groups *their elders believe* experienced after-death appearances that prepared them for Christianity. For instance, the Oglala band of the High Plains Lakota (part of the larger group dubbed Sioux by white explorers) were visited "many generations ago" by young, beneficent, and beautiful Buffalo Cow Woman, "bearing what appeared to be a child." Her gift to them—aiding their communication with a caring fatherly Almighty—was a ritual pipe. Years later when they were introduced to Christianity, Lakota wise woman Lucy Looks Twice (daughter of the widely known Sioux visionary Black Elk) says their Jesuit priest accepted that it was the Blessed Virgin who had come as Buffalo Cow Woman, adding *"and that was what we* [Lakota] *always thought."*

Her father, Black Elk, Lucy says (her testimony is found in Michael F. Steltenkamp's *Black Elk: Holy Man of the Oglala*),[1] saw "all [Sioux] Indian ceremonies"—including the purifying Sun Dance where men fast for three days from food and water, some even shedding blood—as "connected to Christianity." He claimed, his daughter remembers, that from the foundation laid by the Virgin's appearance as Buffalo Cow Woman, the Lakota "knew, somehow, that in the future our Lord Jesus Christ would come one day to his people" and in the Sun Dance "they somehow already practiced the faith they would later know fully."

Farfetched as this story sounds, there is a similar, more mysterious, story told among the Toltec, a very different religious group found in the Vera Cruz area of Mexico. Scholar Janet Barber, IHM, tells me that Toltec priest, culture hero, teacher, and political leader from around 900 A.D., Quetzalcoatl (literally either "precious" or "feathered" serpent), "many seriously believe was St. Thomas the Apostle," which would, of course, have to mean this saint made a prolonged after-death appearance. Barber agrees that could be, or it could also have been the still-living St. Thomas, if he taught an earlier people, the Olmec, and those teachings percolated down into Toltec culture.

In either case, Quetzalcoatl definitely, "planted the seeds of the gospel," as Catholic documents put such things, including forbidding human sacrifice as practiced by the Toltec's neighbors, the Aztecs.

Seemingly defeated by evil, Quetzalcoatl had to leave the area, but prophesied he would return in a certain year, which in western reckoning is 1519, the precise year when missionaries appeared accompanying Cortez. They were puzzled, Barber says, by the many seemingly Christian aspects of the areas' religions, such as baptism and confession.

Of course, these possible appearances of Jesus' mother and his apostle Thomas are shadowy events from the mysterious realms of legend and myth whose truths cannot be validated—or maybe grasped—by twentieth century research methods.

Someone about whom we know more is visionary Black Elk. He lived until 1950—the era of fast cars, milk shakes, and post-World War II consumerism. Born in the era of tepees, horse and foot transportation, buffalo hunts—and sometimes famines—under leaders like Red Cloud, Crazy Horse, and Sitting Bull, Black Elk as a young teenager scalped one of Custer's dead soldiers at the Little Big Horn battle in 1876. He was there, on the fringe of the slaughter, at the massacre of his people at Wounded Knee in December 1890. Between these events, during the years 1886-1889 he traveled in Europe in Buffalo Bill's Wild West Show.

An innately spiritual individual, he had visions from the time he was about five. These were often of spirits, perhaps angels,[2] in the form of animals but he also saw venerable people, such as spiritual "grandfathers," who may have been dead elders of his people. Such experiences opened Black Elk to God's gift of curing the sick and cheering the downhearted as a Lakota medicine man. They were also the foundation, he said, for his later work as a Christian leader.

With intellectual dishonesty all too common where Catholicism is concerned, poet John G. Neihardt (probably because he favored Hindu Vedanta and Spiritualism over Christianity; see appendix for more details), in the book *Black Elk Speaks* wrote of Nick Black Elk's early life and Lakota spirituality without so much as a footnote to acknowledge that this saintly man chose to live the last fifty to sixty years of his life—carrying out duties like those of today's deacons—as a Christian leader of his people.

One of his fellow Indians even today recalls Black Elk as a very special man of prayer who always had a rosary within reach. The Oglala Sioux's children, trained by their father, were faith-filled, too. Once, for instance, son Nick, Jr., had a hemorrhage, bleeding from the nose. His sister, Lucy, recalled years later "he was dying." The family knelt and prayed the rosary and appealed to the compassionate heart of Jesus.

Suddenly the dying boy asked they seek the prayers of St. Therese. This was done. The boy not only recovered, but confided to Lucy he had seen Therese, insisting, "I know it was her."

When Black Elk himself (his age cannot be precisely determined, but he was somewhere in his mid-eighties, his daughter thought) sensed his life was over, he told Lucy not to mourn because "you know I will be happy." While asking that Lucy and her husband, Leo, never let a single day pass after his death without praying for him (which shows the holy man's humility, that he thought he might still need further purification), he also reassured Lucy:

Do not worry. There is a man who comes to see me every day at three o'clock. He is from overseas, and he comes in to pray with me. So I pray with him. He is a sacred man.

Lucy explained to Michigan anthropology professor Jesuit Michael F. Steltenkamp (from whose book cited earlier I take all quotes on Black Elk in this chapter) that "when he was living my father always used the phrase *wicasa wakan* when speaking about a Blackrobe [Jesuit] priest. And that's the phrase he used in talking about that visitor—*wicasa wakan.* So he might have been a Blackrobe who visited him."

Nick Black Elk was staying at the time with his son Ben. Was this a local, foreign-born priest who somehow found time to visit Nick every afternoon on the reservation, where homes are scattered and drives between them often long, or was it some dead Jesuit saint? While I wonder if some after-death appearances are hallucinatory, if it was St. Ignatius himself who turned up to pray with Black Elk daily, it wouldn't surprise me. I think Black Elk that holy.

And so do the Sioux.

When Black Elk died on August 17, 1950, people leaving his wake saw a striking phenomena in the sky. Far surpassing any Northern lights, to both Indians and non-Indian missionaries it was a "heavenly display, a celestial presentation ... a celebration" of the dead man's holiness.

And even that was not the end of Nick Black Elk. His daughter told Steltenkamp that after her father's death, people did not forget him. Individuals would get up and speak of Black Elk either at church or in other gatherings as a man of God whose prayerfulness and example should be imitated. Lucy also reported "people would feel *that he was present in our chapel or meeting house*" [italics mine]. She, herself, and her family, she confided, often experienced her father's help. As an example, she spoke of something that had happened very recently. Her brother Ben had died and a memorial gathering was planned for him, when suddenly Lucy's son was taken to the hospital, close to death. She wondered what to do: Cancel or postpone her brother's memorial or go on with it? "All of a sudden, something came to me," she said "like a flash—like somebody speaking to me clearly." She was told to go on with the gathering since it was for a good purpose, people gathering to pray and express their regard for their Catholic faith and Lord. And suddenly Lucy recalled vividly the time her father "had two coffins in church and still preached, even though those two coffins held his own children." She says, "I know it was my father speaking to me ..."

Endnotes

1. University of Oklahoma Press, 1993.
2. For those who question if angels ever take the form of animals, I refer you to the well-authenticated rescue several times from would-be assassins of St. John Bosco by Grigio, a "dog" whose ability to walk through walls, refusal to eat, and appearance when needed "out of nowhere" in places far from each other made many witnesses certain that the wolf-like beast was actually an angel.

Chapter Twenty-two

SOME TOP-RANKING (HASIDIC) GENERALS IN GOD ALMIGHTY'S ARMY

The Bratzlav sect of Hasidic Jews believse in "concrete personal guidance through the teachings of a rebbe." In their case, a dead leader, believing (to quote Rabbi Rosenfeld speaking in Herbert Weiner's *9 1/2 Mystics)* "better a dead rebbe who is alive, than a live rebbe who is dead."

An idea in perfect agreement with Christian saints like Auschwitz martyr of charity Maximilian Kolbe, who taught, "while we are alive we can only work [for God] with one hand, lest we fall ourselves; after our death, we can work with two." Or as Weiner puts it, once safely with God the holy person "no longer has the limitations of the human condition" and is completely at God's disposal to help others.

Jewish groups who accept this—some Reform Jews even question whether there is life after death—point to evidence like the very rational Joseph Karo from the seventeenth-century, "author of a legal work which still guides the Orthodox world of our day." Karo was "regularly visited by a preacher from the higher world."

Jews of this kind—mostly Orthodox—also believe, as do some Moslems and Christians, that through their "merits" the holy dead—both those whose holiness is recognized and those whose sanctity is known to God alone—can intercede with God to win favors such as "protection" for the living. Furthermore Hasidic Jews believe God may send the holy dead to rescue the living at times—whether the holy person knew those helped personally or not.

In 1814 in Poland, the book *In Praise of the Baal Shem Tov* was published in Hebrew. The Baal Shem Tov—literally "the spiritual Master of the Good Name"—is the eighteenth-century holy man considered the founder of modern Hasidic Judaism. (A reaction to the academic formalism of rabbinical

Judaism of the day, the Baal Shem Tov's movement emphasized the mercy of God and encouraged a joyous response through music and dance.) This very important book for Hasidic Jews and those of us interested in saints and mysticism was put together by the son-in-law of the man who had been scribe to the Baal Shem Tov and consists of anecdotes collected from the scribe and others close to the Hasidic holy man, who'd been dead only some fifty years.

Today available in English, the book is rich with anecdotes that most people dismiss as pious legends, but which those familiar with authenticated lives of even some recent saints find worth careful consideration. Among the stories of the Besht (as the Baal Shem Tov is sometimes called) and his holy circle is one of his brother-in-law, Rabbi Gershon.

In brief: Rabbi Gershon was caught in the water when the ship he was traveling on resumed sail. A fine swimmer who once rescued a drowning man, he swam after the vessel and caught up to it, but those aboard did not hear his cries while the ship's high side, coated in pitch, was too slippery for him to climb. Finally he began to drown and, no longer able to speak, anguished that he was unable to properly make a last confession. As he agonized that he would be denied heaven for this failure—the Besht might have rebuked such a lack of faith in God's mercy!—he is quoted as saying:

> Immediately someone appeared on the ship and saw me. He put out a small boat. He pulled me out of the water, brought me to the ship, and threw me into it. I went down to the stern of the boat and lay there for about two hours. I was vomiting because of all the water that I had swallowed. I lay there until I rested a little, and then I put on my clothes.

However when he went to look for his rescuer whom he calls an Ishmaelite (probably meaning an Arab), he found no such person on the boat. Finally he concluded that "probably it was Elijah the Prophet."

No one can insist you believe the dead Jewish prophet rescued the Polish rabbi. If you point out that in those two hours while the rabbi was vomiting, his rescuer might have jumped in his little boat and rowed away, who can argue with you? But from the fact that Rabbi Gershon even thought of being rescued by Elijah, it is clear that Hasidic Judaism has a living belief in the after-death appearance of holy "rescuers."

As for the great Baal Shem Tov himself, let me say he simply had all the gifts you ever found in a great mystic, whatever your faith background: simplicity, purity, compassion, humility, humor, holy wisdom that reads minds and hearts, and spiritual vision that saw things happening afar. Naturally he worked miracles and healed the sick. He also bilocated into people's dreams, was luminous in prayer, a near-inedic at times, and used to see the dead "in droves" coming for his prayers. Centered around this figure are other early Hasidic holy men, such as Rabbi Abraham—called "the Angel" for his great piety—who died at age thirty-six in 1776.

Another rabbi asked Rabbi Abraham if he ever saw his dead father, also a holy rabbi named Rabbi Dov Ber of Mezhirich, but known even before his death in 1772 simply as "The Great Maggid"—that is, Great Preacher and Spiritual Storyteller:

"Yes."

"In dreams? Or are you awake?"

"He comes in my dreams. We talk and then when I wake up, he talks to me while I'm awake."

This dialogue provides the background to an interesting story. A wealthy man caused Rabbi Abraham a lot of grief. So this friend of God complained to his dead father. The Great Maggid said he would summon the man to his son's house of study (part of a synagogue).

The dead man sent a living messenger to the wealthy man. When he said, "The Great Maggid summons you," the wealthy man snorted, "What do you mean 'summons me'? He's dead!"

"Nevertheless he's calling you," his visitor (perhaps holy himself?) said calmly.

When the pair arrived at the house of study, there was the dead rabbi sitting at the head of the table, dressed just as he had been when alive.

The rich man got a scolding but—apparently a person with true gall—continued to protest and excuse himself. Finally the Great Maggid snorted, "Take him home!"

Home they went. Only then did it hit the wealthy man that he had been summoned by a holy dead man to whom he had given nothing but lip. He fainted.

Revived, he was taken to Rabbi Abraham, who smiled and said, "Probably my father summoned him."

"How do you know?"

"Oh, he told me he would."

World War I brought many people to God, but spawned a postwar culture in which influential writers and thinkers no longer found faith relevant. The next generation, shaped by those thinkers, touched off the much more barbarous World War II, which ripped the mask of "civilization" from the face of Europe. After the Holocaust of the Jews; the attempted genocide of that ancient people from India, the Gypsies; and plans to wipe out the Slavic races through sterilization and forced labor; when the war ended with the great fireballs over Nagasaki and Hiroshima, it seemed only "mature" to many to set "childish" ideas of a loving God aside.

Where was God when the people of Israel fed Hitler's chimneys, Jews asked in anguish and anger in books like Andre Schwarz-Bart's *The Last of the Just* and Elie Wiesel's *Night*? Evil seemed stronger than love or goodness to those who wrote and read such works. Many influential Christians, too, anguished over the Holocaust and Hiroshima. Strident voices announced, "God is dead."

Softer voices, sometimes half-embarrassed whispers, maintaining that God was there—weeping over victim and perpetrator alike—during all the horrors men of free will created and visited on others, were drowned out or shouted down. But they have persisted and occasionally been recognized.[1]

In 1982 a book by Holocaust survivor Yaffa Eliach won the Catholic *Christopher Award* given to books that "light a candle" in human darkness. Dr. Eliach, professor of history and literature in the Department of Judaic Studies at Brooklyn College and founding director of the Center for Holocaust Studies, experienced the horrors of the Holocaust firsthand. When the slaughter of Jews of her Polish town began in 1941, Yaffa, then a little girl, would have died with

236 relatives had she not been plucked to safety by a non-Jewish woman. In 1944, Yaffa's mother returned alive only to be murdered with her infant by another Polish neighbor, who screamed, "This is for Jesus Christ" as he fired.

Turning "despair into hope and death into life"—what she has called "the burden of survival"—the pages of Dr. Eliach's book *Hasidic Tales of the Holocaust* are permeated with a healing sense of God's presence although telling the Holocaust stories of Hasidic Jews. God's interventions in their lives during those terrible days included appearances by the dead. Here three examples from Dr. Eliach's highly recommended book, beginning with the rescue (slightly condensed) of two holy rabbis:

The rabbi of Belz, Rabbi Aaron Rokeach, and his brother Mordechai, the Rabbi of Bielgory, were smuggled out of the Bochnia ghetto in May 1943. In charge of the rescue operation was a brave Hungarian officer who was handsomely rewarded for his bold plan.

According to his plan, the high-ranking Hungarian officer would be traveling in the service of the Hungarian Army. His "mission" would be to bring back to Hungary from Poland for interrogation two prominent generals captured on the eastern front. The two captured generals would be none other than the Grand Rabbi of Belz and his brother.

The Hungarian officer made all the necessary arrangements at the various border checkpoints both in Poland and Hungary. All the forged documents were in perfect order, as were the various license plates he prepared for his car. The only possible problem was the fact that he had forgotten to bring along two sets of Russian uniforms. When he realized his error, it was too late to go back. However, the Hungarian officer had confidence in his plan....

With the two "generals" in his backseat, both clean-shaven and dressed in civilian clothing, the brave Hungarian officer successfully passed the first checkpoint. As he passed each additional checkpoint, his confidence grew and he merrily sang Hungarian songs.... He even left his two illustrious passengers alone in the parked car while he entered a bar to have a few drinks.

When he returned he could not find the car ... only to discover that the car was parked in precisely the same spot where he had left it. But it was shrouded in a heavy mist as if to conceal it.... He crossed himself, for now he was sure that all he had been told about his two passengers was indeed true.

... At the first major checkpoint in Hungary, the officer did not foresee any mishaps. As they stopped at the barrier, he presented all the necessary papers.... The guard ... checked their names against a list in his possession. "Sorry, I can't let you pass. I have no order by my superiors to expect the arrival of two captive generals...."

"Check with your superior," the Hungarian officer suggested in a commanding voice. The superior appeared moments later. He apologized for the inconvenience, but he confirmed the young soldier's statement. He had no instructions to allow the passage of two captured Russian generals. "Where are your uniforms?" he asked the gentlemen in the backseat. They remained silent.

"They are under strict orders to speak to no one except at headquarters. How long do you expect us to wait at this godforsaken place?" The Hungarian officer continued speaking in a confident tone while he tried to figure out what had gone wrong and work out an alternative plan.

Just then out of the mist appeared three Hungarian generals mounted on beautiful horses. They ordered the border guards, both the junior officer and his superior, to let the captive generals through. As the car crossed the border, the three mounted Hungarian generals saluted the two "generals" in the car. Once more the car was on its way to freedom....

The Hungarian officer was bewildered. "I know all the high officers in the Hungarian Army, but I must frankly admit to you I did not recognize the three high-ranking military men who came to our rescue at the border."

"We did," responded the Rabbi of Bielgory. "They were our father, Rabbi Issacher Dov Baer (1859–1927), our grandfather, Rabbi Joshua (1825–94) and our great-grandfather, Rabbi Shalom the Seraph (1799–1855), all top-ranking generals in God Almighty's Army!"

Another case chronicled by Dr. Eliach where dead holy family members saved the living took place in a concentration camp near Vienna. Ignac Grunsweig was a teenaged, Czechoslovakian Jew who had already lived through a number of these hells-on-earth when he arrived at Mauthausen in the winter of 1945, a survivor of one of those end-of-war death-marches where camp prisoners were driven like cattle ahead of the advancing Allied forces. When a "selection" was made upon arrival, picking out living skeletons for transport later that day to the gas chamber, Ignac—a bundle of bones—was among the doomed, but saved his life by giving a false I.D. number from a previous camp.

When the death trucks had left with the condemned, back in his barrack that night Ignac dreamed of prewar days. In his dream:

He was a young yeshiva student, going to visit his grandfather, the Dolha Rabbi, Rabbi Asher Zelig Grunsweig [of Carpathian Russia]. It was Sabbath afternoon at dusk. The little house was filled with twilight shadows and the special tranquil Sabbath spirit permeated each corner....

It was time to eat the third Sabbath meal. While Grandmother set the table, he and Grandfather washed their hands from the special big copper cup with two huge handles. Grandfather made the blessing over the two loaves of hallah. It was warm [in the house].... They were singing zemirot, traditional Sabbath songs. Grandfather was stressing the importance of the third meal, telling him that it is the most spiritual and mystical of the Sabbath meals. He who becomes imbued with its spirit will be spared the battles of Gog and Magog. "Remember what our sages say, 'Whoever observes the three Sabbath meals will be saved from the suffering to precede the coming of the Messiah, the rule of Purgatory.'"

Grandfather was caressing Ignac's head while he spoke to him in his good and gentle voice. "You will grow up, my child, and will survive the suffering that precedes the coming of the Messiah and the rule of ... Purgatory. But you must always attempt to observe the third Sabbath meal, for its merit will protect you."

This dream was so real that when Ignac woke, he could still feel his holy grandfather's hands on his head and even smell his grandmother's good bread. The day's nightmare began at once. But night after night the same dream refreshed his soul. Taking the dream to heart, he disciplined himself each day to hide one crumb of bread from his starvation-level rations. With these seven crumbs, week after week on the Sabbath he celebrated the third "meal."

The prophecy of his grandfather—who was known during his life for his scholarship and holiness—came true months later on May 6, when the camp was liberated by Allied forces. That this was a true after-death appearance is at least possible, for the holy rabbi had perished, with others of the family, at Auschwitz.

Another holy rabbi memorialized in *Hasidic Tales of the Holocaust*, the grand Rabbi of Bobov, Rabbi Ben-Zion Halberstam, had a special love for young people. Each Sabbath at the rabbi's house in the Ukraine many men and boys congregated to welcome the Lord's Day with singing and dancing.

Then the Nazis arrived.

On July 25, 1941, the rabbi and his family were among two thousand Jews arrested. Four days later, the rabbi, dressed in his tall fur hat, was striding toward the open pits in the forest where the Nazis and Ukrainian collaborators were waiting to kill the entire group.

Urged to escape, the holy man said calmly, "One does not run away from the sounds of the Messiah's footsteps."

A short time later he was with God.

He was not a "survivor," but something greater: One who faces the worst that evil can devise and triumphs in spirit, entering the next life with the palm of victory.

Fourteen-year-old Moshe, one of those young boys who, in another world of peace and joy, had gathered at the rabbi's to worship God with joyous prayer and music, did not know of the rabbi's death as he himself—sole survivor of his large family—struggled to stay alive during the next four years as a slave laborer, first at Auschwitz and then, in 1944, at Mauthausen. He felt certain though that the rabbi was guiding him and watching over him even amidst the intolerably harsh realities of the camp. The image of the rabbi as he had seen him on many Friday night visits to the rabbi's house was constantly before Moshe's eyes. In the bleakest moments in camp, in spite of physical exhaustion from his slave labor at the granite quarry or at the subterranean aircraft factory, in moments of despair and hunger, he felt the presence of the rabbi next to him. The rabbi's soothing voice comforted him and commanded him to live.

Wherever Moshe went, he felt the Bobover Rabbi guiding his steps, almost as if the rabbi were pulling him and pushing him, often in directions opposite those he would have chosen to follow.

In prewar days, Moshe's favorite melody of the rabbi's songs was the one to which the rabbi chanted the holy Zohar, the mystical *Book of Splendor.* Any time life in the camps ground the teenager down to where his humanity began to slip away, he would concentrate on the rabbi's Zohar melody. Unfailingly this would produce "warm, human tears" that rekindled his spiritual fire.

Then a bitterly cold winter decimated the ranks of the camp inmates through exposure, starvation, and disease. The growing fourteen-year-old was simply a bag of bones by December 1944, when the prisoners were stripped of their filthy, thin clothes and sent into showers as part of a delousing regimen.

Suddenly the naked men were ordered out on the parade ground, into what Eliach calls "a howling December wind." A difference had been discovered between the overseer's list and the number of actual bodies he had counted entering the showers. As the source of this discrepancy was determined, naked, starving men stood in this weather over an hour while frost formed on their bodies. People collapsed and died. But the diabolical "count" continued. Moshe felt himself freezing into a pillar of ice that was about to topple over.

Suddenly he felt the Rabbi of Bobov, Rabbi Ben-Zion Halberstam, supporting him. The rabbi's reassuring voice rang in his ears: "Don't fall, my young friend, don't stumble! You must survive! A Hasid must sing, a Hasid must dance; it is the secret of our survival!" The rabbi's melody was burning in his head ... but his frozen lips could not utter a single sound. Then slowly his lips began to move. A note forced its way through the colorless lips. It was followed by another and another, individual notes strung together into the ... melody. Like burning coals, the tune scorched his lips and set his body aflame. One foot began to move, to free itself from its chains of frost. The ice crackled; one foot began to dance. The other foot tore itself away from the clinging ice. The snow became red as skin from the sole of Moshe's foot remained grafted to the ice. Bones, muscles, and sinews began to step in the snow, to dance to the rabbi's [tune]....

Yaffa Eliach
Hasidic Tales of the Holocaust

When that period of horror was over, many lay dead on the ground. Young Moshe walked away.

Years later, a rabbi himself in Monsey, New York, when he told this story of the Bobov rabbi's care from beyond the death pit, Moshe's eyes glittered with tears.

Endnote

1. Christian examples include concentration camp survivor Protestant Corrie ten Boom's *The Hiding Place*, Michel Carrouge's *Le Pere Jacques: "Au Revoir Les Enfants,"* Buchenwald survivor Jacques Lusseyran's *And There was Light*, and my own *A Man for Others* on Auschwitz martyr of charity Maximilian Kolbe.

Chapter Twenty-three

THAT BOSCO BUNCH

Saints—like grapes—grow in bunches, the first group in Christianity formed of the motley crew surrounding Jesus Christ. Shaping up those fellows required the Savior to make any number of after-death appearances and finally drench them in his own Holy Spirit.

Christ's apostles went out and formed holy groups of their own. In the early Church many groups carried each other to heaven, such as the forty Roman soldiers martyred together for refusing to worship the emperor.

Families make up other holy clusters. St. Bernard of Clairvaux led thirty-one friends and relatives—including his uncle and four brothers—to the first Cistercian monastery in 1112.[1] Among Bernard's immediate family are nine official saints. More recently, the parents of St. Therese of Lisieux, and her sister Leonie are candidates for beatification.

Less known are the Ledochowska family from the same nineteenth and twentieth centuries era. Their uncle Miecislaus a cardinal, three children of Count Antony Ledochowska were special souls: Vladimer, who became superior general of the Jesuits; Saint Mary Theresa, who founded the Sisters of St. Peter Claver; and Blessed Julia, who founded an order of Ursulines.

Cities experience outbreaks of holiness. From the late 1500s through the first half of the 1600s, Lima, Peru, was known as the "city of saints." Included are St. Martin de Porres, St. Rose of Lima, St. Francis Solanus, Blessed John Massias, and the archbishop, St. Turibus.

Religious orders experience outbreaks, too: In twentieth century Los Angeles, three Claretian priests and a Brother spurred each other to holiness, while leading many others in that direction. Effects from the lives of Father Aloysius Ellacuria, Father Thomas Matin, Father Frank Ambrosi, and Brother Salvatore Azzarello—the last two dying in the 1990s—are still visible.

Groups have found holiness around particular ways of becoming holy: St. Ignatius Loyola and his first six Jesuits—four of the seven canonized—introduced Ignatius' "Spiritual Exercises" and Ignatian discernment to their church.

In many women's orders, the foundress is beatified or canonized; but these officially recognized saints are merely the most notable in a cluster. For instance, among the women who joined St. Madeleine Sophie Barat in founding the Society of the Sacred Heart, pioneer missionary to the United States Philippine Duchesne (1769-1852) is canonized, but a dozen others are equally holy. The same can be said of Mother Cabrini's spiritual daughters.

Some official saints, others never publicly recognized, members of these groups guide and encourage each other to holiness in life. And go right on, with God's permission, doing the same after some of them are dead. Let's look at after-death appearances in a representative spiritual family, the Salesians of St. John Bosco and their women's branch, the Daughters of Mary Help of Christians.

In this family, everything radiates from John Bosco—the holy priest who strolled, dead, into the infirmary (see prologue), encouraging one nun and healing another. "He was a spiritual magnet," explains Blessed Louis Guanella, who as a young priest lived with Bosco for almost three years. "I didn't suffer as much when my parents died as I did on leaving Don Bosco," Guanella claimed, citing how much he benefited from Bosco's "example of so much virtue," as well as from the saint's direct spiritual guidance.

Guanella is echoed by thousands—yes, thousands. Don Bosco's is a veritable spiritual army comprising in its ranks all those educated by him, or by his spiritual sons and daughters. Among this group, roughly a hundred are "Servants of God"; that is, they lived such holy lives that they are under study for possible beatification; at least six are Venerables; several have been beatified, including past pupils Michael Rua and Philip Rinaldi, spiritual sons Louis Orione and Guanella, and some pupils of Bosco's spiritual sons and daughters. Bosco's spiritual daughter and cofoundress, Mother Mazzarello, is canonized; as is his spiritual son, Dominic Savio; confessor, St. John Cafasso; several helpers in the saint's work for young people, such as St. Leonard Murialdo (sometime director of one of Bosco's playground-catechetical centers); and, on the outermost fringe of this bunch are various priests who joined Bosco in mutually supporting each other's apostolates, such as St. John Cottolengo, whom Bosco helped financially. Now a sampling of this family's after-death appearances.

Back in John Bosco's seminary days, he formed a deep spiritual friendship with a more introverted classmate, mild, otherworldly Louis Comollo. Brawnier and earthier, greathearted John was still struggling with aggressive tendencies. In short, he was not yet the great saint he would become.

John and Louis spent free hours in long, intimate conversations, while walking in the Piedmont countryside. In one of those talks John was startled when Louis confided he thought he would not live much longer.

"But are you ill?" John's handsome face was all concern.

"No, not yet." Louis explained that he felt his love for God "carrying me away" and found himself unable to resist.

John did not consider Louis a nut. Maybe from his reading on the saints he knew that some have literally died of love. At any rate, he took Louis' confidence seriously. So seriously that they did something that Bosco learned the hard way was most unwise. In their youthful enthusiasm, they agreed Louis should try to get God to send him back to tell John if he went straight to heaven.

Not long after this Louis Comollo caught some trifling illness and died. Picking up Bosco's own account:

It was the night ... after his burial. I was sleeping with twenty other theology students in the south dormitory.... I was in bed but not asleep, and I was thinking about our promise. Almost as though I had a premonition of what was about to take place, I was strangely afraid.

At the stroke of midnight, I heard a dull sound at the end of the corridor. As it drew nearer, it became sharper, more lugubrious and louder. It sounded [successively] like the rumble of a heavy cart drawn by many horses, a railroad train, or like the boom of a cannon. I cannot adequately describe it except as a composite crashing sound so vibrant[2] and, somehow, so violent that it terrified and rendered me speechless.

As it drew closer to our dormitory door, the very walls, ceiling and floor of the corridor reechoed as with the roar of crashing steel slabs being shaken with great force. And yet the rumble gave no clue as to where it came from. It was like trying to pinpoint the position of a locomotive by the trail of smoke it leaves in the air.

All in the dormitory were startled but nobody dared say a word. I was petrified. The din was getting closer and ever more frightening, but still it sounded outside the dormitory. Then the door was flung open, the roar grew in intensity, and a slim, flickering, multicolored light, which seemed to modulate with the sound, pierced the darkness. Abruptly all noise ceased, the light flared more brilliantly and Comollo's voice was clearly heard. It was frailer than it had been when he was alive. Three times in succession he called out: "Bosco! Bosco! Bosco! I'm saved!"

At that very moment a light flooded the entire dormitory and the sounds, which had ceased, were again heard ever louder. It was almost as though a thunderbolt had struck the house and it was collapsing. Immediately again all noise ceased and the light vanished. My fellow seminarians leaped out of bed and fled wildly in all directions. A number huddled together in a corner of the room to boost their courage. Others grouped themselves around the dormitory prefect, Father Joseph Fiorito of Rivoli.

They spent the night this way, eagerly awaiting dawn. All had heard the noise; several heard the voice, but not the words themselves. They kept asking one other what the noise and the voice could have meant. Sitting on my bed, I told them to calm down, assuring them that I had clearly heard the words, "I am saved." A number had heard the voice directly above my head and this became the accepted version at the seminary for a long time afterward.

I was so shaken and frightened that, at the moment, I would rather have died. As far as I can remember, this was the first time that I really was afraid. This too was the beginning of an illness that brought me to the edge of the grave and left me in such weak health that I did not fully recover until many years later....

Bosco later wrote a biography of Louis Comollo which he had read and corrected regarding this unforgettable event by those there that night; so the account rests not just on his say-so. That is certainly important, since John seems to have suffered a mild nervous breakdown, which could suggest that the experience was a momentary psychotic episode, rather than objective reality. With these other witnesses, that "explanation" must be set aside.

Why did Comollo's return shake Bosco so? The saint's own comment was "whenever we attempt to breach the supernatural, especially when it is unnecessary for our eternal salvation, we are bound to suffer ... [unpleasant] consequences." In that view, we can theorize that one reason God let Louis return was to scare the pants off his friend, so he'd realize such visits are to be initiated by God, not by "pacts" between buddies.

Years later, as a full-fledged saint, Bosco frequently spoke to the dead who came to his slum room to guide and encourage his backbreaking labors as "the friend of poor kids." For instance, as a young priest living in rented rooms next to a brothel and tavern (with his widowed mother to protect his reputation), John received another visit from Louis Comollo.

We know this because his mother just had to tell someone about a strange experience, and bent the ear of a kid named James Bellia. Mama Margaret, as the boys called her with affection, confided to James that she woke once before dawn, and heard her son talking to someone in his room. At times he seemed to reply to questions. At other times he asked them. She strained to listen but could catch no words. The front door, she knew, was secured. Nor would John bring visitors traipsing through their small quarters in the middle of the night. Eventually the conversation ceased.

When her son opened his door sometime later, his mother peeked in and observed that the closet-less room had no one else in it. Margaret shared her son's slum kids awe about that almost bare bedroom-study with its plain iron bedstead, sensing that extraordinary things went on in there. Both Margaret and the boys knew if they asked for particulars, Bosco would detour the conversation with a joke or pleasantry. But this morning Margaret could not contain herself. Looking her son squarely in the face, she said, "Who did I hear you talking to last night?"

Saints keep a low profile in a world only too quick to credit them for God's works. Still it was Margaret—widowed when this youngest son was only two—who set John firmly on the path to God and taught him most of his wise educational system.

To her he said simply, "That was Louis Comollo."

"But he's dead," she protested. "He's been dead for *years!*"

"Yes," her son admitted, "but I was talking to him."

End conversation. But her mother's eye observed that, however matter-of-factly her son spoke, his face was flushed, his eyes glittering. For the next few days, he was somewhat abstracted, almost "distraught," with emotion he kept to himself.

As the years went on, for their spiritual benefit, Don Bosco began to narrate to his youngsters and his first crop of homegrown adult spiritual sons what he called "dreams," but which he privately admitted to some of the older group were "much more." Even to the boys at times he made offhand, equivocal remarks such as "as you know, dreams come in one's sleep. So during the night hours ... while I was in my room—whether reading or pacing back and forth or resting in bed, I am not sure—I began dreaming." These experiences, which often contained symbolic imagery and language like certain Biblical parables, always had a guide. Sometimes this was Jesus or his mother. Those instances Bosco would humbly cover up by saying something like "a distinguished man" instead of "Jesus."

But many guides were dead people he had known well. Louis Colle, for instance, was the saintly young son of a family that was very generous to Don Bosco's works. After dying a holy death, this youth, Bosco's intimates testified, "used to appear to Don Bosco to reveal secret things to him."

It was Louis Colle and angels who guided Don Bosco through one of his great prophetic visions (narrated by the saint in 1885 to encourage some of his closest associates). That night, Louis and the angels showed Bosco the future of his little band of Salesians, revealing they would work—as they do—in places such as Australia, the center of Africa, and the Middle East. In another visit in 1883, Louis Colle took Don Bosco on a mystical visit to all the South American tribes his sons would serve, the "travelers" sitting peacefully under a tree with cannibals. Such visits assisted Don Bosco in planning for the future.

At other times Louis Colle's visits, it appears, were much more personal matters, such as to encourage his parents, who as "Cooperators"—lay people involved in the Salesians' ministries—were also part of Bosco's spiritual family. For instance, on the day Louis died in 1881, while Don Bosco was hearing confessions he had what he called "a distraction." Actually a momentary vision, he saw Louis "in a very beautiful garden" with other boys. With this image came the ineffable assurance that Louis was happily in heaven, a consolation he passed on to the young man's family.

On May 27, 1881, as Don Bosco was saying Mass for the Colles, Louis appeared to the priest at the Consecration and later again, "bathed in light, beautiful ... (radiating) joy and well-being." Following the service, the dead youth appeared a third time in the sacristy where Don Bosco was saying some prayers of thanksgiving. With him this time were several other "Bosco boys" who had since died. Don Bosco asked Louis' advice on how to console the Colle family.

Among Louis' answers was to encourage them to "make friends with the Blessed," that is, I take it, with the saints in heaven.

Because in other visits the dead boy says how much he loves his parents and how he prays for and is "waiting" for them, one day Bosco groused, "Why don't you let your parents see you? They love you so much."

"Yes, I know they love me," the dead boy answered, "but God's permission is needed for them to see me. If I spoke to them, my words would not have the same efficacy as when they are relayed through you." Does he mean they might become troubled about whether they were hallucinating? Possibly. People who know their grief makes them vulnerable might well trust a saint's experiences more than their own.

Bosco did not accept seeing Louis credulously. He pondered and undoubtedly sought guidance. Finally he wrote to the boy's mother:

When I reflect upon these appearances and *study them through and through* [italics mine], I feel that they are not at all tricks of the imagination, but real. All that I see in them is clearly in conformity with the Spirit of God. Undoubtedly, Louis is in heaven. As far as the frequency of these visions [*Note: they were occurring often*] I do not know what God has in mind. I only know that Louis advises me and teaches me things I did not know about Theology and science.

Some of Louis' teachings the saint jotted down (always from memory, naturally); some were recorded by spiritual sons, to whom Bosco narrated what took place. Too long to give in full, I extract a bit of dialogue from one example:

"Are you happy, Louis?"
"Very!"
"Are you dead or alive?"
"My body is dead, but I am alive!"
"Isn't it your body that I see?"
"No."
"Your soul, then?"
"No."
"Your spirit?"
"No."
"Then what am I looking at?"
"Just an apparition."
"How can an apparition speak?"
"Through God's power."
"Where is your soul, then?"
"It stands before God and in Him. Your eyes cannot see it."
"How do you see us?"
"We see all things in God—the past, the present, the future as though in a mirror."
"What do you do in heaven?"
"I give thanks always to God—to Him who created me; to Him who is master of life and death; to Him who is the beginning and end of all. Thanks! Praises! Alleluia!"

(Contrast Louis' role to that of St. Therese of Lisieux, who seems to have a different role than continual praise; the reader may find new meaning in the term "many mansions"—or Catholic, Jewish, and Hindu saints' references to "levels" of heaven.)

Quoting again from *Dreams, Visions, & Prophecies of Don Bosco:*

During Don Bosco's journey to France in 1883, Louis appeared to him many times. On March 4 ... he accompanied Don Bosco by train from Cannes to Toulon and discoursed in Latin on the wonderful works of God. He even turned his attention to the skies and gave him some facts of astronomy that the saint never knew before. He told Don Bosco: "If you were to go by express from earth to the sun, you would reach it after 350 years! And to cross the sun's face you would need just as long a time. Each nebula out there is fifty million times larger than our sun, and its light needs ten million years to reach us."

When Louis kept giving him these astronomical figures, Don Bosco cried: "Enough, Louis, enough! My poor mind cannot keep up with you."

"And yet," replied Louis, "this is only the beginning of God's greatness."

Margaret Bosco guided her fatherless son toward becoming a saint primarily by example. Among the thousands of youngsters Don Bosco befriended in his boarding facilities, trade schools, workshops, and playgrounds, a number of spiritual sons, in turn, modeled on the priest who cooked for them, tailored clothes for them, played with them, tutored them, and lovingly formed their souls. Thousands of "Bosco's boys" became devout priests—in the Salesians, in other orders, and at least 2,500 in the diocesan priesthood. Many more thousands grew into good family men.

Some of those Bosco mentored died as boys or teenagers. From this latter group, God also sent individuals to show the saint what he should do next, what the future held for him, and the precise state of soul of each youth under his charge (so he could help those amenable to change). In one vision, two boys—the saint later identified one as a past pupil named Valfre—were his guides. And in another six boys, now in heaven, returned in celestially white garments to enlighten Bosco on the spiritual condition of his charges of the moment.

Among Bosco's boys who returned after death is St. Dominic Savio (1842–1857). His goal "to become a saint," under Don Bosco's tutelage, when Savio died at fifteen, there was no difficulty establishing the teenager's virtues were heroic. In 1876, in a "visit" lasting much of the night, Dominic let his onetime mentor see that the next decade would be a tough one for Bosco, predicted developments in the Salesian order, and revealed the future of some individuals. The dead saint even showed Bosco lists of all the boys in his care—and some the youth apostle didn't know yet, but would meet later—divided into three groups on the basis of their spiritual condition.

When this moving experience with his dead spiritual son was over, Don Bosco grabbed his pen and wrote down as many as he could recall of the predictions made during that long night so he could see, as time passed, if these things really occurred. Everything proved accurate, even to the dates of eight boys' deaths, none of whom were anywhere near dying at that date.

Dominic's blood father, a country blacksmith brimming with goodness, also profoundly influenced his son. Even though he had many children, in his last years Charles Savio chose to live with Don Bosco, and thus is part of the extended Salesian family. It was to his dad that Dominic made his first after-death appearance:

About a month after Dominic's death, Charles Savio lay in bed one night unable to sleep. The memory of his son for some reason or other, was particularly vivid to him that night. As he stared at the gray ceiling, he gradually grew aware of something odd. The ceiling above him began to glow, dimly at first, and then brightly. Finally it became a circle of light and in the center of the light appeared Dominic, radiant and smiling.

"Dominic! Dominic!" cried Charles. "Where are you? Where are you? Are you in heaven?"

"Yes, Dad, I'm in heaven."

Immediately Charles Savio begged Dominic to pray for his brothers and sisters that they might go to heaven too. Dominic said he would. Charles asked his dead son to pray for his parents. Again Dominic said he would. Then the radiant teenager disappeared, the light faded, and the ceiling went back to its ordinary gray.

Years later when the elder Savio was living with Don Bosco, the saint many times questioned Dominic's father about this, as did others. Always the devout blacksmith maintained that he was not asleep when Dominic came to him; furthermore, he insisted he was so stirred that he was unable to fall asleep "for a long while afterward." He had never had any experience like that before—asleep or awake—and even though he would have loved to see Dominic again, it never happened.

In 1935, when Don Bosco and Charles Savio were long dead, a Salesian nun, Eusebia Palomino lay near death in Valverde del Camino, a village in the mountains of Spain's southern Andalusia region. Unknown to the world, she was venerated by those who had contact with her as a holy woman with extraordinary charisms. Now, after those at her bedside thought her dead, Sister Eusebia revived unexpectedly. She said she had seen Dominic Savio. At this time, Dominic had been dead almost eighty years, was from another country, and had been neither beatified nor canonized.

The following year, also in Spain, Consuela Adelantado, a little girl studying with Salesian sisters, double-fractured her left elbow, with dislocated bone splinters, as the translated report rather awkwardly puts it. Twenty-one days after the accident the elbow showed no signs of healing.

Then she had a dream.

A priest she did not know came to her and told her to make a novena for the prayers of Dominic Savio. If she had Dominic praying for her, the priest assured her, she would be playing the piano again by the following Friday.

Consuela's family, not overly religious, were skeptical. But when she told the dream to her Salesian teachers, they were interested. Curious as to who this priest that appeared in the child's dream might have been, the nuns showed her a picture of St. John Bosco.

Consuela shook her head, "No, not him."

Scurrying about, the nuns dug up photos of other Salesian priests. Consuela kept nodding "no." Finally someone showed the schoolgirl a picture of Don Bosco's onetime pupil, and Dominic Savio's Salesian boarding-school pal, John Cagliero.

"That's him!"

This caused a mild hubbub among the sisters, for dead Cagliero, a missionary leader and the first Salesian cardinal, had been very closely associated during his lifetime with the Salesians' women's branch. He had also worked hard to push along the beatification of his old school chum, Dominic, but died with that task unaccomplished.

Quite excited, sisters and student began the novena.

The dead Salesian cardinal had promised that Consuela would play the piano Friday. Thursday night—seven days into the novena—the Salesian infirmarian looking after the little girl began trying to "push" the miracle. If you've ever been to a healing service you may have seen this sort of thing—someone so determined that another be healed immediately that, unable to leave it to God, they get into the act themselves, ripping away crutches and ordering someone to walk, causing the individual to crumple to the floor. It's sad, but also comical because of the implication one can order God around this way.

In this case the infirmarian was still working on Consuela—who was equally fired up—at three o'clock Friday morning. A Salesian writing from original testimonies says, "the only result of their labors was a red and dangerously swollen arm, and great pain."

At 4:00 A.M., worn out and sobbing in her pain, Consuela pleaded with Dominic Savio to do what the cardinal said he would do. In answer a huge invisible weight seemed to fall from her arm. She raised it. No pain. She examined it under light: no more wound, no swelling—nothing but a perfectly normal arm.

In her joy the schoolgirl kept swinging and moving her elbow until 6:30, when she went to Mass. That same day she was indeed playing the piano.

Comparing before and after X-ray photos of her arm, medical men agreed the healing was "instantaneous, complete and perfect," a cure accepted by the Church for Dominic's beatification. So what Cardinal Cagliero could not accomplish for his fellow Salesian and boyhood friend as a prince of the Church, he managed to pull off as a humble messenger from heaven.

With Don Bosco my starting point, I have worked down three generations. But Bosco was helped along by those before him as well. A number of those individuals, too, God sent back to guide or encourage the youth worker. We know, for instance, that six years after her death, Bosco's saintly mother, Margaret, was part of a guiding vision he had one night. In August 1860, Margaret came to her son in a more personal way. In this dream or vision, he seemed to be—or was—walking near the shrine of Our Lady of Consolation in Turin, the North Italian city which was his headquarters. Suddenly he met his mother, who looked beautiful.

"But aren't you dead?" he gasped.

"I died but I'm alive."

The son asked if she were happy and was assured she was very happy. After asking her questions about various boys who had died and herself, Don Bosco begged, "Tell me what it is you enjoy in heaven."

The dead woman protested that she could not explain, a statement similar to that of many saints. (The revived Sister Eusebia Palomino, pressed to explain her experience of heaven, said in exasperation, "If St. Paul couldn't do it, how can I?")

"Well just give me an idea of it—a glimmer," Margaret Bosco's middle-aged son wheedled his mother.

In life, every time John found a few bucks, with which Mama Margaret could replace her threadbare dress, she took it willingly, *promised* she would get herself "something nice"—and promptly spent the money on some needy boy. Now she appeared in heavenly glory garbed in magnificent robes no money can buy.

... She began to sing a song of love to God that was indescribably sweet and went straight to the heart, filling it and carrying it away with love. It sounded as if a thousand voices and a thousand tones—from the deepest bass to the highest soprano—had all been blended together masterfully, delicately, and harmoniously to form one single voice, notwithstanding the variety of tones and the pitch of the voices ranging from loud to the barely perceptible. Don Bosco was so enchanted ... he was out of his senses and ... no longer able to tell or ask his mother anything.

When Mama Margaret [ended her song] ... she turned to him and said: "I'll be waiting for you...."

Then she was gone.

"Come to heaven with me," Bosco whispered in many a tough slum boy's ear. Even gang leaders proved open to that invitation because of the genuine love in the words as much as because he could outrun them, outplay them, outwit them, and smilingly hammer a nail into the wall with his bare hand to impress even the dimmest that here was a *man*. In his lifetime Bosco turned thousands of lives in new directions, at the cost of great opposition, attack, and labor so arduous that occasionally he fell asleep standing up. "We'll rest in heaven," he often encouraged his overtasked helpers. And Bosco certainly has not made the number of after-death appearances of someone like Therese, who wanted to "work 'till the end of time."

But Don Bosco has at times interrupted his heroically earned rest to come as God's messenger to members of his spiritual family. Betania, Venezuela visionary Maria Esperanza says it was he who told her when she'd meet her husband. I'm guessing Don Bosco also appeared to his "right hand" man and first successor, Blessed Michael Rua. But in Rua we have a saint so self-effacing he wouldn't even sleep in Don Bosco's bed after he inherited his mentor's room, but bedded down on the couch instead. No use looking to Rua for any testimonies. A good reminder, actually, that all the after-death appearances to saints we know about are only "the tip of an iceberg" hidden in God's depths.

Fortunately there are cures. People who are cured will almost always give you most of the details. From the healing of Sister Giovanna, we know of Bosco's two visits to Sister Teresa Valse-Pantellini. In addition, Don Bosco appeared twice in numinous dreams to a nun, unquestionably dying in 1938 of a duodenal ulcer, announcing her cure. Those bending over her bed shook their heads, since even as she gasped out Don Bosco's promise of a cure, she was in the throes of death. But cured she was, with a sudden great shudder, as if her body were hit by lightning.

As Spain in the middle 1930s edged toward civil war, the Salesians' fourth successor to Don Bosco, Blessed Philip Rinaldi, recalled what Don Bosco had told him fifty years earlier: Much blood would be shed in that country after Bosco's death—some of it Salesian. Was it the dead Bosco who told Sister Eusebia? No one knows. But she knew all about the horrors to come—even that her close friend, Sister Carmen, would be martyred, and that Valverde, where they worked, would be attacked.

When the Salesian sisters quaked as they hid out from threatened attack, Sister Eusebia soothed "nothing will happen *this* time." But seeing what was coming, with her confessor's permission, she quietly offered God her life[3] for the country.

When she made her sacrificial vow, Don Bosco came to her one night accompanied by Michael Rua. Rua—the reticent miracle worker with the wry little smile—had a paper in his hand, which he presented to Don Bosco. This was probably the offering of Eusebia. Then the two dead leaders of her order discussed in front of the humble little cook whether what she was doing was in keeping with the Salesian spirit. Their conclusion: that Sister Eusebia was doing "the will of God" comforted her that she was "on the right path."

Eusebia died on February 10, 1935, having seen Dominic Savio, the Virgin Mary, and Jesus during her final days. After her death, the town of Valverde was saved in a way that, witnesses insist, was both "miraculous" and had Sister Eusebia's stamp on it.

Until the present, Valverdeans—including members of the Salesian family—have experienced miracles attributed to the meek, smiling little nun who said on her deathbed, "I will come back and take my little walks here!"

Back in 1887 in South America, missionary Bishop John Cagliero lay recuperating from broken ribs when a supernatural voice told him to get up and go assist Don Bosco on his deathbed. The young bishop painfully straddled a mule to the coast, hobbled aboard a ship and arrived in time to comfort his spiritual father, as Bosco had so often comforted impetuous John. With Cagliero came thirty-four-year-old Sister Angela Vallese. Angela had been only twenty-three on November 14, 1877, when, at the command of St. Mary Mazzarello, she led the first group of six Salesian nuns to Uruguay, then into Patagonia.

Don Bosco died on January 31, 1888. That November Angela headed the third Salesian women's expedition to Tierra del Fuego—a bleak, lawless area at the remote southernmost tip of Chile. Another twenty-five hard years and in 1913 Sister Angela made the arduous trip to Italy again to attend a council of Salesian leaders. To her disappointment, her superiors cancelled her return to Chile. She proved their assessment of her condition correct by dying the next August 17. Angela Vallese, too, then appeared to a number of people. Among them was Salesian Monsignor Joseph Fagnano.

While he was on board ship in the latter half of February 1916 on his way from Ushuaia, the southernmost city in the world, to Punta Arenas, he saw before him a vision of Angela surrounded by a great light. She made several predictions to him about the Mission and when she had finished, she exclaimed, "Oh blessed Tierra del Fuego!"

Less holy than Angela, but still a noteworthy individual in the generation that clustered around St. John Bosco and St. Mary Mazzarello, was Sister Louise Arecco of Mornese, Italy. Remember how Louise at her death came to Mother Mazzarello before it was known that Louise was dead? Louise also made a second after-death appearance to Mary.

On this occasion, Mary was traveling with Father Cagliero in Italy. Not feeling well, she lay down for a rest, only to hear someone groan. Thinking it was another sister who was also ill, she drew back the curtain that gave her bed some privacy, only to see Sister Louise.

Carefully she explained later that Louise was not exactly "in the flesh," but that there was no doubt it was she. Like the true mother she had always been to Louise (who came from a messy background), Mary immediately questioned her spiritual daughter as to whether she was saved, how much spiritual work she had left to do before she could enter heaven, etc. Satisfied that Louise would be done with her purgation by the coming Easter, the foundress of the Salesian sisters quizzed Louise, "Tell me, what in me works against the glory of God?"

Dead she may have been, but Louise squirmed in front of her mentor and refused.

Mary cajoled.

Insisted.

Finally Louise told her.

Emboldened, Mary wanted to know what should be corrected in their community?

Louise was not hesitant on that one. She pointed out something that didn't seem so harmful, but was a wedge opening the nuns to worse things.

When she left, there was no more rest for Mary. Wide-awake and energized, she headed for the chapel to help Louise's after-death work with some prayers.

On the morning of February 24, 1910, Michael Rua, who first met Don Bosco when he was seven and had now for many years been head of the Salesians, confided to his associates a curious dream. Although fifty-seven years dead, Rua's saintly brother Louis—claimed by Don Bosco to be equal in sanctity to the canonized Aloysius Gonzaga—had come to Michael. Louis told his Salesian Brother that he was going to die and he had come to take him to heaven. Six weeks later on April 6, Michael Rua died. Did Louis Rua come *that* day? If so, tight-mouthed Rua kept it to himself.

Rua's right-hand man, Philip Rinaldi, a late vocation gently nudged into the priesthood by Bosco—who seems to have known Philip, too, would one day head the Salesians—was a fatherly man very much like his beloved Don Bosco. A troubled young nun once told him she would not mind dying young, in order to have the much-older Father Rinaldi still alive and able to help her in her last moments.

"Well," he smiled, "if you die before me, count on my being there. Should I go before you, then I will ask the Lord to let me come assist you just the same." And in 1925, while giving a talk, Father Rinaldi said of St. Therese's desire to spend her heaven doing good, "I, too, would like such a grace from the Lord: To do good upon earth while also in heaven. Wouldn't you?"

Affable, great-hearted Father Rinaldi died December 5, 1931. He did indeed do good from heaven, obtaining during World War II what Church authorities call "a great miracle" for a nun machine-gunned in the face by enemy planes. Such favors have led to Rinaldi's beatification. As to the nun who wanted his help at her death, I can't find out what happened.

But this I do know. Where the bonds between people are woven in God—whether the dead return visibly or not—there is no breaking the life-giving connection between those in heaven and those on earth.

Endnotes

1. An offshoot of the Benedictines, it was more rigorous.
2. This sound is also described relating to supernatural events in some Hindu sources, so it is apparently a universal phenomenon.
3. Such acts, traditional in the Church all the way back to Paul in Scripture, are always done in union with Christ's sacrifice since this, Catholics believe, is what gives them their value.

EPILOGUE

In writing these pages, I have dipped my pail in a mere hundred seventy-five years of the stream of time. Its living waters rush on, filled with the universe's abundant life—including after-death appearances of saints and mystics. May such visits remind us not only that there is a greater life after life but that it is God's love which makes this so and sends us his messengers.

APPENDIX:
ON MISREPRESENTING
BLACK ELK AND SÉANCES

The popular book *Black Elk Speaks* by John G. Neihardt has given many people a very positive picture of shamanistic religion with the accompanying suggestion that shamanism was superior to the Christianity enforced upon a betrayed, beaten people by their conquerors. Because of the book's importance (it is found in many school curricula), it is right to note that due to Neihardt's strong anti-Christian bias, he presented Black Elk's early spiritual experiences as if those were his entire spirituality. By omission of the fact that Black Elk chose to spend the majority of his adult life as a Catholic evangelist/catechist, Neihardt misrepresented completely the Lakota Sioux Catholic holy man's attitude toward his shamanistic past. Far from mourning over the lost faith of shamanism, as Neihardt presents Black Elk, the Indian Christian catechist (who had no way to check on Neihardt's depiction of him, since he did not know how to read), taught his people that in shamanism God was preparing the Lakota Sioux for Christianity. To Black Elk, his conversion then was a move forward spiritually into more truth, more light, more—not less—of every spiritual good. Michael F. Steltenkamp's book (p. 251) gives an authentic picture of Black Elk's spirituality based on the choices and events of his entire life and the records of Steltenkamp's personal interviews with Black Elk's family and associates.

Neihardt seems to have had an anti-Christian bias from very early since at age sixteen in 1897, he had already published a long poem based on Hindu Vedanta philosophy.

More interesting data on Neihardt's bias against Christianity turned up as I wrote this book. A reporter for *The Los Angeles Times* (who wishes anonymity) shared with me that around 1975, she attended séances started in the early to mid-1960s by Neihardt on his Midwestern farm. Born in 1881, Neihardt was almost eighty in 1960, so his involvement in groups antithetical to Christianity had been lifelong. He had died by 1975 but his daughter, having inherited her father's unconventional spiritual allegiances (the group was also "into" flying saucers), was continuing her father's Spiritualist sessions. Black Elk was spoken of at these meetings (as Neihardt had portrayed him, that is, without even a whisper regarding the Indian's Christianity). And allegedly the Lakota Sioux was among the visiting spirits summoned up by the séance leader. All these spirits communicated by "knocks" so nothing was seen, no voice heard, nor any other evidence offered—beyond this easily fraudulent or suggestion-induced phenomenon—to indicate a true after-death appearance. That the saintly Black Elk could have been summoned up at a séance is, to this writer, unthinkable.

Holy people—living or dead—respond only to God's call. Both holy Protestants like minister John G. Lake and Catholics like St. John Bosco have attended séances to uncover the truth and found no real after-death appearances. Lake found the "spirit" of a dead member of his flock was willing to discuss many trivial things but not her fervent faith in Jesus Christ. A spirit was present all right, the holy Protestant concluded, but not the dead girl's. Instead, Lake was certain, a dark spirit was posing as the dead child. Why? To lead her grieving parents away from God, in whom alone is found true consolation and peace. Asked by a bishop to attend a highly "successful" séance, St. John Bosco's holy presence totally disabled the "spirits," so that nothing could take place, the medium complained, again indicating that—whether simple foolishness, fraud, or "of darkness"—there was nothing there of God.

INDEX